THE VNR
REAL ESTATE
DICTIONARY

THE VNR REAL ESTATE DICTIONARY

DAVID M. BROWNSTONE

IRENE M. FRANCK

A HUDSON GROUP BOOK

VAN NOSTRAND REINHOLD COMPANY
NEW YORK   CINCINNATI   ATLANTA   DALLAS   SAN FRANCISCO
LONDON   TORONTO   MELBOURNE

Van Nostrand Reinhold Company Regional Offices:
New York   Cincinnati   Atlanta   Dallas   San Francisco

Van Nostrand Reinhold Company International Offices:
London   Toronto   Melbourne

Copyright © 1981 by Litton Educational Publishing, Inc.

Library of Congress Catalog Card Number: 80-29661
ISBN: 0-442-25856-9

All rights reserved. No part of this work covered by the copyright hereon may be reproduced or used in any form or by any means—graphic, electronic, or mechanical, including photocopying, recording, taping, or information storage and retrieval systems—without permission of the publisher.

Manufactured in the United States of America

Published by Van Nostrand Reinhold Company
135 West 50th Street, New York, N.Y. 10020

Published simultaneously in Canada by Van Nostrand Reinhold Ltd.

15 14 13 12 11 10 9 8 7 6 5 4 3 2 1

Library of Congress Cataloging in Publication Data

Brownstone, David M.
 The VNR real estate dictionary.

 "A Hudson Group book."
 1. Real estate business—Dictionaries. I. Franck, Irene M., joint author. II. Title.
HD1365.B76   333.33′03′21   80-29661
ISBN 0-442-25856-9

Preface

The special language of real estate continues to grow and change. New financing arrangements, construction materials and techniques, laws and regulations, and an ever growing and always changing body of colloquial terms continually create new language that must be understood by everyone concerned with real estate. Older terms, even those coming from the large body of common law that underlies the entire field, change and develop over the years, as new situations and approaches affect them. The result has been a growing need for a clear, concise, up-to-date real estate dictionary, which supplies definitions for key words and phrases needed by all those involved in any way with the real estate field.

This dictionary is an attempt to respond to that need. It defines and explains terms drawn from all the areas that make up the special language of real estate, including real estate transactions, financing, law, accounting, construction, architecture, management, government regulation, personal financial planning, taxation, and investment. Throughout, we have included practical examples to illustrate current usage.

The *VNR Real Estate Dictionary* is for real estate brokers and agents, lawyers, investors, bankers, lenders, appraisers, teachers, librarians, and library users—in short, for everyone who has an interest in the field of real estate and who needs a clear, concise dictionary written in easy-to-understand business English.

In pursuit of concision and clarity, we have often consolidated several related terms into one usable definition, rather than define several forms of the same term. We have also quite often briefly defined terms that might otherwise have been cross-referenced, while ensuring that key words in those brief definitions will lead interested readers to wider definitions. Where two or more terms are synonymous, in general, the most commonly used term is defined, and the less commonly used terms are cross-referenced.

The alphabetizing style we have chosen is "letter by letter" rather than "word by word." This method should enable readers to find desired words and phrases quickly and easily.

Many commonly encountered terms have quite different meanings in different contexts. Sometimes these differ from each other, as well as from non-real-estate usages. For such terms, we have numbered the various meanings in order of importance, giving the most general meaning first, except where a narrow meaning is the one most often encountered.

Please note that some of the terms and definitions in this book are also found in the authors' *VNR Dictionary of Business and Finance* and *VNR Investor's Dictionary*, as these are overarching terms used in many kinds of business applications. In some instances, we have used definitions interchangeably. In others, we have defined a widely used business term in its real estate applications and with real estate-oriented practical examples. Approximately 60 percent of the terms herein defined are not to be found in the two previously published dictionaries. Some 15-25 percent of the terms herein are general terms redefined for this work. Ten to 15 percent of the work is composed of terms interchangeable with those in the previous works.

This dictionary is by its very nature selective, reflecting the authors' decisions regarding which terms will prove most useful to its users. While including as many new terms as possible, we have tried to select mainly those terms of lasting value and to exclude the jargon of the moment.

DAVID M. BROWNSTONE
IRENE M. FRANCK

THE VNR
REAL ESTATE
DICTIONARY

A

AAA tenant: A commercial tenant possessed of prestige and financial stability; a tenant so highly regarded by lenders as to have positive impact on a decision to finance a real estate project, such as an office building or suburban mall. Although some credit rating organizations rate companies and their debt obligations by letter, such designations have no real relationship to the AAA designation of tenants.

abandonment: The total, irrevocable, and voluntary giving up of any property and of all possible rights to that property. Once abandoned, the property becomes the possession of the first to claim it. There must be both intent to abandon and an overt act of abandonment, as when the owner of a building leaves it with clear intent never to return, the owner of a right to drill for oil or gas under a lease specifically relinquishes that right and permanently leaves an occupied site, the possessor of a homestead leaves it with clear intent to leave it forever, or the owner of a right to easement ceases to use that easement for a considerable time and with clear intent not to use that right to easement in the future. Absence from a property, for however long, does not by itself constitute legal abandonment.

abatement: 1. A decrease; for example, a decrease in real property taxes due to correction of an assessment error, or a decrease in rent due when rented premises are unavailable because of fire or other natural causes stated in the lease. **2.** The total destruction of a plaintiff's cause of action at law, but leaving the plaintiff the ability to commence another cause of action based on the same set of facts. **3.** In law, the unlawful possession of real property in an estate by one who is not a rightful heir, to the detriment of rightful heirs.

abeyance: The condition of a property capable of being owned, but in which no ownership interest currently exists, as when a property has been taken by the state for unpaid taxes, but has not yet been sold to a new owner, or when the property of an involuntary bankrupt is in the hands of a bankruptcy court.

ab initio: Latin for *from the beginning*, describing the legal status of a condition or transaction, whether by its very nature or constructed from subsequent matters; for example, as applied to a contract that is void from the start, or to a legal entry later construed to have been a trespass from the start, due to the subsequent actions of the trespasser.

abode: One's dwelling place; often but not always also one's legal domicile; usually a place in which one can legally be served with legal process and from which one can legally vote, but one which may fall short of domicile status for some legal purposes. In modern practice, the line between abode, legal residence, and domicile, is a fine one, and the three terms are usually synonymous, in law and general usage.

above the line: 1. Describing any normal, customary item on an accounting statement; unusual items are described as *below the line*. **2.** In marketing, describing costs for advertising, while other sales promotion costs are called *below the line*.

abrogation: The destruction or repeal of an existing law, whether by legislative, judicial, or executive act, or by practice.

absentee ownership: 1. The ownership of wealth-producing assets by those who neither work nor manage those assets; for example, a landlord who resides elsewhere and hires someone else to manage owned property; sometimes used as a term of opprobrium by local people and tenants who feel that absentee owners care little about them, but only about profits. **2.** The ownership of real property somewhere considerably distant from one's main residence, which is occupied relatively infrequently; taxing authorities may disqualify some kinds of such absentee owners from favorable tax treatment accorded owner-occupiers.

absolute: That which is complete, final, irrevocable at law, and carrying no encumbrances or conditions. The word is often used merely for emphasis, but more precisely refers to a large number of definable matters, such as an absolute sale, which is a sale consummated in full at the moment of formal agreement and without conditions; or an absolute title, estate, or property, which all refer to unconditional and unencumbered interests or states of ownership.

absorbed costs: Any additional, determinable cost which might either be passed on whole to the buyer or paid by the seller, but which is paid by the seller, such as postage or handling charges.

absorption rate: The rate at which any market will buy up goods offered for sale in that market; in real estate, the rate at which properties offered for sale or lease will be bought in a given geographical area.

abstract: A written summary of the contents of a longer work, such as a brief digest of a legal decision or of any other document or set of documents.

abstract of title: A summary statement of all transactions affecting title to land, all interests held by anyone in that land, and all liens, charges, or other claims upon that land. It is a basic document needed by all purchasers of land.

abutment: 1. That portion of one property which touches an adjacent property. **2.** A supporting major substructural element of a bridge, such as the structure anchoring one end of a bridge.

abutting: Lying next to and touching another property; synonymous with adjacent and adjoining.

AC: See alternating current.

accelerated depreciation: Any method of calculating depreciation of land, buildings, or other fixed assets so that the stated value of the asset diminishes faster than if it lost its value in equal proportions, period after period, as is the case when *straight line depreciation* is used. It is used widely as a tax avoidance device, especially in real estate and generally throughout American industry.

acceleration clause: A clause in a debt instrument, such as a mortgage, which makes the entire amount of the debt due and payable on demand if the conditions stated in the clause are not met. For example, the entire amount of a mortgage may become immediately due if a single payment of interest or principal is missed.

acceptance: Agreement to a proffered transaction with intent to carry through that transaction. Acceptance is usually expressed and indicated by acts such as signing a contract, registering a deed, or accepting an application and first check from an insured. It may be implied, conditional, or partial, and provable by the acts of one alleged to have accepted, as when one moves to take possession of property which has been auctioned and allegedly bought with the twitch of a purchaser's eyebrow or the wave of a hand.

access: 1. The legal right to move freely to and from one's privately owned land from public land, even if the way lies through other privately owned land. **2.** The legal right to enter one's own property for purposes of inspection and display to prospective tenants, even if it is in the possession of another, such as a current tenant.

access door: A door which is not primarily used for traffic within or to and from a structure, but rather is used relatively infrequently for reaching internal portions of the structure, such as a door leading to a central air conditioning unit or water tank.

accession: The legal right to that which naturally accretes or is added by others to owned property; for example, built-in furniture added to leased premises which then legally becomes part of those premises and the property of their owner; or valuable mineral-bearing deposits that accrete on the banks of a stream on owned property and become part of that property.

accessory structure: A building auxiliary to a main building on a property, standing separately and not part of that main structure, such as a barn or garage.

accident insurance: 1. Insurance against claims of others who allege the insured's involvement in claimant's accidents; a kind of liability insurance. **2.** Insurance covering an insured for damages to person or property stemming from an accident; for example, worker's compensation.

accommodation paper: A debt instrument which is co-signed by one who does not receive the borrowings, but who is signing as guarantor that the borrower will repay or, if not, that the co-signer will repay the debt.

accommodation party: One who signs a debt instrument and undertakes co-liability for borrowings while not receiving any of the proceeds of those borrowings.

account: 1. A written record of transactions, kept in one or more ledgers and usually, though not always, expressed in money or money equivalents. **2.** A customer, such as one who has a bank or brokerage account, or one who regularly buys and is extended some kind of business credit.

accountant: One who practices accounting, such as a Certified Public Accountant or public accountant.

account executive: An employee responsible for handling the relationship between a firm and one or more of its clients; in real estate, used primarily as a synonym for salesperson.

accounting: 1. Reporting, classifying, summarizing, and interpreting transactions, partly or wholly of a financial nature. **2.** Any formal report of an entity's transactions during a specific period, usually including a summary of the entity's current status as of the beginning of the period.

accounting period: Any period for which an accounting is prepared, usually monthly, quarterly, and yearly.

accounting practice: 1. The professional practice of a Certified Public Accountant or public accountant. **2.** The normal and generally accepted practices of accountants regarding commonly encountered professional matters.

accounts payable: Money a firm owes others for goods purchased and not yet paid for; does not include such obligations as notes, bonds, and other debts.

accounts receivable: Money owed a firm by its customers for goods purchased and not yet paid for; does not include income from such sources as investments and bank deposits.

accretion: In general, any gradual increase in size, as in the value of stocks and bonds held. In real estate, a gradual increase in the size of land held abutting a body of water, through deposits by action of that water.

accrual: 1. The process of adding to and accumulating. Also refers to anything that is added to and accumulates. **2.** In accounting, continuous or periodic change in the amount of any account, including increases and decreases, income and expenses. Also refers to the specific account item that is changed by the process of accrual.

accrual basis: An accounting method which records income and expenses for accounting purposes when they are earned and incurred, rather than on a cash basis, when they are actually received and spent. For example, on the accrual basis, goods bought are charged against the day they are actually bought rather than the day they are paid for, which may be considerably later; goods sold are recorded as income, minus any necessary reserves for uncollectibles, when sold rather than when the money due for them is collected.

accrue: 1. To increase, accumulate, and accrete over some extended period of time. **2.** In accounting, to record accruals in the appropriate accounts.

accrued: Describing any item which, for accounting purposes, has been earned or incurred but which has not yet been received or spent.

accrued depreciation: The amount of depreciation that has accumulated since an asset was acquired; for appraisal purposes, the difference between replacement cost and current appraisal value; for tax purposes, a record of depreciation taken, which depends on the method of depreciation selected.

accrued expense: An expense incurred and recorded in one accounting period which is due and payable in a future accounting period, under an accrual basis accounting method.

accrued income: Income earned and recorded in one accounting period which is to be actually received in a future accounting period, under an accrual basis accounting method.

accrued interest: Interest earned that is not yet due and payable, as with fixed interest bonds earning interest every day which is payable quarterly or semiannually.

accumulated depreciation: See accrued depreciation.

acknowledgment: A declaration by the signer of a document made to an official, usually a notary public, stating that the signature on the document is authentic and that the document was freely signed; also the official's declaration that such a declaration has been made and personally witnessed by the official.

acoustical: Relating to sound; in real estate, normally used to describe materials that absorb sound, such as cork and some kinds of tiles.

acquisition: 1. The process of gaining ownership of anything. Also that which is acquired. **2.** In business, the process of gaining full or partial but controlling ownership of a business entity. Also the business entity which is acquired.

acquisition cost: The total of all direct costs incurred by the purchaser of an asset, such as a real estate property, including the purchase price and such associated costs as lawyer's closing fees and transfer taxes, but not including time and other overhead costs.

acquittance: A document that completely discharges a financial debt or other performance obligation; usually issued upon settlement of a financial obligation.

acre: A land measure equalling 43,560 square feet, 4,840 square yards, or 160 square rods, however shaped. In metric equivalents, it is 4,407 square meters.

acreage allotment: The amount of land that a farm may use for production of a specific crop; part of the national farm price support program, which seeks to limit supply in order to keep prices at minimum specified levels.

acre foot: That volume of a stated material, such as water, that will cover one acre one foot deep, constituting 43,560 cubic feet.

acronym: A word constructed from the first letters of a series of related words, such as OSHA for Occupational Safety and Health Administration.

action: The pursuit of a claimed legal right by any kind of legal process in a court of law. Also refers to the legal proceeding itself.

action to quiet title: A legal action in which one states legal title in land, states that another has claimed some kind of title to that land, and sues to remove that other's claim to title.

act of God: An event beyond control or planning; usually a cataclysmic natural event such as earthquake, famine, flood, and pestilence, which precludes contracted performance without penalty or is a stated exception to insurance coverages.

actual notice: The possession of direct knowledge. In law, the possession of notice may change one's claim to title; for example, prior knowledge of a valid claim to title may make one's current claim to title invalid or subject to that prior claim. Notice construed by statute or court may function as actual notice does.

actuary: An insurance mathematics and statistics expert, whose work includes the setting of insurance premiums through the calculation of all the kinds of risks involved.

addendum: Something added in writing or print, usually to a document, such as a book or contract. An addendum is often used to correct a minor error or omission in such a document.

addition: A construction added to an existing structure, such as a second floor or attached garage later added to an existing building. Occasionally, documents will use the term to describe unattached structures, and such uses will be binding as to the aims of the document even though it is an unusual use; for example, an insurance policy describing an unattached building as an addition and insuring it as such will be binding upon the insurer.

additional deposit: See deposit.

add-on interest: Interest that is payable on the total amount loaned as if the loan were repayable in a single lump sum at the end of the loan period, even though the loan is actually repayable in installments during the loan period, the net effect being to almost double the amount of interest paid. For example, a loan of $1,200 at 12% interest, payable in 12 equal $100 installments, with interest payable on balanced outstanding balance, or $12 the first month, $11 the second month, and so on, has a total interest payment of $78; but if the add-on interest method is used, the total interest payable is 12% of the whole $1,200, or $144, nearly twice as much.

address of record: An address stated for legal purposes, such as a legal residence statement for tax and voting purposes, or an address stated for purposes of legal notification under the terms of a contract.

ad hoc: On a one time basis. For example, an ad hoc committee is one formed for a single purpose, to be dissolved after that purpose has been achieved or abandoned; an ad hoc rule is one adopted for a single situation and is not intended to set any precedents.

adjacent: See abutting.

adjoining: See abutting.

adjudication: The judgment or decree of a court, usually after the completion of the legal process as to an action.

adjusted basis: For Federal income tax purposes, the basis used to determine gain or loss on sale or depreciation of a fixed asset, consisting of original cost, plus improvements and other capital additions minus depreciation and other diminutions of capital.

adjuster: One who examines, evaluates, and negotiates settlement of insurance claims. Adjusters are usually employed directly or indirectly by insurance companies to assess and settle claims on behalf of those insurers.

adjusting entry: A change in existing accounting records to correct entries or to modify them to reflect changing circumstances, such as reserves for bad debts, uncollectibles, accruals, and writeoffs.

adjustment: 1. In a real estate sale, an item of expense or income other than the stated selling price, acting to alter the net selling price. **2.** Any satisfaction of a claim, as in the settlement of an insurance claim. **3.** Any necessary change, as in an adjusting entry in accounting.

administration: 1. The management of matters, businesses, and other organizations. **2.** The organizational entity created to accomplish the work of managing matters, companies, and other organizations. **3.** In law, the process of managing an estate.

administrative agency: A governmental body set up to administer a specific law or laws, such as the Securities and Exchange Commission, charged with administration of Federal securities laws.

administrative discretion: Power to act as one's own judgment indicates within the framework of legislative intention indicated by statute and supporting material. For example, state and Federal anti-discrimination agencies may issue regulations regarding alleged discriminatory practices in the rental and sale of real estate, and individual administrators may take action within the framework of statutes and regulations.

administrative expenses: Expenses incurred to accomplish the management of matters and organizations. In business, the expenses of management as management, rather than by specific productive functions.

administrative law: The body of law created by the interplay between statutes, administrative agencies, and the courts, in areas of government regulation of the lives of its citizens and their organizations. Composed of statutes and their interpretation, in contrast with common law, which is composed of cases and their development.

administrator: One who manages matters and organizations. In business, an executive in charge of some aspect of management. In law, one who manages an estate.

adobe: A building material made of clay and straw, usually formed into large bricks or blocks; widely used in the American Southwest.

ad valorem tax: A tax computed on the basis of the value of the taxed item; usually expressed as a percentage of that value. Examples are many excise, most property, and all value-added taxes.

advance: 1. A partial payment of funds committed by a lender to a builder under the terms of a construction loan; the lender usually makes periodic payments to the builder as the work progresses, which are also known as progress payments. **2.** Any payment made before it is legally due; for example, a repayable loan to an employee or a non-returnable forward payment to a salesperson, to be repaid later out of earnings, if any.

advance commitment: A financing commitment by a lender in advance of the time set for execution of a commitment, and in contemplation of the meeting of certain stated terms by the borrower, such as completion of all or part of construction.

advance refunding: An offer by a bond issuer to bondholders at favorable rates, to forestall early redemption of the old bonds. Treasury bondholders often take advantage of advance refunding offers.

adverse claim: A claim of title by the possessor of real property against the claims of others recognized by law as the owners of that property; aimed at securing a change of legally recognized title; for example, a claim by one in occupancy of real estate as against a receiver in bankruptcy.

adverse possession: Legally acceptable assertion of title to real property by one claiming title because of open, adverse, and clearly claimed right as against the rights of all others, and actual, continuous physical possession of the property for the minimum length of time specified in the applicable statute.

adverse user: One who makes a legally acceptable assertion of the right to limited use of another's real property, as in the development of an easement across another's land, after continuous, adverse, open use for the statutory period, with the knowledge of but without the permission of the land's owner.

advertise: To announce something publicly, especially aiming to sell, purchase, or hire goods or services.

advertised bidding: A mode of obtaining bids to perform contracts, in which the purchaser publicly solicits bids for the work to be performed. Bidders for the contracts must respond with very specific and detailed proposals in competition with all other bidders. This mode of contracting is widely used by governmental bodies and is often required by law; it is seldom used by private industry.

advertising manager: The employee responsible for overseeing a company's advertising activities. Depending on the company, this manager may run the company's advertising department as if it were an in-house advertising agency, or may mainly work as liaison with outside advertising agencies.

advisory fee: A kind of consulting fee, usually a fee paid to a registered investment advisor for investment advisory services rendered.

aeolian soil: Soil created by the deposit and accretion of wind-blown solid materials, such as the ash and other materials generated by a volcano.

aerial map: A map created by use of photos taken from the air; sometimes describing a planetary map using photos taken from space vehicles.

affidavit: A written statement as to facts, sworn to or otherwise affirmed by its maker before someone legally authorized to administer and verify that oath or affirmation.

affidavit of ownership: See affidavit of title.

affidavit of title: A sworn statement, in writing and witnessed by a notary public or other authorized official, stating that a conveyor of property has clear and defect-free title to convey.

affirmative action: Action undertaken, by employers, unions, and others concerned with employment and equal economic opportunity, to reduce discrimination against minority groups and women. The basic statute mandating such actions is the Equal Opportunity Act of 1972, since followed by other administrative and legal actions.

affirmative marketing: Action by realtors to comply with government statutes and regulations requiring that minorities be informed of available housing and that realtor procedures and attitudes combine to afford fair housing opportunities to all; goes considerably beyond passive non-discrimination against minority group members seeking housing, recognizing a positive obligation on the part of those handling the rental and sale of housing to ensure that minority groups in their communities are aware of housing opportunities and will be treated fairly when attempting to secure housing.

A-frame: A kind of building, characterized and described by its front framing, which is in the form of an A; a widely used single family or vacation residence form, particularly in the field of relatively inexpensive, wholly or partly pre-fabricated structures.

after-acquired: In law, something acquired after the occurrence of the event or transaction which makes it possible for the later acquisition to take place; for example, the passage of good title some time after a transaction in which a seller tried to pass title but could not because it was defective, the defect being cured later and title then passing legally without need of any further transaction.

after date: Describing when a debt is due to be repaid, a specific time after it is incurred; for example, a note payable 90 days after the date on which it was executed and the money loaned is described as payable "90 days after date."

after sight: Describing when a debt is due to be repaid, a specific time after legal presentation and acceptance of the debt instrument; for example, for a note that is payable "30 days after sight," the debt is due 30 days after acceptance of the note.

age-life depreciation: An appraisal method applying straight line depreciation to a structure's anticipated life; for example, a building acquired for $100,000, with an anticipated physical life of 50 years might be appraised each year at $2,000 less, if this depreciation method were used exclusively. As a practical matter, other factors, such as location and maintenance, affect appraisal considerably.

agency: 1. A relationship in which one party, the agent, acts for or represents another, the principal, under authority granted by the principal, the parties then entering into a fiduciary relationship. In this relationship the agent is legally bound to exercise all due care and to represent the best interests of the principal, untainted by personal considerations or by representation of the possibly adverse interests of others. An agency may be express or implied, written or oral, exclusive or shared, general or limited. 2. A business organization, mainly engaged in the representation of others; for example, an insurance selling organization that represents and handles business for an insurance company.

agency agreement: A formal and written contract between principal and agent, setting forth all terms and conditions of the agency arrangement; for example, the agreement between an insurance company and one of its general agents.

agency contract: See agency agreement.

agent: 1. One who sells property, goods, and services for others, as do real estate and insurance agents, and who therefore legally has fiduciary relationships with those represented. **2.** One who acts for or represents another in a series of transactions over a period of time; a formal business relationship usually governed in every major way by the provisions of an agency contract.

agreement of sale: See contract.

agribusiness: See farm.

agricultural land: Generally indicating land used primarily for agriculture; of practical significance in jurisdictions where zoning laws and other applicable statutes specifically treat this kind of land differently than they do other kinds of land.

agricultural lien: A lien held by a lender on specific crops, as provided by statute in some states.

agriculture: Farming to produce crops and animals. Until recently, it has always referred to working the land, but now also refers to working the sea, using such techniques as hydroponics.

AIA: See American Institute of Architects.

AICPA: See American Institute of Certified Public Accountants.

AIREA: See American Institute of Real Estate Appraisers.

air rights: Proprietary rights to air space above owned land. Often leased or sold to others for building purposes, as in the instance of apartment buildings over bridge approaches in some major cities.

air space: The volume of air above an owner's property and the space it occupies; theoretically part of that property out to the limit of Earth's air envelope, but practically an ownership defined by a series of overlapping statutes and regulations, and by public policy.

alcove: A portion of a room; usually recessed or partly separated by partitions from the balance of the room.

alienation: The act of conveyance of real property from one to another; does not apply to passage by action of law or to any involuntary passage, such as by a defaulting borrower to a lender.

alienation clause: A clause in a loan agreement, allowing the lender to demand immediate payment in full of outstanding balances due on conveyance of a property to another; most commonly encountered in mortgages.

allegation: A statement in a pleading by a party to an action, specifying all or part of that which the party will attempt to prove; in common modern usage, the term has come to mean any charge or statement directed against another.

alley: A passageway between buildings that is a public right of way but is narrower than a street and usually unsuitable for the passage of vehicles; often used to describe a private right of way of the same nature.

allocate: 1. To distribute according to a plan or set of rules, as in distribution of scarce commodities by government in time of emergency. **2.** To distribute expenditures and revenues according to function among various accounts in an accounting system. For example, the direct costs attributable to order processing may be distributed among the various products for which orders were processed.

allocation: See allotment.

allodial: That system of real property ownership that vests absolute ownership in private individuals; contrasts with feudal and other state ownerships, which vest absolute ownership in the state. An estate in land so held is called an allodium.

allodium: See allodial.

allotment: Distribution according to a plan or set of rules; in real estate, the amount of funds made available for mortgages in a period by such institutional investors as pension funds and insurance companies.

allowance: 1. In real estate accounting and management practice, a reserve set aside for possible losses incurred on future sale of real property. **2.** A sum granted by an employer for reimburseable employee expenses, as in a mileage allowance for real estate sellers. **3.** An amount taken off a debt to offset claims by the debtor for such matters as defects in the quality or quantity of goods delivered.

all-risk insurance: See comprehensive insurance.

alluvion: Soil or other material deposited at the edge of any body of water by action of the water, such as sand on a sea beach, or topsoil in a delta; sometimes called alluvium. The process of depositing such materials is accretion; while accretion is the process and alluvion the result, the two terms are commonly used as synonyms.

alluvium: See alluvion.

ALTA: See American Land Title Association.

alteration: A change within an existing structure, which although substantial, does not add to or substantially change the size or shape of the structure, as might an addition; for example, the removal or modification of existing internal partitions or plumbing.

altered check: A check that has undergone unauthorized change after issuance, usually by addition or erasure, so that such matters as payees, amounts, and dates have been materially altered.

alternating current (AC): Electrical current that constantly reverses the direction of its flow within a circuit; in contrast with direct current (DC) which does not; the two kinds of current are incompatible.

amenity: 1. A natural or manmade object or circumstance that enhances the enjoyment and desirability of, but is not necessary for the use of, residential property, such as a lake, stream, pool, view, or playing field. **2.** A restraint on a property owner due to an easement or grant, barring the doing of something which might otherwise have been rightfully incident to ownership, but for the existence of the restraint; often called a negative easement and part of the law of easements.

American Institute of Architects (AIA): The main national professional association of architects in the United States; all registered architects are eligible for membership.

American Institute of Certified Public Accountants (AICPA): The main national professional association of certified public accountants; all certified public accountants are eligible for membership. This organization is active in setting standards and defining ethical practices. In some states, public accountants have similar status and their own professional organizations.

American Institute of Real Estate Appraisers (AIREA): A national association of real estate appraisers; an affiliate of the National Association of Realtors.®

American Land Title Association (ALTA): A national association of those concerned with title insurance and title insurance law, including title insurance agents, abstracters, and attorneys.

amicus curiae: Latin for *a friend of the court;* one who is not a party to a case before a court, but who volunteers discussion or argument of a matter before the court; usually an attorney on a matter of law.

amortization: 1. The reduction and ultimate wiping out of an amount over a specified period, as in retirement of a mortgage debt through installment repayments that include both interest and principal until the full debt is repaid. **2.** The process of writing off the premium on a bond bought above par. **3.** The reduction and ultimate wiping out of the stated value of a fixed asset over a specified period, including all forms of depreciation, write-offs, and depletion of assets of limited life; of special tax significance in the form of accelerated depreciation.

amortization schedule: 1. A table showing the mathematics of amortization, as the obligation or asset is gradually reduced and eliminated. **2.** A table showing the mathematics of amortization as the premium paid on a bond is gradually reduced.

amortized loan: A loan repaid in equal installments over the life of the loan, each payment containing both interest and principal repayments; interest is high and principal repayment low at the start of the period, with principal repayments high and interest low toward the end of the period. Home mortgage loans are usually made on this basis.

ampere: A standard measure of the amount of flow of an electric current.

anchor bolt: A large fastener primarily used to attach wooden to masonry constructions, such as a door sill to a masonry wall.

anchor lease: See anchor tenant.

anchor tenant: A prime tenant, such as a substantial department store, in a shopping center or mall; other tenants, usually called satellite tenants, are drawn to the center by the promise of consumer traffic generated by the prime or anchor tenant.

angle: A geometrical construct used in surveying, which relates two lines to each other as they meet or would meet if extended. The relationship between the two lines is expressed in degrees, in minutes at 60 minutes to a degree, and seconds at 60 seconds to a minute. The maximum number of degrees in an angle is 360, which is a full circle; a right angle is 90 degrees.

angle iron: A right-angled strip of iron used for several kinds of fastening and support purposes in construction.

annexation: 1. The process of attaching or joining one thing to another; in real estate, usually the joinder of a smaller to a larger primary thing, as in the joining of plumbing hardware to a building, creating a fixture that in law becomes part of the building. 2. The taking of additional territory by a government, as when a city takes an adjoining suburb, with the consent of the suburb, or a country takes one of its neighbors, with or without that neighbor's consent.

annual audit: Thorough examination of a firm's books and records for a year's activities, usually by outside accountants.

annual closing: The closing of a firm's books for the fiscal year, including the posting of closing entries in those books.

annualize: 1. To derive an annual rate from partial figures. For example, under certain conditions costs incurred in one month can be multiplied by twelve to get a projected annual rate of expenditure. 2. In taxation, to compute for tax purposes when operations are taxable for only part of a year, as in a change from a fiscal to a calendar year on a one-time basis.

annual report: A formal report of a firm's operating results for the year and its year-end financial condition, containing a balance sheet, operating statement, auditor's report, and often other financial materials and management comments; submitted by the board of directors to the firm's stockholders and often to other interested parties.

annuity: A sum paid periodically in equal installments to annuitants under terms of an insurance policy or bequest. It is usually a form of retirement insurance, in which the insured buys an insurance policy, making periodic premium payments, a single lump sum payment, or some combination of both; then on maturity of the policy the insured receives payments in one of several alternative payment modes. In the recently introduced variable annuity, insureds may receive payment in shares of an annuity fund that varies with the fortunes of the securities in which it is invested.

antedate: To date a document earlier than the real date on which it is executed, as in dating a gift earlier than the actual date of its giving, to qualify for favorable, and often illegal, tax treatment.

anticipation: 1. Any expectation of change; generally used to describe the impact of events and reactions to them on stock market fluctuations, consumer buying patterns, and other economic trends. **2.** In accounting, recording costs and revenues before they actually occur, as in recording all proceeds from a multi-year magazine subscription as if they had already been received, even though payment is yearly.

anticipatory breach: A breach of contract occurring before other parties have obligations to perform under the terms of that contract, such as a direct statement of intent not to perform, or bankruptcy clearly making it impossible to perform.

apartment: A rental unit within a multi-unit residence; occupants of apartments pay rent to the apartment building owners, who are responsible for providing communal services such as heat and light.

apartment hotel: A multi-unit residence which often includes apartments and hotel rooms, and which usually makes several hotel services, such as cleaning and linen services, available to tenants.

apartment house: See apartment.

appeal: An attempt to secure a hearing in a higher court, after adjudication by a lower court and exhaustion of all other relevant processes, asking overturn of the lower court's decision.

apportionment: Any proportional division, as in the division of taxes, pending utility bills, insurance premiums, and other such overlapping matters between buyer and seller on closing a real estate sale and conveyance; or the division of a tax levied among those who must pay it, according to rules developed by the taxing authority.

appraisal: The development of a formal estimate of value of any real or personal property, usually by an appraiser and in writing; also refers to the document so produced. Income-producing properties are usually appraised using the *income approach*, a method that evaluates a property by estimating its anticipated future earnings and comparing them to the probable yields of other properties, and then setting a value equivalent to the values of these other properties. Residential properties are usually appraised using the *market data approach*, a method that evaluates a property by analyzing other similar properties recently sold. The *cost approach,* which focuses on cost of reproduction, is sometimes used to crosscheck and supplement the other methods, and in the evaluation of nonprofit and public properties.

appraisal correlation: The process of appraising a property in light of all three major approaches—income, market, and cost—in order to reach the most balanced appraisal possible.

appraisal report: A formal document of appraisal submitted by an appraiser. Such a report may be written or oral, and of any length, but normally is in writing and includes supporting documents and all relevant facts about the property being appraised and the appraisal approaches used.

appraised value: The estimated value of real or personal property set by an appraiser; often a value set in contemplation of sale in an attempt to determine fair market value; also an estimate made by taxing authorities for purposes of fixing taxes on real property.

appraiser: One who sets value on properties for a wide variety of legal, taxing, and transacting purposes; who is generally recognized as an expert in the kinds of properties being appraised; and who often possesses such credentials as a course of study, professional certification, and professional society membership.

appreciation: 1. An increase in the value of any property. **2.** An increase in the value of a fixed asset over its book value. **3.** An increase in the market price of a security.

appreciation participation mortgage: A mortgage in which the mortgage lender shares in the appreciation of a property mortgaged if and when that property is eventually sold, and on which the lender takes proportionally less interest; for example, a mortgage carrying an interest rate of 10%, rather than the 15% that is the current going rate for mortgages at the time the mortgage loan is made, with the right to take one third of any appreciation in the property mortgaged on eventual sale of property.

apprentice: One who is in the process of learning a trade while employed in that trade, usually for a fixed period. Certification to practice that trade often depends on satisfactory completion of the apprenticeship period.

apprenticeship training: The training of relatively unskilled workers to become skilled tradespeople, in prograns sponsored by government, labor, and industry, often as part of affirmative action programs developed in compliance with Federal and state anti-discrimination laws.

appropriation: 1. An expenditure authorized by legislative act for the accomplishment of a public purpose. **2.** The taking of private property for public purposes, as in the exercise of the right of eminent domain, with or without current or future payment for that taking.

approval sale: See trial sale.

appurtenance: Something legally belonging with and to real property being conveyed, though not necessarily attached to that property, such as a barn, easement, plant, or tree that is part of the ownership interest being conveyed, but not the main property, which may be land or land and a main building.

appurtenant: See appurtenance.

aquatic rights: Fishing, navigational, and subsurface rights held by individuals in a body of water and the land in which it stands or flows.

aqueduct: A substantial construction built to act as a conduit for water.

aquifer: A water-bearing subsurface formation, usually of rock, through which ground water moves.

arbitrage: The practice of buying something in one market and simultaneously selling it in another or the same market, with the aim of taking advantage of price differences, often quite small, existing at the moment of purchase and sale. The usual objects of arbitrage include currencies, securities, mortgages, precious metals, and several kinds of futures, including mortgage futures.

arbitration: A dispute-settling process, in which the parties in dispute submit their cases to a third party, either a single arbitrator or a panel, for a settlement that will be binding upon the parties. Arbitration is usually voluntary and written into contracts, such as construction and lease contracts.

arbitrator: One who functions to settle disputes between parties and whose decision will be binding upon those parties.

arbor: A sheltered place in a garden; usually constructed of some kind of latticework, on which climbing plants grow.

arcade: A covered passage, with retail establishments along its sides; often a series of covered arches open at both ends. The arcade is a European and North American version of the covered bazaar, and the forerunner of the modern covered shopping mall.

arch: A structural component, curved or pointed at the top, forming the upper end of an aperture, such as a doorway, or used as a structural support, as in an aqueduct.

architect: A licensed professional in the field of architecture, who designs and often supervises the construction of all kinds of structures.

architectural control: The regulation of structural design by government; often embodied in local law requiring review by a local governmental body of several significant aspects of a proposed structure, including its design, before that body grants necessary approval to go ahead with construction.

architectural drawings: Drawings and supporting data prepared by an architect as part of the workup or contract in connection with a proposed structure, and including detailed plans for land and structure.

architectural review board: An agency of local government, charged with reviewing the quality and appropriateness of the designs of proposed structures, in terms of local standards and existing structures.

architecture: 1. The art, science, and practice of building. **2.** That which is built by humans, describing the entire range of constructions, from a single small building to all the edifices of humankind. **3.** A style of building, described by school, period, or place, such as in the international style, of the Colonial period, Islamic, or Roman.

Are: A measure of area in the metric system, equal to 100 square meters. One hundred ares equals one hectare, the basic metric unit of land measure, or 2.471 acres.

area: 1. The surface of real property, measured as if the property were level; rolling land therefore actually contains more surface than flat land, but is measured as if the hills were not bulging but flattened. **2.** Any portion of any surface, and used as a loose substitute for more specific designations, such as neighborhood, region, town, or community.

area zoning: See zoning.

arm's-length: Describing a transaction engaged in by parties who are absolutely independent of each other as regards the transaction. For example, wholly unrelated buyers and sellers can deal with each other at arm's-length.

arrears: Debts such as installment payments, rent, and bond interest, which are owing and past due but unpaid on their normal and acceptable payment dates. Occasionally used to describe debts which are due, but not yet overdue.

Art Deco: An architectural and design style, also called Moderne, originating in the 1920's and 1930's, which features sleek, streamlined surfaces; basic geometric shapes, such as chevrons, zigzags, and octagons, as design motifs; and in public buildings, often a tall section balanced by low sections.

arterial highway: Any substantial highway serving as a main through route, or artery, for traffic.

artery: See arterial highway.

artesian well: A well, usually quite deep, drilled through a non-water-bearing formation into a subsurface body of water, which then rises to the surface due to internal pressure without need for pumping.

articles of association: A document embodying an agreement between those forming a company under the common law, that company in legal effect being a partnership rather than a corporation.

articles of incorporation: A document embodying an agreement between those forming a private corporation under the general corporation law, which is a statute specifying the limited liability of corporate shareholders and otherwise defining the special nature of that form of doing business.

articles of partnership: A document agreed to and signed by parties forming and organizing a co-partnership.

asbestos: A mineral widely used for fireproofing buildings for many years, but now rarely used in new construction; in recent years understood to be a very dangerous source of carcinogens, and now being replaced in many older buildings.

as is: Describing a sale made without any express or implied warranty; usually describes merchandise for sale, and is not always a bar to recovery under United States consumer protection laws.

asking price: The price at which anything is offered for sale; usually used in real estate and other substantial transactions to mean that the price being asked is negotiable, rather than firm.

assemblage: The acquisition of several contiguous properties on which a single realty project can be developed; often a long, complex, and secret process, with the potential developer trying to acquire many or all of the properties before current owners realize that a project is being planned, and therefore raise their asking prices greatly.

assessed value: The value placed on real and personal property by government for property tax purposes, based on an appraisal of the fair market value of the property and a governmental decision as to how much of that value will be the standard set for taxing purposes. Some states require that all property be taxed at full appraised fair market value; others allow values to be stated in fractions, with state administration setting standards, aimed at producing approximately equal statewide property tax rates.

assessment: 1. A tax on real property, whether a recurring tax or a special tax for a single property-related purpose, such as sewers or sidewalks. **2.** The process of determining the assessed valuation of property as a basis for a tax to be levied. **3.** An amount levied by such companies as banks, insurance companies, and stock companies on shareholders and other parties holding some form of ownership interest, to compensate for such matters as unanticipated losses and impaired capital positions. **4.** The amount of damages set to be paid to the winner of a lawsuit. **5.** Any special and temporary charge levied by an organization on its members.

assessment base: See tax base.

assessment ratio: The ratio of assessed value to full appraised fair market value set by taxing authorities; for example, a taxing district setting a 60% ratio would state the value of a $100,000 property as $60,000, and would tax accordingly, with state administrative bodies attempting to equalize actual tax rates in all districts.

assessment roll: A list showing all taxable properties in a taxing district, and their assessed values.

assessor: A taxing district official responsible for appraisal and assessment of taxable properties within that district.

asset: 1. Any owned item that can be converted into cash. In the widest sense, anything of value. **2.** In accounting, any source of wealth that can produce future value for its owner, including both intangible and tangible items, such as real property and cash.

asset value: The per-share value of an investment company, arrived at by dividing book value by the number of shares outstanding.

assignee: One to whom legal rights belonging to a contracting party have been transferred, as in the transfer of rights to collect a debt or receive purchased property.

assignment: The act of transferring to a third party legal rights belonging to one who is party to a contract, the transfer in all respects taking on the character of a contract superseding the previous contract between the original parties. In real estate, leases and contracts are usually assignable unless specifically prohibited by the existing lease or contract; in practice, however, many such assignments are barred.

assignor: One who possesses legal rights arising from a contract and transfers those rights to some other party. The assignor may be a party to the original contract or a previous assignee who is transferring the rights once again.

association: 1. Any group of persons joining together for a common purpose. **2.** An unincorporated organization, functioning much like a corporation, but without a corporate charter or the protections and obligations afforded corporations under the general corporation law.

assumption: The taking over of an existing obligation by a new obligor, as when a new property owner takes over existing contracts and mortgages relating to the newly acquired property.

assumption fee: See assumption of mortgage.

assumption of mortgage: The taking over of an existing mortgage by a new property owner. Such an assumption often, but not always, requires the consent of the mortgage lender; where such consent is required, the lender may charge an assumption fee to the new owner, and may renegotiate mortgage terms.

at-risk rules: In tax law, statutory limitation on the extent to which losses may be deducted from income; no more may be deducted than was "at risk," the real value of the investment serving as the deduction limit.

at sight: Describing a negotiable instrument, such as a bank draft, on which payment is due immediately on presentation.

at sufferance: A tenancy by one who is holding over a terminated tenancy, without the consent of the landlord, and who may be evicted at any time, or in the time specified by statute, which is usually 30 days.

attachment: A court order authorizing seizure by legal authorities of property belonging to the defendant in a legal action. The seized property may be physically seized and held safe, as with cash, paintings, and other small portable items; may be held in place with a lien against its sale, as with realty; or may be frozen as with a bank account with the defendant unable to draw upon it. If the defendant loses the lawsuit, the attached property may then be used to satisfy damages and expenses.

attest: 1. To affirm, verbally or in writing, the truth of a statement or the existence of a fact. **2.** To witness, and to sign a statement that verifies the signing of a document by another. **3.** To certify that a document copy is genuine; usually done by a court officer licensed to fulfill this function. **4.** To offer a professional opinion supporting stated facts and opinions, as when an accountant verifies a financial statement.

attestation: The formal and written witnessing of a document's signing by another, at the request of the other.

attic: The upper enclosed portion of a building, directly below the roof; it is often but not always wholly or partially finished and usable.

attorney in fact: A status conferred by the signing of a valid power of attorney, by which one empowers another to act as his or her attorney for purposes specified in the document.

attorney of record: That attorney on record, in the documents relating to a specific case, as representing a party in that case, and to whom service of process and other communications are to be directed.

attornment: An explicit acknowledgment by an existing tenant of leasehold obligations to a new owner; such a statement of obligations has been rendered unnecessary by statute in most states, the old lease automatically transferring to the new owner.

attractive nuisance: In law, a set of circumstances that may be attractive and dangerous to young children, obliging the creator of those circumstances to take reasonable precautions to protect children from resulting danger; for example, a property owner is obliged to safely cover an old well near a public right of way on which children walk to school.

auction: Any sale to two or more potential buyers in which those buyers bid against each other, with whatever is being sold going to the highest bidder. Property at auction is often described as being "on the block."

auctioneer: One who conducts an auction, offering goods for sale, taking bids, and ultimately selling to the highest bidder.

audit: To examine and substantiate the accuracy, completeness, and internal consistency of books of account and the transactions recorded in them by one professionally qualified to do so. Also refers to the examination and substantiation process.

audit trail: In accounting records and computer systems, references from entries back to the source materials from which the entries were generated; used in a wide variety of applications, including tax examinations.

avails: See net avails.

average: 1. An arithmetic mean, found by adding two or more items and dividing their sum by the number of items. **2.** Any number expressing the center or typifying a set of numbers of which it is part, such as a median, weighted average, or moving average.

award: To make a judgment in favor of a party or parties. Examples include a sum given to one party in a dispute involving a construction contract; damages given a plaintiff by judge or jury; or the giving of a job to the lowest of several bidders. Also the judgment, sum, or job so given.

B

baby bond: A bond originally valued at less than $1,000, sometimes at as little as $10; calculated by issuers to appeal to very small investors. These bonds are not routinely accepted for sale or as collateral by banks and brokers, requiring specific agreement to handle.

backdate: To date a document earlier than its actual date of execution; for example, to date contributions as if they were given on December 31 of one year, rather than on January 2 of the next year, in an attempt to evade timely income tax payments on the money given.

back end income: See negative shelter.

backfill: Material used to replace excavated material; for example, earth and gravel used to fill in the remaining excavation after a foundation has been built.

backing: Material attached to and supporting facing material, such as masonry behind facing brick or rough wood behind finished panelling.

back taxes: Taxes previously due, and now overdue and unpaid; for example, property taxes due which may ultimately result in forced sale by government to satisfy those taxes.

back-to-back: In real estate, describing a set of connected transactions, in which the taking over of a partial obligation is made part of the new obligation. For example, a back-to-back lease involves the lessor's assumption of a lessee's existing lease, usually as an inducement to sign a new lease in a different location; or a back-to-back financing arrangement may involve any of several means of connecting the sale of an existing property to the purchase of a new property.

backup offer: A second or subsequent offer to buy, knowingly made after another offer has been made and accepted by a seller, which is to become a firm and current offer if the prior sale falls through.

bad faith: Intent to deceive or defraud, usually in relation to a contract; often applied to the state of mind of one committing a willful breach of contract, beyond honest mistake or simple negligence.

bad title: Title that is so defective or otherwise encumbered that it cannot be transferred.

bailee: One who holds property for another, and returns that property after specified purposes are accomplished, such as a freight shipper, broker, or bank.

bailment: The delivery of property to be held in trust by one for another, and the creation of an express or implied contractual relationship between owner and bailee, in such areas as banking, transporting, warehousing, and rental-purchase agreements.

bailor: One who entrusts property to another for the accomplishment of specific purposes, and to whom that property is to be returned after those purposes are accomplished.

balance: 1. The plus or minus total in an account after all debits and credits have been added and subtracted within that account. **2.** The amount needed to equalize credits and debits in an account. **3.** To equalize credits and debits in an account.

balance due: That sum still due and unpaid on a debt obligation; usually an installment debt obligation or one on which a partial payment has been made, to be followed by full payment.

balance sheet: A financial statement, indicating the financial condition of a business or other organization as of a specific time, including all assets, liabilities, and ownership equities. Balance sheets vary in size and the amount of detail included, from the closely detailed statements of some small businesses to the summary statements of major corporations.

balcony: 1. A platform attached to and projecting from an upper floor of a building; usually has a railing or some other protective device, and sometimes is fully roofed and enclosed. **2.** An upper seating area in a theatre, projecting over the main floor; theatres may have several balconies.

balloon: 1. A kind of payment, occurring at the end of a period of debt obligation, which is larger than previous periodic payments; for example, a personal or mortgage loan arrangement in which periodic payments account for 50% of repayment due over a period of years, with the final 50%—the balloon—due in one payment at the end of the period. A balloon mortgage is a standard mortgage form, and was much used in the United States until the advent of the Great Depression of the 1930's, then to be superseded by the fixed-term mortgage characteristic of the next 50 years. **2.** In finance, a far overpriced item of value, such as a security, market, or company; usually so much overpriced in relation to its underlying values that some form of manipulation is suspected.

bank: 1. Any organization lending, handling, holding, investing, or otherwise servicing money and other instruments of and claims to value; includes commercial, savings, mortgage, and investment banks, savings and loan associations, trust companies, credit unions, and government banks of several kinds. **2.** To place money or other instruments of value in the hands of a banking organization for saving or holding purposes.

bank account: Money deposited in a bank for saving or holding. In a checking account the money is payable on demand; in a savings account, payable on notice to the bank of intent to withdraw funds, a requirement that is generally waived by the bank; in a time deposit, sometimes called a long term savings account, payable at a stated time after deposit has been made.

bank check: A check by a bank drawn on itself; usually used by bank customers as a means of cashless payment or in transferring funds.

bank draft: A check to a specific payee drawn by a bank on its own funds on deposit with another bank. For example, a bill rendered in Swiss francs to an American may be paid by a bank draft purchased in the United States by the American, sent to Switzerland, and cashed there with a correspondent bank of the American bank that issued the bank draft.

banker's acceptance: A negotiable time draft or bill of exchange traded in money markets. These instruments usually originate in international trade, resulting from export or import transactions in which a bank accepts an obligation to pay the seller if the buyer defaults; they also originate in domestic shipping transactions and in the storage of staples in the United States and abroad.

bank failure: The temporary or permanent closing of a bank because it is unable to meet the withdrawal demands of its depositors; such failures may be "hidden," when the failing bank is taken over by another bank that is able to meet depositors' demands. After the widespread bank failures following the stock market crash of 1929, a combination of regulation and Federal deposit insurance has served to minimize depositor losses from bank failure.

bank holding company: Any company owning a controlling interest in one or more banks. Such companies are regulated by applicable Federal laws; they may and often do engage in non-banking activities under conditions specified by law and the regulating authorities.

bank money order: A money order sold by banks, usually for a somewhat smaller fee than a postal money order. It is a kind of cashier's check, and a negotiable instrument that may be signed by many successive endorsers.

bankrupt: Describing a corporation or individual who has been declared to be in a state of bankruptcy by court proceeding. Often used more loosely to describe a person or firm that is insolvent, whether or not so declared by the courts; used even more generally, it describes something of no further value, such as a bankrupt policy.

bankruptcy: The condition of a debtor who has been declared insolvent by court proceeding, and whose financial affairs are being administered by the court through a receiver or trustee. Bankruptcy may be voluntary, when applied for and granted to an insolvent debtor by the court, or may be involuntary, when petitioned for by creditors and granted by the court. Businesses and individuals going into voluntary bankruptcy often use the court as a shield against their creditors while they attempt to solve their financial difficulties.

bankruptcy clause: A widely used contractual provision allowing a party to terminate a contract if another party to the contract becomes legally bankrupt; encountered in many sales, rental, and loan contracts in real estate.

Banks for Cooperatives: A Federal lending agency established by the Farm Credit Act of 1933, consisting of a central bank and twelve district banks that loan money to farm cooperatives.

bar: All those who are licensed to practice law; originally referring to that portion of the courtroom in which an action at law physically took place, which was literally separated by a bar from that portion occupied by the general public.

bargain: 1. A contract or agreement, as in "to strike a bargain." **2.** To negotiate a contract or agreement. **3.** Anything bought or sold at a price significantly below what it would normally command in its market.

bargain and sale deed: A document of sale conveying whatever title is possessed in real property by the seller to the buyer, while not guaranteeing clear title; a form sometimes used by those possessing, but not holding title to, property they hold by force of law, such as court officers and fiduciaries. The form can also be used to convey personal property.

bargain counter: A market in which a wide range of properties are for sale at prices considerably below what professionals in the field think is their fair market value.

bargain hunter: 1. A buyer who looks and waits for bargain counter properties, and then buys as low as is considered possible. **2.** Anyone searching for a bargain in any market.

bargaining power: The relative strengths and weaknesses of parties in any bargaining situation, such as the buyer and seller in a real estate transaction. For example, when a buyer and seller are bargaining over a parcel of land to complete assemblage of a plot for an office building or shopping center, and both know the parcel is crucial to the buyer, the seller's bargaining power is large, and the buyer's bargaining power is small.

barn: A spacious outbuilding, used for a wide variety of productive purposes, including storage and shelter.

baroque: Elaborately ornamented; from the European period 1550–1700, but now more generally describing any structure thought to be highly ornamented, and sometimes used as synonymous with over-ornamented.

base: 1. The lowest load-bearing portion of a construction, such as a column or wall. **2.** The primary ingredient in a substance, such as rubber in a "rubber-based" paint.

baseboard: A strip of wood or other protective material running across the bottom of a wall and touching the floor.

baseboard heating: A heating mode in which the heat is conveyed into a room through units placed at the joinder of walls and floors, replacing the baseboards that would otherwise be placed there.

base fee: See fee simple conditional.

base line: Any line serving as a starting point for measurement; for example, a line used as a starting point for the development of a structure, or the line used as starting point for measuring a road.

base map: A map containing some drawings and often some information, upon which other drawings and information are then placed; for example, a county map from which many maps, serving different purposes, can be developed.

base period: The time period chosen to serve as a yardstick for measuring changes, such as a year chosen to serve as the basis for an escalator clause in a rental agreement. For example, choosing 1980 as such a base year would mean that 1980 would be set at a given value, such as 100; if costs being measured rose 10% in 1981 in relation to 1980 costs, the 1981 index would be 110, and rentals would be raised as specified by contract.

base rent: A minimum rent, in rental agreements providing that rentals will vary as stated variables change; for example, as the lessee's gross sales fluctuate, or the lessor's costs rise.

basic cost: See basis.

basis: **1.** In Federal tax law, the cost of property to a taxpayer plus improvements and minus depreciation, providing in final or adjusted form the main figure to be deducted from the selling price to arrive at the taxable gain on sale of the property. **2.** For purposes of computing depreciation, the cost of property plus improvements. **3.** The rate of interest paid on bonds and other debt securities; also the current annual rate of return on stocks, expressed as the relation of current dividends to current market prices.

basis point: One hundredth of one percent; used to express changes in interest rates and in the yields of stocks and bonds, which often change only slightly, and must be expressed in fractions of a percent.

basket loans: A miscellany of kinds of loans not normally permitted by law to be made by lending institutions, but which some state laws allow, up to a small percentage of all loans outstanding; for example, some kinds of second mortgage loans.

batten: Strips of material used to cover construction joints, mainly for cosmetic purposes.

bay: 1. Any space between walls or columns in a building; for example, an unfinished building area into which may be built several rooms, or an open compartment in an outbuilding such as a barn. **2.** A body of water partly surrounded by land, opening out into a larger body of water, such as an ocean, lake, or river.

bay window: A window or group of windows projecting outward from a building wall; usually curved, and creating a baylike effect when seen from inside the building.

beach: That portion of a shore lying between the high and low water marks; more commonly used to describe any body of shoreline consisting mainly of sand and gravel.

beam: A large structural component, usually of wood, steel, or stone, and load-bearing, although some beams serve aesthetic rather than functional purposes.

bearer: One who has physical possession of negotiable instruments, such as notes, bills, and bonds. If such instruments are payable to their bearer, that is if ownership is transferred by a mere change of physical possession, then the bearer is in law the owner of those negotiable instruments. For other types of instruments, the bearer is not necessarily the owner at law.

bearer bond: A bond payable to its bearer, carrying coupons that are clipped and presented to the bond issuer for interest payments. A bearer bond can be transferred without endorsement, by simple transfer of physical possession.

bearing wall: A wall supporting part of a structure's weight, as distinguished from a wall serving only as a partitioning device; sometimes called a load-bearing wall.

Beaux-Arts Classicism: An architectural style used in many public buildings, such as libraries, theaters, and bank branches, of the early part of the 20th century; characterized by a domed central section and classical ornamentation.

bed: A body serving to contain and support other bodies. Examples include a river bed, over which the river's water flows; a bed of sand, into which slates are placed to form a walk; or a bed of concrete, into which are placed load-bearing steel supporting beams.

bedrock: A formation of solid rock, capable of supporting heavy loads, such as buildings and bridge supports; may be found at surface or subsurface levels.

bedroom community: A community possessing little or no commerce and industry of its own, from which most of those employed commute to jobs in other communities; often a residential suburb of a city.

below the line: 1. Unusual items, such as major one-time costs and revenues, which are shown separately on accounting statements; such items are described as *below the line,* while customary items are *above the line.* **2.** In marketing, sales promotion costs other than advertising are *below the line,* while advertising is *above the line.*

bench: The judiciary; originally that portion of the courtroom occupied by judges.

benchmark: A reference point, from which calculations and predictions stem, such as a permanent boundary or elevation marker, or a major court decision which provides a basis for evaluating probable future court decisions on closely equivalent matters.

beneficial interest: Benefits stemming from an interest in an estate not involving control or ownership, such as the interest of one left a legacy under the terms of a will.

beneficial use: The legal right to benefit stemming from the use and enjoyment of property, for pleasure or profit, going beyond the right to occupy or possess that property, and including enjoyment of light and air and the right to access.

beneficiary: One who is legally entitled to benefit from a will, trust, insurance policy, or contract. A beneficiary may benefit from property legally held by another, as in many trusts, or may hold ownership of the property, as in a lump sum payment of all proceeds of a life insurance policy to survivors.

benefit of bargain rule: The legal rule allowing a purchaser who has been defrauded to collect damages larger than those actually suffered, up to the difference between the real and represented values of the property sold.

bequest: A gift of personal property conveyed by the terms of a will; in contrast, a willed gift of real property is called a devise.

Better Business Bureau: A private organization sponsored by business owners to foster ethical business practices among its members and in the entire business community; in many communities, a major handler and source of adjustment of consumer complaints directed against local businesses.

betterment: Spending that increases the value of a fixed asset in terms of operating efficiencies and useful life, rather than spending that maintains a fixed asset at present levels. Minor repair of an existing roof is simply maintenance; a new roof that substantially adds to the value of the building is betterment; similarly, replacement of an old gravel driveway with a new asphalt driveway is betterment.

bias: 1. A tendency to select and interpret data based on preconceived conclusions. **2.** Systematic error in a statistical test, usually resulting from invalid selection of test groups. **3.** A synonym for discrimination.

bid: 1. An offer to buy immediately at a specific price; for example, to buy a property for sale at an auction. **2.** A formal quotation of the price a seller will require to do a job for a potential purchaser; often part of a formal private or public procedure in which contractors competitively submit prices and specifications.

big ticket: In selling, a colloquial description of a high priced item or a large sale.

bilateral contract: A two-party contract, in which both parties are required to perform promised acts; for example, a sale of real property, in which the seller delivers title to the buyer, and the buyer delivers money to the seller.

bill: 1. A written, formal statement of specifics. Two of the many kinds of bills important in commerce are the bill of exchange and bill of sale. **2.** A list of charges, as in an invoice for goods and services. **3.** A piece of paper money, such as a dollar bill.

bill of exchange: A written, unconditional order from one party instructing a second party to pay a specific amount of money to a third party. The order may be to pay on demand or at a specified future time.

bill of sale: A document signed by a seller passing title to personal property sold; usually a receipt for money paid by the buyer.

binder: 1. A written agreement between a buyer and seller, evidencing their intention to go to contract on the sale of real property; usually accompanied by a relatively small "good faith" or "earnest money" payment. **2.** An interim agreement, oral or written, between an insurance company or its authorized agent and the insured, setting up an interim insurance policy and providing coverage; its extension is subject to full acceptance by the insurer on terms indicated by the insurer's formal documents.

binder agreement: See memorandum of agreement.

bird dog: A real estate seller who functions primarily as a scout, finding properties for sale and then turning over selling activities to other sellers.

blank check: 1. A check signed by its maker but with key information, such as payee or amount, omitted. **2.** A colloquial expression of the delegation of virtually unlimited responsibility or agency to another, as in "He has a blank check" to do something.

blanket bond: See fidelity bond.

blanket insurance policy: An insurance policy covering a group of related items, rather than a single item. Buildings and their contents are often covered by blanket policies, as are such related items as a fleet of company cars.

blanket mortgage: A mortgage loan secured by more than one property, and which encumbers all properties so mortgaged. The mortgagees must pay bank the entire amount of the mortgage before any of the properties are mortgage-free.

blighted area: An area in seriously deteriorated condition, usually, but not always, a city slum area, in which the conditions of life are difficult, the physical condition of much of the housing stock is very bad and worsening, and real estate is worth very little and is almost impossible to sell at any price; often characterized by the flight of its realty owners, who in many instances abandon buildings and let them pass to municipal ownership for nonpayment of taxes.

blind pool partnership: In real estate investment, a limited partnership in which none of the assets to be acquired by the partnership are known to the investor at the time of purchase of the limited partnership interest.

BLM: See Bureau of Land Management.

blockbusting: The creation of an atmosphere of fear and hysteria in a community by real estate speculators, aiming to force homeowners of a certain race or group to sell at low prices, followed by quick resale at inflated prices to homeowners of another race or group; most commonly employed to dislodge white homeowners and victimize black homeowners.

blue laws: Laws prohibiting some kinds of activities on Sundays, including restrictions on the kinds of businesses allowed to open, the hours of operation, and the kinds of goods that can be sold.

blueprint: **1.** A detailed plan of any kind. **2.** A reproduction of a set of detailed architectural or other construction plans, in the form of white print and lines on a blue background.

blue sky: Statements unsupported by facts or contrary to facts, and made with intent to deceive or defraud; "that has a lot of blue sky in it" is a common reaction to what is perceived as an over-imaginative sales approach.

Blue Sky laws: State securities laws aimed at the regulation of many aspects of securities industry practice and procedure, from the issuance of new securities to day-to-day procedures in the industry, with particular attention to questions of fraud and deceptive practices; real estate securities and syndications are regulated under these laws, as well as under applicable Federal laws.

board foot: A piece of lumber one foot long; a standard measure of lumber length. For example, a piece of lumber four feet long is four board feet long, whatever its other dimensions.

boarding house: A residence offering lodging and meals to others for a fee; once a very widely used kind of modest residential hotel, but now less frequently encountered.

board of directors: A group elected by a corporation's stockholders as the chief policymaking body of the corporation. The board of directors is responsible to the stockholders for the overall direction and control of the corporation and usually selects all major corporate officers.

board of equalization: See equalization.

board of trade: An organization composed of member businesses, usually in a geographical area, which promotes group business and community interests.

boiler plate: A popular term for all standard clauses in legal documents, such as contracts and wills; sometimes used more loosely to describe any conventional often-encountered body of language.

boiler room: Any firm that uses high pressure selling tactics deceptively and often fraudulently to sell such investments as land and securities. Sales are usually made by phone out of minimally equipped offices, using techniques that are specifically prohibited by the securities laws.

bona fide: 1. In good faith; applies to one who contracts, holds, buys, or sells, innocent of any knowledge or intent that could be construed as bad faith or fraudulent intent. **2.** A popular term for guarantees of good faith, as when one party to an agreement wants to see the other party's "bona fides" before proceeding to agreement.

bond: 1. An interest-bearing debt instrument issued by a government or a corporation, which promises to pay specific sums at named times, with interest paid in installments and principal paid in a lump sum. **2.** An instrument pledging one as surety for another, as when a bonding company issues a surety bond to cover work to be performed by a contractor, or a bail bondsman issues a bond pledging payment of bail set in a criminal proceeding. **3.** Any stipulated amount that must be paid by a specified date. **4.** Describing taxable goods held pending payment of taxes or duties; such goods are described as being held "in bond."

bond circular: An advertisement offering bonds for sale, which fully describes the nature of the bonds being offered and any conditions attached to the offer; usually placed by banks, bond brokers, and bond underwriting syndicates.

bond discount: The difference between the face amount of a bond, or kind of bond, and any lower price at which it is actually sold.

bond dividend: A dividend issued by a corporation to its stockholders in the form of corporate bonds.

bonded debt: The amount of debt in the form of bonds being carried by an entity, as indicated by the total amount of bonds outstanding.

bonded warehouse: A government-licensed warehouse that holds taxable goods pending payment of customs duties and other taxes due.

bond fund: 1. A mutual fund specializing in bond trading. **2.** A special fund set up by government to handle the proceeds of a bond issue.

bondholder: The owner of a bond and therefore the one to whom payment is owed. Ownership is evidenced by either the simple holding of bearer bonds or being the named owner of registered bonds.

bonding company: A company in the business of providing surety bonds.

bond market: A general term for all markets in which bonds are traded, including both stock exchanges listing bonds traded on those exchanges and the major over-the-counter transactions occurring between institutions.

bond premium: The difference between the face amount of a bond, or kind of bond, and any higher price at which it is actually sold.

bond ratings: Evaluation systems established by private companies to assess the investment quality or relative risk of bonds offered for sale. Moody's and Standard and Poor's are the two main bond risk evaluators. The Moody's system rates on a scale from Aaa to C; the Standard and Poor's scale runs from AAA to D.

bonus: 1. Anything freely given over and above what is due under the terms of a contractual relationship, as in a Christmas bonus given to employees, or the leaving of tools or furniture free by a seller for a buyer in a home sale. **2.** In real estate loan agreements, sometimes used to describe premium payments, the addition of a fixed sum to be paid by one party to another on top of normal contract terms. For example, a lender in a tight money market may add a "point" to a mortgage loan, forcing the borrower to pay one extra percent of the entire amount loaned, payable immediately upon execution of the loan agreement.

book: 1. To enter a transaction into a book of account. 2. A shorthand term for book value.

book cost: See book value.

book depreciation: The amount of depreciation showing on the books of an asset's owner, up to a specified date; may be straight line or any of the several varieties of accelerated depreciation, and often will be different from the mode of depreciation chosen for tax purposes.

bookkeeper: One who handles a business' books of accounts on a day-to-day basis, short of broader accounting responsibility, such as preparing summary financial statements.

bookkeeping: The handling of all or part of a business' books of account, but stopping short of such accounting responsibilities as preparing summary financial statements and designing accounting systems. In practice, many bookkeeping and accounting functions are often difficult to separate.

book of account: Any record that is part of an accounting system, including both transaction records in permanent form and supporting papers, such as memoranda and invoices.

book of original entry: Any journal or other record of the day-to-day transactions of a business, kept in permanent form and serving as a source of entries into an accounting system.

book value: 1. The net assets of a business, derived by subtracting all liabilities from all assets. The book value of a share of common stock consists of net assets minus the value of all preferred stock outstanding divided by the number of shares of common stock outstanding. 2. The net value of an asset, or a kind of asset, as carried on the books of accounts of a business entity, such as the book value of a company car; also called carrying value.

boot: An additional compensation given to balance a trade; in real estate taxation, money or property beyond the properties involved in an otherwise tax-free exchange or reorganization of like properties. Taxing authorities may construe some or all of the proceeds of such additional payments to overbalance the trade in favor of the party receiving them, and may treat the overbalancing amount as taxable gain on the transaction.

borough: A subdivision of a municipality, sometimes providing some aspects of communal service to its residents.

borrowing: The process of getting a loan from others with a promise to repay, usually within a certain period at a specified rate of interest.

borrowing power: The extent to which a borrower may secure loans; always an estimate, and one that changes depending upon factors beyond the power of the borrower to control.

bottom land: Land located in a fertile valley, usually one created by and currently containing a waterway.

bottom line: The net of profit or loss; use of the term has expanded to include any result thought to be final, or to refer generally to the financial result of any endeavor, whether or not it is subject to accounting procedures. It is sometimes used as synonymous with "ultimate result."

boundary: The place where two properties meet, along which a line can be drawn.

breach of contract: Failure by a contracting party to do or allow to be done something that is required by the terms of the contract; or clear renunciation of the contract before it goes into effect. Such failure or renunciation can lead to invalidation of the contract and to the assessment of damages; called breach of covenant when the contract is in the form of a covenant.

breach of covenant: See breach of contract.

break even: To conclude any commercial transaction with neither profit or loss; often used narrowly, to describe only the money factors in the transaction, failing to take into account many very real costs, such as overhead.

breezeway: A covered passageway between two related buildings, such as a house and a garage, which is open to the outdoors on any two of its sides.

brick: A building block of baked clay containing small quantities of iron. The iron causes the baked brick to be red; other substances can be used as pigments to produce brick of different colors.

bridge: A structure built over a ravine, stream, or other depression or watercourse, facilitating passage.

bridge financing: See gap financing.

bridging: Wood or metal strips used to brace floor joists, thus spreading the impact of weight placed on the joists.

brief: A written document submitted to a court on a pending matter and serving as a basis for argument to be presented to the court on that matter.

British Thermal Unit (BTU): A standard measure of heat quantity which is the amount of heat needed to raise the temperature of one pound of water by one degree on the Fahrenheit scale, starting at approximately 39.2 degrees Fahrenheit; used in measuring and designating air conditioning and heating system capacities.

broadside: A piece of advertising matter, consisting of a single sheet of paper that contains the entire advertising message. The sheet of paper is often, but not always, folded down to a smaller size for ease of distribution.

brochure: A booklet devoted to advertising matter, often illustrated, printed on expensive paper, and using a good deal of display type.

50 broker

Brochures vary widely in size and style, ranging from a small, folded broadside to a substantial booklet virtually indistinguishable from a small book.

broker: One engaged in the business of bringing buyers and sellers together for a fee, who acts as a limited agent for purposes of purchase or sale. A broker acts in another's name, as distinguished from commission merchants or factors, who act in their own names, buying and selling goods belonging to others. A broker is an agent, as distinguished from a middleman, who brings parties together, but not as agent for any of them. There are many kinds of specialist brokers, including stock, insurance, real estate, commodities, ship, money, and mortgage brokers.

brokerage: 1. Fees to brokers for transactions arranged between buyers and sellers; such fees may take many forms, including percentage commissions, fixed fees per transaction, and a wide variety of special arrangements in specific situations. **2.** A business run by a broker or brokers.

brokerage commission: Compensation received by a broker for services rendered; in real estate, including compensation for such services as listing, selling, renting as agent, and handling such transactions as mortgage loan placements.

broker-dealer: See dealer.

broker's insurance: Business insurance against liabilities arising from the agency relationship between broker and client, such as negligent handling of property or contracts.

broom clean: Describing the state in which leased or sold premises are to be left by lessor or seller, and literally meaning swept and clear of accumulations.

brownstone: A house faced with brownish sandstone; usually part of a row of like houses built near the turn of the twentieth century in a major American city. New York City, for example, has thousands of such row houses, which are highly prized for their basic soundness of construction and spaciousness.

BTU: See British Thermal Unit.

budget: 1. Any formal estimate of future income and costs. A budget is a primary financial planning tool for public and private purposes. The operating budget, usually prepared from year to year, functions as both a forecasting device and a performance yardstick; the capital budget functions to forecast expenses and consequent capital needs. **2.** To estimate future income and to attempt to establish a spending plan that conforms with income estimates.

budgeting: The formal process of developing a budget. In business organizations, budget development is often a process involving a series of formal estimates made by every responsible member of management, the working of those estimates into coherent company-wide forecasts, a series of refining and reworking steps, and ultimately the production of the budget as a primary working took for all of management.

budget period: The time covered by a budget. Operating budgets are normally developed on an annual basis, with results stated monthly and the budget reviewed quarterly, annually, or at any time variances from forecasts cause management to undertake a special review. The period of a capital budget varies with the projects budgeted.

buffer zone: A strip of land separating two developed properties, usually left wholly or mainly undeveloped; commonly used to separate two incompatibly used properties and often set aside by agreement between a developer and local zoning officials.

buildable area: The land area actually available for building upon, after subtracting green space, setbacks, access, and other such areas required by law to be set aside.

builder: One professionally engaged in the construction of buildings, taking as his or her province the entire building enterprise, rather than a single aspect of that enterprise. An architect or general contractor may also from time to time control an entire building enterprise, and be, in that instance, a builder. More generally, sometimes used to refer to anyone involved in construction.

builder's risk insurance: Interim insurance purchased by a builder, and covering fire and other risks intrinsic to building construction; the amount insured increases as the value of the building grows.

building: In law, a structure built by humans, of durable materials, and intended for some kind of human use or convenience. The structure may be enclosed and have a roof, but need not have either to be considered a building; a wide variety of structures may be considered buildings, depending upon the context in which they are being considered. In common use, an enclosed permanent structure.

building and loan association: An early form of and name for what has become the savings and loan association. As early "building associations" began to focus more and more on the savings function, the general name for this kind of banking organization changed as well.

building block: A cube of any material used in construction, such as brick or adobe.

building codes: A set of local laws and regulations controlling all substantial construction activities within each jurisdiction. Building codes cover most kinds of new construction, modifications of existing construction, and associated activities, such as service roads and water supply, and often require the filing of specifications and the granting of official approval for even relatively small modifications. Different codes regulate the several kinds of construction and construction-related activities and hazards, such as those involving electricity, fire, and water supply.

building line: The actual construction boundary on a property, beyond which no construction may by law and regulation be built.

building loan: See construction loan.

building permit: An authorization granted by local authorities to a builder to pursue construction activities; usually necessary before any such activities may begin, and dependent upon satisfying those authorities that planned construction will meet all local zoning, land use, and building code requirements.

building society: See building and loan association.

building standards: The work standards used in a construction by its builder, or in maintenance and alteration by its owner, such as the kinds and grades of materials to be used in the construction of internal partitions and in electrical fixtures.

building trades: The series of skilled trades represented in the construction industry, including such trades as bricklaying, carpentry, plumbing, and structural steelwork.

build-to-suit: A lease in which the owner agrees to customize the premises to be leased as specified in the lease; usually part of a long term lease.

built-ins: Items which under some circumstances might be movable personal property, such as bookcases, appliances, and furniture, but which are attached to or literally built into a structure; such items are considered part of that structure, their title passing on sale of the structure.

bulkhead: 1. A retaining wall along a waterfront. **2.** A cover over a vertical shaft within a structure, such as an airshaft, stairwell, or elevator shaft.

bulk sale: 1. The sale of any large, unpackaged quantity of goods. **2.** The sale of most or all of the assets or stock of a business, to avoid creditors or as part of a bankruptcy proceeding. Such sales to avoid creditors are prohibited by law.

Bulk Sales Act: A kind of statute aimed at the prohibition of secret bulk sales of assets or stocks by businesses to avoid the claims of creditors.

bulk zoning: See zoning.

bundle of rights: All those rights incident to ownership of real property; in practice, used as synonymous with ownership.

bungalow: A small one or one-and-a-half story residence.

Bureau of Land Management (BLM): An administrative agency of the Federal Government, part of the Department of Interior, which is responsible for administration of those Federal lands outside the national park and forest system.

business: 1. Any gainful activity. The gain sought is generally commercial or financial, but the term is so broad that it includes activities engaged in for personal development and emotional gain. **2.** An organization engaged in any form of commerce. **3.** An amount of trade engaged in, as in "Total business for the day was $1,000."

business day: Any day other than Saturdays, Sundays, and holidays; of significance in construing time periods set in such contracts as leases and loans agreements, as the question of default is affected by the meaning of the term.

business ethics: An attempt to apply the highest ethical standards of the larger community to the business community; business ethics are in no way different from any other ethical conception, and constructs in this area vary as widely as they do in the larger community.

business failure: A firm that ceases doing business primarily because of inability to meet its obligations. Failure may be involuntary, as in foreclosures, assignments, and attachments; or it may be voluntary, as in cessation of business leaving unpaid debts or making an agreement to pay part of creditors' claims.

business firm: An organization doing business for profit and organized as a corporation, partnership, or individual proprietorship.

business insurance: Any kind of insurance taken by a business for business purposes, including such insurance on property and the conduct of business as fire, casualty, theft, credit, and business interruption, as well as such business-related insurance as life, health, and accident.

business interruption insurance: Insurance covering an insured against losses caused by cessation of business, usually in addition to coverage for direct damage to property; for example, a sum paid to the owners of a restaurant for a proportion of profits lost by inability to do business caused by a fire, between the time the fire occurred and the time the restaurant reopened after repairs.

business law: See commercial law.

business risk: For credit and investment purposes, an estimate of the skills and performance of management, of such marketplace factors as relative prices and the strength of competition, and of the over-all conduct of and prospects for the business.

business trust: See Massachusetts trust.

buyer's market: Any market in which supply exceeds demand, giving buyers leverage over sellers in such areas as prices, quality guarantees, and delivery timing.

buying in: A bidding technique in which the bidder makes a lower-than-cost bid to get a job, hoping to secure through that job other, more profitable jobs or to develop billings in excess of estimates during the course of the job.

bylaws: 1. The rules of a corporation, governing the conduct of its own internal affairs and supplementing the articles of incorporation. **2.** Generally, any set of rules adopted by an organization to govern the conduct of its own internal affairs.

bypass: A road skirting a heavily travelled area, such as a city or a town center, and designed to allow through traffic to move past that area more easily.

C

cabinet work: Finely finished carpentry; mainly interior detail and furniture.

caisson: A strongly built, watertight construction, in which construction workers operate, either under water or in conditions made dangerous by the presence of unstable surrounding materials; also called a cofferdam.

calking: See caulking.

call: 1. A natural boundary marker mentioned or described in a survey. **2.** A demand for payment, as when a mortgage or other lender exercises a contractual right to demand acccelerated payment of balances due; or when a seller demands payment of the balance due on the purchase of capital stock.

callable bond: A bond that may be redeemed by its issuer at any time before maturity, usually with a premium payment to the bondholder at the time of redemption. The "callable" feature of the bond is specified by the terms of the issue, often on the face of the bond itself.

call loan: A demand loan, which either lender or borrower may terminate at will and without notice. In the securities industry, it is a standand form of loan from bank to stockbroker, amounting to a special line of credit on which interest is computed daily at that day's rate.

camber: The degree of slight arching built into a structural component, such as a floor or girder; aimed at preventing the development of a sag and consequent concavity.

canal: An artificial waterway, used for irrigation or transportation; often built to connect natural waterways.

cancellation: 1. The legal termination of an instrument or agreement on maturity or completion, such as the termination of an insurance policy pursuant to the terms of the contract, whether before or at the end of the term covered by the contract, or the retirement of a debt instrument upon payment in full. **2.** The termination of an order for good or services, often prior to fulfillment of that order.

cancellation clause: A contract provision allowing termination of the contract by a party, usually under specified circumstances.

cantilever: A projecting structure or structural support that is itself anchored and supported only at one end; two such structures joined at their projecting ends are often used form a cantilever bridge.

cantilever bridge: See cantilever.

canvassing: Searching for sales or listing prospects by means of calls on those who might be prospects; sometimes used as a synonym for selling.

capacity: 1. The legal qualification of one to do a thing, such as make a legally binding contract or collect a loan; for example, one who has been judged mentally incompetent lacks the capacity in law to make a valid contract. **2.** The presumed ability of a loan applicant to repay the amount sought, in the judgment of the lender. **3.** In extractive industries, the amount of material that can be extracted in a given period by present equipment, such as the amount of coal or oil a mine or well can produce in twenty-four hours.

Cape Cod House: A heat-efficient, relatively small, box-like house developed to withstand New England winters; one to two stories high, with steeply pitched roof and often dormers; also called a *salt box*.

capital: 1. Any kind of tangible wealth that is or can be used to produce more wealth. In this sense, money invested to start a business is capital. Intangibles, such as a good reputation of one starting a business, are often loosely called capital, but the term is then stretched so far as to make it lose its useful meaning. **2.** The net worth of a business. **3.** Amounts invested by shareholders in a business, called *paid-in capital*.

capital account: 1. An account or group of accounts indicating ownership equities. They are designated proprietorship, partnership, or capital stock accounts, depending on the business' form of organization. **2.** Any fixed asset account.

capital asset: Any asset held and used for the production of goods and services, including fixed assets, such as land, plant, raw materials sources, and reserves; investments in owned and affiliated companies; and some long term intangibles, such as patents.

capital budget: A budget or part of a budget which handles the acquiring and financing of capital assets. Capital budgets may be developed by private organizations or governments; may be short term or long term; and may be financed out of current revenues or debt instruments or both.

capital coefficient: The amount of new capital investment needed to produce one new unit of output capacity. The figure can be derived for a whole economy or any portion of an economy, and it varies widely from enterprise to enterprise and industry to industry.

capital expenditure 1. An expenditure to acquire capital assets. **2.** In accounting, an expenditure which wholly or mainly benefits future accounting periods rather than the current period.

capital flow: The movement of funds in and out of an enterprise, as recorded in a cash flow statement.

capital gains: The profits realized from a sale or exchange of capital assets, usually realty or securities. Long term capital gains are given preferred treatment for tax purposes, since they are taxed at substantially lower rates than short term gains, which are treated as ordinary income for income tax purposes.

capital goods: Capital in the form of fixed assets used to produce goods, such as plant, equipment, and rolling stock. The term is used to describe the assets themselves, rather than the amount or kinds of funds used to acquire them.

capital improvement: A permanent addition or major repair that adds to the efficiency, anticipated life, or value of a property. For tax purposes, the line between substantial repairs and capital improvements is sometimes a fine one; the tax difference can be significant, as the cost of capital improvements must be deducted over a period of years, while repairs are deductible in the year expenses were incurred.

capital-intensive: Describing any kind of business or economic unit that requires large amounts of capital investments relative to the number of people employed in it. For example, the nuclear industry requires far more investment per employee than the garment industry. The nuclear industry is then described as capital-intensive, while the garment industry is described as the opposite—labor-intensive.

capital investment: See capital expenditure.

capitalization: The total value of a corporation's stocks, bonds, and surpluses. The term includes stocks, normally carried at par rather than market value, and bonds and debentures carried at their face values, but does not include other debts, such as bank loans.

capitalization rate (cap rate): A ratio used in evaluating the worth of property, when using the income approach, in which an assumption is made as to the percentage of yield a property should return, compared with other similar properties in similar circumstances; that percentage is then used to evaluate the total worth of the property. This method is also used in evaluating the worth of a potential investment, in terms of anticipated yield. For example, assuming a yield or anticipated yield of 10%, a yield of $10,000 a year, actual or anticipated, results in an evaluation of $100,000; assumption of a 15% yield results in an evaluation of $150,000.

capitalize: To carry forward capital expenditures for accounting purposes. Investments in the acquisition of capital assets then appear as expenditures in future profit and loss statements, and are associated then with any benefits derived from those assets.

capitalized expense: An expense charged to a capital asset account which would normally be charged to a current account and would appear on the current profit and loss statement; for example, tax and interest payments on a plant being built but not yet in operation.

capitalized value: The current value of assets that will yield future earnings, derived by projecting both anticipated earnings and interest on the money invested as if it had been borrowed forward over the life of the asset.

capital loss: A loss stemming from sale of a capital asset, other than a personal residence, at less than its seller's basis, or adjusted cost for tax purposes.

capital market: The long term debt obligations market, dealing in long term loans and bonds, with the proceeds of the obligations normally used to finance the purchase of capital assets. The distinction between long and short term loan markets tends to blur in modern practice, as most major lending institutions engage in both long and short term financing, with financing "packages" often including loans in several forms and of varying durations.

capital stock: The ownership stock in a business, representing the equity held by its owners. Not all of the capital stock need be distributed; some may be held in the business. Sometimes stock issued and outstanding is bought back, wholly or in part, by a business.

cap rate: See capitalization rate.

carport: A roofed but open-sided structure, functioning as a vehicle shelter, standing free or attached to another structure.

carrot financing: Financial arrangements that include built-in incentives for completion of a construction project ahead of schedule or under budget.

carrybacks: For business income tax purposes, those current operating losses that can be used to offset profits from preceding years, thereby diminishing taxes for those years.

carryforwards: For business income tax purposes, those current operating losses that cannot be absorbed as carrybacks to diminish taxes on income of previous years, but can be used as deductions carrying over and thrown forward into succeeding years.

carrying charge: Any normal and repeated charge stemming from asset ownership, such as interest charged by brokers on margin accounts and charges for warehousing goods.

carrying cost: The cost of holding an asset, such as inventory or equipment, for a given period, including both actual costs, such as maintenance and warehousing, and opportunity costs, such as the interest that might have been earned at current rates on money tied up in inventory and spent in warehousing.

carrying value: See book value.

carryover provision: A clause in a real estate listing contract, providing that the seller will pay a broker commissions on a sale resulting from an introduction to a prospective buyer arranged by the broker; usually requiring physical inspection accompanied by the broker and specifying an extension period, such as 90 days; also called an estender provision. Some such clauses provide automatic renewal of existing listing agreements unless terminated by seller or broker; but such automatic renewals may not be legally enforceable.

carryovers: See carrybacks and carryforwards.

case law: The body of law formed by preceding cases and therefore possessing value as precedents for use in deciding current cases, as distinguished from the body of law formed by laws, regulations, and other sources. In practice, cases, statutes, regulations, and other sources form an intertwined body of law.

casement window: A hinged window that opens outward.

cash: 1. Money in any form that can be directly and immediately used as legal tender, including paper money and coins. **2.** For accounting purposes, anything immediately usable or almost immediately convertible into legal tender, including paper money, coins, checks, net bank balances, and some other negotiable instruments. **3.** To turn a negotiable instrument of any kind into cash, as in cashing a bond.

cash assets: Assets that either are in ready cash form, such as currency and coins on hand, or can be easily turned into cash while continuing business as usual, such as bank deposits and trade acceptances.

cash basis: An accounting method that records and keeps books on the basis of when cash is received and spent, rather than accruing income and expenditures. While most individuals operate on a cash basis, most businesses are on an accrual basis.

cashbook: A book in which cash transactions are recorded.

cash budget: An income and expenditure estimate based solely upon cash receipts and cash spent for a certain period. In a cash budget, nothing is accrued or in any way deferred.

cash equivalent: What something would be worth if immediately converted into cash. The term is normally encountered in a sale or exchange in which items that are paid for in ways other than money are valued by the transacting parties at agreed-upon levels.

cash flow: 1. The movement of cash into, through, and out of an entity. Cash flow may be traced for an individual or an entity, as well as for a single property or product, a line of products, or a group of properties. **2.** The actual cash flowing into or leaving an income-producing real estate property in a given period, composed of net operating income in cash or cash equivalents minus loan interest and principal repayments, and without accounting for depreciation. Such cash flow can be positive (plus) or negative (minus), and is not synonymous with profit or loss for tax or other business statement purposes, which must take other factors into account. It is called pretax cash flow when no allowance is made for cash payments of income tax, and net cash flow when such allowance is made.

cash flow statement: A statement accounting for the movement of cash through an entity during a specific period.

cashier: 1. One who directly handles and records receipts and expenditures for a business. **2.** In banking, an officer in charge of the bank's funds, who is directly responsible for all disbursements and must personally authorize them.

cashier's check: A bank's check, signed by a cashier of the bank, and functioning as a direct obligation of the bank. Cashier's checks are issued for many purposes, including deposit transfers, bill payments, and loans.

cash on delivery (COD): The payment terms of a purchase in which buyer and seller agree that payment will be made in cash immediately upon delivery and acceptance of the goods, with completion of delivery contingent upon cash payment.

cash sale: A sale paid for immediately in cash, either at the point of sale or on delivery, as in most non-credit retail stores. **2.** A sale paid for soon after delivery, often within a specified 30 day period, as in many industrial sales.

casing: An outer covering, such as the outer wall or "skin" of a building.

casualty insurance: A now somewhat outdated term, generally describing all the kinds of insurance other than life, fire, and marine insurance; now covered by multiple line companies, writing all property insurance, including fire and casualty.

catch basin: See cistern.

catwalk: A narrow walkway, usually elevated, used for access to relatively inaccessible areas that are not part of normal traffic patterns.

caulking: The filling of joints or seams to make them watertight; also the material used to fill them.

cause of action: Any set of circumstances recognized by a judicial body as valid for purposes of bringing an action against another at law or equity, whether or not that action will ultimately be successful.

causeway: An elevated roadway over land unusable for a road, such as a swamp, or over relatively shallow water.

caveat emptor: Latin for "let the buyer beware," an underlying theme in commercial transactions of all kinds. This maxim places the burden of prudence on the buyer, except for specific warranties or misrepresentations made by the seller. To some extent, consumer-oriented statutes and court decisions have redistributed burdens in this area, resulting in the creation of a large number of implied warranties binding on sellers, so that caveat emptor now has rather limited significance.

caveat venditor: Latin for "let the seller beware," placing the burden of truthful representation on the seller. Short of specific and willful misrepresentation, caveat emptor has been the far stronger maxim in the marketplace; but recent legislative and judicial trends have created a large number of implied warranties binding upon sellers, which to some extent have changed the balance between caveat venditor and caveat emptor.

CBD: See central business district.

CD: See certificate of deposit.

cease and desist order: An order issued by an administrative body with quasi-legal powers, such as the Federal Trade Commission, demanding that a particular activity be stopped.

ceiling price: The maximum price that may legally be charged on an item covered by government-imposed price controls.

cellar: A subsurface room under a building, used for service mechanisms and storage.

cement: A construction material, consisting of powdered rock, clay, and from time to time other special purpose materials, which when combined with water hardens into a durable, rock-like substance.

cement block: A standard building block formed of molded cement and usually hollow.

cemetery: A burial ground. A single special purpose land use designation; in many jurisdictions tax exempt or otherwise tax advantaged.

central business district (CBD): A prime central city area, in which the main shopping area and other major city functions and assets are located; often the highest business rental price area of the city.

central city: The heart of a major metropolitan area, including the central business district and several surrounding areas, but not necessarily including the entire city that is the core of that metropolitan area.

certificate: A document stating that something has been done or complied with. The document is usually issued by an established public or private institution, such as a government agency or a college, though in the widest sense a "certificate" may be issued by any person or organization for any purpose not specifically covered by existing law.

certificate of beneficial interest: An ownership share in a Massachusetts, or business trust.

certificate of deposit (CD): A receipt for a bank deposit, in certificate rather than passbook form. Time certificates of deposit are payable either on a specific date or after passage of a specific amount of time, can bear interest, and are therefore widely used by companies and institutions as short term investment vehicles. They are also negotiable and widely traded as short term paper in the money market. However, demand certificates of deposit are payable at any time on endorsement and therefore are not available as money market instruments.

certificate of eligibility: A Federal Government certificate, stating that the person named in it is a veteran who is eligible for a Veteran's Administration (VA) mortgage.

certificate of incorporation: A document forming a private corporation signed by the parties so incorporating and filed in the public office of appropriate jurisdiction.

certificate of indebtedness: The short term promissory note of a corporation or institution, unsecured by specific property but generally interpreted as carrying the same obligation as a bond. There is some question about whether it operates as a lien prior to the liens of general creditors or whether it is merely an unsecured promissory note that is no more than equal to the claims of other general creditors.

certificate of insurance: A document issued by an insurer, stating that a specified insurance policy is in effect for a named insured.

certificate of occupancy: An official document certifying that a building is in compliance with applicable ordinances and regulations and may therefore be occupied and otherwise used.

certificate of public convenience and necessity: A license or permit issued by government, authorizing the business operations of utilities, communications companies, transportation companies, and other regulated businesses serving the public.

certificate of purchase: See certificate of sale.

certificate of sale: An official document verifying the purchase of a property by a successful bidder at a sale conducted by a court or governmental body.

certificate of title: A formal opinion issued by a title company or attorney as to the current title status of a property, after study of relevant public title, court, tax, and regulatory records. This opinion does not certify title, which may be flawed for many reasons not on the public record and for defects in the public records themselves; only a title insurance policy accomplishes complete protection.

certified check: A check drawn on a depositor's account which a bank endorses and accepts, usually on the face of the check, after first setting aside enough of the depositor's funds to cover the check. The check then becomes a bank obligation, backed by the full resources of the bank, and short of bank failure will be paid, if properly endorsed, on presentation. Certified checks are widely used as payment in transactions requiring sure immediate payment of large amounts of money and immediate passage of title, as in many securities and real estate transactions.

certified copy: A copy of a document, such as a deed or birth certificate, held by a public official, signed and certified as a copy by that official.

Certified Property Manager (CPM): A professional certification issued by the Institute of Real Estate Management.

certified public accountant (CPA): An accountant holding a state license to practice public accountancy, granted after passing a written examination and other examining procedures. This license is not necessary for the practice of accountancy, but no uncertified person may use the title "certified public accountant" in those states issuing this license.

certiorari: A writ issued by an appellate court, calling for review of the action of a lower court or other lower judicial body, bringing all records of the lower court action into the appellate court; used by an appellate court to force review of a lower court action in place of adjudication of an appeal, when the appellate court is not satisfied that appropriate appeal has been made and wants to review a case fully.

cestui que trust: One who holds a beneficial interest in a trust, but not legal title to that trust, such as a beneficiary who gets money distributed by a trustee.

chain of title: The public and official history of title to real property, as far back as public title records can be traced. Establishing an unbroken chain of title is essential to the enjoyment of clear title by a present owner, as a break in the validity of a chain of ownerships will invalidate all subsequent ownerships, including that of the present owner, and will make it impossible to pass title without court action to clear or "quiet" title.

chain store: A retail store that is part of a group of commonly owned, centrally managed stores, usually having quite a similar look. Some examples of chains are the Woolworth, J.C. Penney, Grand Union, A & P, and Safeway stores.

chalet: An architectural style adapted for areas of heavy snowfall, featuring weather-resistant construction and heavy eaves; originating in the Alps and found now in many mountain and ski resort areas.

chamber of commerce: An organization formed for the stated purpose of promoting the interests of the business community it represents. Chambers of commerce operate in cities, and in regional, state, and national groupings.

change of venue: A change of the location at which a pending legal case is to be tried; for example, the move of a scheduled trial from one Federal district court to another, or from a state court to a Federal court.

change order: A formal instruction from one in charge of construction to a contractor, authorizing changes in an agreed upon contract; often involving a change in pricing as well.

charge off: See write off.

charter: A document issued by government, defining and granting the basic legal rights and obligations of corporations and other private and public organizations. A charter, which is a grant of government, should not be confused with articles of incorporation or association, which are private documents.

charter of accounts: In accounting, a list, classification, and systematized organization of a company's accounts, including names, numbers, and other identifying information.

Chateauesque: See Victorian.

chattel: Any personal property, except for freehold title to real estate, including both movable and fixed items of property. For example, clothing, dogs, automobiles, and real estate leases are chattels, while wholly owned real estate is not.

chattel mortgage: A mortgage loan using chattels, such as vehicles and paintings, as security for the loan. If there is default on repayment of the loan, the chattels become the property of the lender. Chattel mortgages are substantially similar to real estate mortgages.

chattel real: A legal interest in real property, such as a leasehold interest, that is less than that of a freehold, and which therefore is treated as personal property in the law, unless otherwise provided by statute or judicial construction of a will.

check: 1. A draft or order drawn on funds belonging to the drawer and on deposit with a banking organization. Checks are payable on demand. **2.** A twenty-four square mile section, as designated by government survey.

checking account: See bank account.

chimney: A structure containing a passageway or flue for venting smoke from a building's heating and cooking systems, usually elevated above the roof level of the building.

chose: A chattel; a piece of personal property.

chose in action: A personal property right that is not yet physical, but which is recognized at law, and which can be recovered by legal action, such as the right to collect a debt or secure performance of a contract.

churning: In the securities industry, the unethical and sometimes illegal practice of turning over customer accounts faster than necessary for the customer's investment purposes, in order to create brokerage commissions.

cinder block: A building block, usually hollow, containing both cement and cinders as major components.

circumstantial evidence: Indirectly derived evidence, constructed from a consideration of the facts surrounding a case, rather than from direct testimony.

cistern: A container for collecting rain water, especially as runoff from buildings; also called a catch basin.

city planning: See urban planning.

civil action: An action at law involving private rights and wrongs rather than criminal questions. In the widest sense, any action at law that is not a criminal action.

claim: Any demand for payment for any stated legal reason, but most often a demand for payment made by an insured of an insurer under the terms of an insurance policy.

clapboard: Wooden siding on a building in the form of thin strips laid horizontally; one edge of each strip is thicker than the other, and the thicker and thinner edges of pieces are placed in overlapping positions.

class action: An action at law brought by one or more on behalf of a larger number, all alleged by those bringing the class action as being commonly interested and commonly damaged. The class action has been a widely used form of complaint in suits brought against businesses and institutions by such groups as consumers and stockholders.

Classic Revival: See Neoclassic.

clean credit: A letter of credit without significant qualifications placed on the issuing bank's commitment to pay when presented with an undocumented bill drawn on that letter of credit.

clean hands: In law, the equity-derived concept that a party seeking redress or relief must come into court untainted by fraud, dishonesty, or other attitudes or actions that discredit motives as to the matter at issue.

clear: 1. In law, entirely free of any kind of ambiguity, limitation, or encumbrance, as in ownership of a property "free and clear." **2.** To leave a port with all legal necessities completed and in receipt of all appropriate permissions and papers. **3.** To complete a financial transaction, most often as in the collection of a check that has been passed through a bank clearing house.

clear title: 1. To ensure that title to property is clearly in the hands of its owner, and that property can therefore legally be sold to another; involves examining all relevant records and taking any actions necessary to erase any cloud on the title. **2.** Title to property which is legally clear, and which is therefore capable of being legally transferred to another by its present holder.

client: One for whom professional services are performed, usually for a fee: for example, one who hires a lawyer, or one who hires a real estate broker to sell a house.

close corporation: See closely held corporation.

closed end mortgage: A mortgage specifying that no further money can be borrowed on the property being mortgaged. Some bonds carry the same limitation.

closely held corporation: A company that is owned by a small number of people, all or most of whom are directly involved in the conduct of the business, with very little of its stock in the hands of outsiders.

closing: 1. The consummation of a real estate transaction in which buyer and seller exchange purchase price and deed, and title passes; or in which lender and borrower exchange mortgage and loan. At the time of closing, buyer and seller make agreed-upon adjustments and subsidiary sales, including any separate sales of personal property, as well as allowances for proration of taxes, fuel, rent previously received by the seller, utility bills, and any other overlapping charges and credits. **2.** In accounting, the process of closing the books at the end of an accounting period. **3.** In general business usage, making a sale. In real estate, the term is normally reserved for the formal procedure that passes title or loan.

closing adjustments: See closing.

closing costs: Those costs incurred by buyer and seller in a real estate sale or mortgage that are directly attributable to the transaction, including attorney's fees, title clearing and title insurance fees, recording fees, brokerage commissions, transfer taxes, insurance costs, appraisal and inspection reports, and one-time loan fees.

closing date: In accounting, the date the books of account are closed for accounting purposes, and the date of preparation of all financial statements derived from the books of account.

closing entries: In accounting, a series of entries closing the books as of the end of an accounting period, which serve to balance the books and prepare them to be the basis for preparation of the financial statements.

closing statement: A statement outlining all the specifics of a completed real estate transaction, including all costs and prices directly attributable to the transaction, prepared by an attorney, broker, escrow agent, or bank responsible for preparing such a statement in a given jurisdiction and for the specific transaction.

cloud on title: A potential threat to a clear title. Such claims as tax liens, mortgages, and prior judgments may cloud title and must be settled before the title can be conveyed unencumbered.

cluster development: A housing development with more units per built-up acre than allowed by local zoning laws, but with a body of land set aside for communal use; for example, a development in a one-acre-per-residence zone, containing 50 houses on 25 acres, with 25 acres set aside for communal uses. This kind of development is also sometimes used to amend local zoning intentions, as when local authorities and a developer agree on a development netting more units than would otherwise be allowed by local law.

cluster zoning: A zoning law that allows greater housing unit density in a specified area than previously allowed, in return for the developer setting aside land for community purposes; the net effect over a period of years is normally greater housing unit density in the affected area.

coastal zone: The land and water areas on or near an ocean or major inland body of water shoreline, recognized as a national resource by Federal law, and the object of Federal and state environmental protection efforts.

coast and geodetic survey system: See geodetic system.

COD: See cash on delivery.

code: See codification.

code of ethics: A body of standards of ethical behavior adopted by a group for its members, such as that of the National Association of Realtors.®

codicil: An addition to a will, in some way modifying or explaining that will. A codicil may be drawn at any time and must be executed as formally as the will itself.

codification: The compilation of a body of statutes into a system covering a body of law. The resulting body of law is called a code.

cofferdam: See caisson.

cognovit: See confession of judgment.

coinsurance clause: A provision in most property insurance policies dividing the risk between insurer and insured, usually at an 80-20 ratio. The provision comes into play in the event of a partial loss, as when there is a $40,000 loss on the property really worth $50,000, but which has been insured for only $40,000. In that event, the insurance will pay 80% of the $40,000, or $32,000, rather than the $40,000 of actual loss. If the property had been insured for its real value of $50,000, then 80% would have been $40,000, the amount of the loss.

collapsible corporation: A tax avoidance device, in which a corporation is organized to convert ordinary income from business activities into lower-taxed capital gains; in real estate, often the formation of a corporation to engage in construction, which will be liquidated by sale of its stock to others before the project is entirely completed or sold, but after substantial value has been added to the property owned by the construction firm. The shareholders then attempt to treat the gain they received on the sale of their stock as capital gains, rather than ordinary income; however, tax statutes and regulations preclude this treatment.

collateral: Security for a loan, in the form of real or personal property belonging to the borrower which is formally pledged to the lender, and which can become the property of the lender upon default on the loan. Collateral is property of determinable value that can be fairly readily sold and converted into cash, such as securities, real estate, savings account passbooks, and commodities.

collateral assignment: The assignment of property or rights to another to serve as collateral for a financial obligation; for example, the assignment of bonds to secure a mortgage loan, that assignment ending when the loan is fully paid.

collateralize: To provide collateral as security for a loan. A loan is described as "collateralized" when it has been so secured.

collateral loan: A loan secured by collateral, usually applied to a short term loan in which the collateral security is physically held by the creditor.

collateral trust bonds: Bonds secured by other bonds and sometimes stocks of the issuing company. The securing bonds and stocks are placed in trust as collateral for the bonds being issued.

collateral value: The value of assets pledged as collateral for a loan. In setting collateral value, lenders will consider such factors as the collateral's current market value, its stability, and its convertibility into cash.

collusion: A secret agreement by two or more parties to commit fraud or other illegal actions against others.

collusive bidding: Seemingly competitive bidding carried on by two or more bidders which is actually pursuant to a secret agreement between them to commit fraud by attempting to control bidding to their advantage.

Colonial: See New England Colonial, Southern Colonial, Dutch Colonial.

color of title: An appearance of good title which, although supported by documentary evidence, is in fact insufficient to establish good title, because the evidence is flawed, such as an invalid deed or conveyance.

column: 1. A cylindrical supporting shaft, with base and capital, or head. **2.** A vertically arranged body of figures or digits.

co-maker: One who signs a debt instrument with others and is therefore responsible for repayment, often without being in any way a recipient of the money borrowed.

combination door: A door using panels and screens interchangeably, as the seasons change.

combination window: A window using panels and screens interchangeably, as the seasons change.

commerce: Any and all trade and commercial intercourse between individuals, organizations, peoples, and governments. The term is so wide as to be used synonymously with "business" and "trade."

commercial bank: A bank primarily in the business of holding demand deposits and making business loans. Commercial banks have many other functions, however, including a wide variety of consumer loans, trust functions, finance and securities industry service and selling functions, and a large number of services usually described as "full service banking." Commercial banking is the major form of banking in the United States.

Commercial Code: See Uniform Commercial Code.

commercial law: A very wide and imprecise term generally used to describe all matters in the law relating to commerce, trade, and the people and organizations engaged in commercial practices.

commercial paper: 1. All short term, negotiable debt instruments issued by businesses, including all bills, notes, and acceptances arising from the normal conduct of business. **2.** Short term notes issued by large, well-established, and well-regarded businesses, usually in the $100,000 to $1,000,000 range. Such notes are traded in the money markets, rated by private rating organizations as to their degree of investment safety, and often provide short term, relatively low-cost financing to their issuers.

commercial property: Property classified as usable for commercial purposes, and so zoned by local zoning authorities; such property may be used for residential purposes as well.

commingling: The illegal act of mixing one's own personal or business funds with those of a client; illegal whether or not accompanied by misuse of client funds.

commission: A sum paid by a principal to one acting in some sort of representative capacity. Commissions are usually figured as a percentage of the transaction consummated, such as a sale or rental, although some commissions are fixed fees or combinations of fee and percentage. Both independent representatives, such as real estate brokers, and employees, such as salespeople, are often compensated on a commission basis. In real estate, commissions may legally be payable by a seller to a broker or agent even when the sale is not consummated, when failure to consummate has resulted from such acts of the seller as fraudulent misrepresentation, change of mind, inability to deliver, or title defects; but the facts of each case and the laws of each jurisdiction will govern disposition of a broker's claims.

commission agent: An independent businessperson or company, selling goods for another on a commission basis.

commission plan: A sales compensation plan, in which salespeople are wholly or in major part compensated on the basis of a percentage of sales made. Such plans are often tied to other aspects of compensation, such as non-refundable advances against future commissions and base salaries.

commitment: A promise by a lender to loan a specified amount of money to a borrower for a stated period. When that promise is firm, the promise is legally binding from the time it is made until the end of the stated period, subject only to the borrower's meeting stated terms and providing satisfactory documentation. When the promise is conditional, it depends upon the occurrence of other actions, such as approval by the lender of the borrower, based upon credit verification.

commitment fee: An extra charge by lender to borrower for issuance of a loan commitment; often a means of charging very substantial additional fees in "tight" mortgage markets, and sometimes a means of avoiding state usury statutes.

commitment letter: A letter making a loan commitment, sent by lender to borrower, and specifying all the terms and charges involved in the loan offer being made by the lender.

Commodity Credit Corporation: The bureau of the United States Department of Agriculture responsible for a wide range of farm-support aids, including cash payments, crop purchases, loans to farmers, the management of farm surpluses, and the encouragement of domestic consumption and foreign trade in agricultural commodities.

common area: An area used communally by all the owners or tenants of a building or development, including such public areas as lobbies, hallways, pools, tennis courts, and parks.

common brick: Ordinary building brick, not treated to provide color variations.

common elements: Those portions of a condominium that are owned in common by all the owners of the separately owned units in the condominium, including outer walls, stairways, elevators, and recreation areas.

common expenses: Those expenses shared by the owners of a condominium, including tax, operating, and some special expenses.

common law: That body of law developed in England and other English-speaking countries, which has been built case by case and precedent by precedent, rather than depending upon statutory bases. Much of our civil law, adjusting the private relations between private parties, is based upon the common law. Much of the relationship between private parties and governments is based upon statutes, and upon regulations and cases interpreting those statutes.

common-law trust: See Massachusetts trust.

common stock: An ownership share in a corporation in the form of capital stock which is neither preferred nor in any way limited, and therefore fully shares the risks and opportunities created by corporate operations. It is the standard form of stock ownership in American corporations.

common wall: A wall within a structure, separating two units of that structure, such as two apartments or sets of offices, which are common elements of both and therefore are part of the structure, rather than the property of one or both of those sharing it.

community property: Property owned jointly by wife and husband, which in some states includes all property acquired during marriage but does not include property owned before marriage, nor some kinds of property acquired during marriage but specifically exempted from community property provisions of the law, such as property acquired as a bequest.

company: 1. A very broad term, meaning any business entity, including corporations, partnerships, and sole proprietorships. **2.** A group joining together to pursue common interests for profit.

comparables: Properties close enough in value to properties being evaluated to be used as a basis for judging fair market value, such as properties in similar communities, with similar floor space, taxes, utilities rates, school systems, quality of construction, and states of repair.

compensating balance: An amount kept on deposit by a borrower, in a non-interest-bearing regular account in a bank holding active loans of that borrower. Many commercial banks informally but very firmly require that borrowers keep deposits of approximately 20% of the amounts currently borrowed on deposit. As the deposits do not bear interest, the loans therefore cost considerably more than they seem. For example $100 borrowed at a simple interest of 10% costs $10 in interest. But if $20 must be kept on deposit, the borrower is paying $10 in interest while only $80 is usable, so the real interest rate is 12.5%, or 25% more than it seems.

compensation: 1. Any payment made to satisfy the just claim of another. **2** A popular abbreviation for Worker's Compensation.

competitive bidding: See bid.

competitive price: A price quoted by a seller which realistically reflects the facts of marketplace competition, comparing favorably with, or at least equaling, prices quoted by other sellers for similar goods or services.

complaint: The first pleading of a plaintiff in a civil action, setting forth the facts alleged to constitute a cause of action against the defendant.

completion: In real estate, the finishing of work in progress, as specified by contract or recognized at law through issuance of a completion document, such as a certificate of occupancy.

completion bond: A surety bond, often called a performance bond, which guarantees satisfactory and lien-free performance of a construction contract; may be posted by an owner or developer with a lender, the government, or both, or by a contractor with an owner or developer.

compliance: Action by private parties to comply with government-set rules, regulations, and procedures, usually referring to actions by business to comply with government regulations; for example, to adhere to government-set pollution control, health, and safety regulations.

compliance inspection: An inspection of a site or structure to see that conditions set by law have been complied with, such as an inspection by local regulatory bodies to see that building codes have been met, or by a government or private lender to see that loan conditions have been satisfied.

component construction: See prefabrication.

component depreciation: A mode of depreciation in which the parts of a structure are separately depreciated, rather than being depreciated all together with the basic structure; available for both new and used structures, although taxing authorities have in the main unsuccessfully resisted the use of this mode of depreciation for new buildings. Using this method, considerably more depreciation can be achieved than if all components were depreciated together, because such components as heating systems, roofs, and plumbing depreciate far more quickly than do basic structures.

component financing: See split financing.

composition: An arrangement between a debtor and all creditors to satisfy the entire body of debt outstanding for less than the totals due and on a pro rata basis. For example, a debtor owing a total of $10,000 to five creditors, composed of four $1,000 debts and one $6,000 debt might reach agreement to repay on a 50% basis, and then repay each of the $1,000 debts at $500 and the $6,000 debt and $3,000. Composition is a common-law arrangement between debtor and creditors, arrived at voluntarily and not as part of a bankruptcy settlement.

composition in bankruptcy: Substantially the same arrangement as composition, but arrived at by operation of law in pursuit of a settlement of outstanding debts during bankruptcy.

compound entry: In accounting, a single entry that combines three or more elements; often used to record a series of related transactions, clarifying the nature of those related transactions as a single complex transaction.

compound interest: A system of computing and paying interest that takes the original sum on which interest is to be computed, adds simple interest, and then uses the resulting amount as the basis for the next computation of interest. For example, payment of compound interest on $100 for two years at 5% per year would result in first year interest payment of $5. With the $5 added to the original $100, second year interest would be 5% of $105, or $5.25.

comprehensive insurance: Property insurance covering all risks related to the property insured, except for stated exceptions, such as war and certain natural disasters.

computer listing: The use of a computer memory to store and retrieve real estate listings; widely used for multiple and regional or national network listings.

concession; 1. Any reduction in price, usually offered by a seller as an incentive to buy. A concession may be a simple price reduction on goods for sale; it may be an incentive offered by government to business in the form of a tax reduction, cut rate, or rebate in return for moving into an area; or it may be selective tariff cut or any other move resulting in lower price. **2.** A permission, usually in the form of a lease granted by government or a private owner, granting the right to conduct a given kind of business in a specific area. For example, a stadium management may sell a business the right to sell food at events conducted in the stadium.

concrete: A substance composed of sand and gravel, which when mixed with water forms a cement widely used in construction.

condemnation: 1. The taking of private property by government for public use; a legal process by which government conducts a forced sale to itself of private property, relying upon its power of eminent domain, and without recourse on the part of the private owner, except in those relatively few instances in which the owner is able to challenge the validity of the public purpose. **2.** The taking of private property by government for public health or safety reasons, as when a structure is in imminent danger of collapse, or an area is contaminated by chemical dumping.

condemnation clause: A clause in a real estate sale or lease contract specifying the rights of the parties in the event of condemnation; for example, cancelling a lease in that event and specifying the shares of the condemnation payment to which lessor and lessee are entitled.

conditional fee: See fee simple conditional.

conditional sale: A sale in which the buyer takes possession of goods at the time of sale, but must meet certain conditions before actually receiving title to the goods. A typical form of conditional sale is the credit purchase, in which the buyer takes possession of goods on sale and agrees to pay for them over a period of time, usually in fixed installments. The seller retains title, which passes only if the buyer completes payment. If the buyer defaults on payment according to the terms of the sales contract, the seller may reclaim possession of the good.

condo: See condominium.

condominium: A housing unit, usually an apartment in a multiple occupancy building, which is separately owned, just as if it were a single family house standing alone. It may be purchased, sold, mortgaged, and in all other ways handled as any other wholly-owned building. Condominium owners also own a share of communally used elements, such as land or land lease, lobbies, basements, stairs, roof, heating, and cooling systems.

condominium owners' association: An association composed of all those owning interests in a condominium, which serves as a governing and managing body, usually through an elected board of directors. The association is responsible for all communal areas, as well as for such matters as collection and disbursement of charges and assessments.

conductor: Any electricity-conducting material; usually a material that conducts well, such as metal. Almost all materials are to some degree capable of conducting electricity.

conduit: 1. A natural or artificial channel for conducting fluids, such as water. **2.** A channel or tube used for protecting electrical wiring.

confession of judgment: In real estate, a debtor's written admission of debt, allowing adverse judgment without recourse to legal action by the creditor; a clause commonly found in debt and lease instruments; also called a cognovit.

confirmation: A document expressly validating a previously made oral or in some other way voidable purchase, agreement, or contract. For example, a telephone order for goods must often be followed by a written confirmation, signed by the ordering party.

confirmed credit: Credit that cannot be withdrawn or altered in any way, usually in the form of a letter of credit.

confiscation: The taking of property without compensation by government. A government may confiscate the property of its own citizens or may confiscate property in its control belonging to the citizens of other countries or to other governments.

conflict of interest: Any contradiction existing between the responsibilities created by a position of trust and the other interests of the holder of that position. For example, a government official awarding public contracts who has a substantial stock interest in a company bidding for those contracts has a clear conflict of interest.

conglomerate: A large, diversified organization, doing business in a number of more or less unrelated areas. A conglomerate usually acquires many of the unrelated portions of its operations, instead of developing them from the kinds of business it originally conducted. An example is the International Telephone and Telegraph Corporation, which does business in dozens of areas unrelated to its communications activities.

consent decree: An agreement between parties to an action at law, entered by the court in the form of a legally binding decision. A consent decree is normally an agreement by the defendant to meet certain demands of the plaintiff.

consent order: See consent decree.

consequential losses: Indirect losses, such as the damages caused by the water used to put out a fire, which are recoverable from insurances.

conservation: A term used to describe a wide variety of theories and practices aimed at preserving or restoring the physical environment and at saving depletable natural resources, including such human-made resources as historic and beautiful structures, and such natural resources as parks, wildlife refuges, oil, coal, clean water, clean air, timber, and metal ores.

conservator: One appointed by a court to guard and protect the property of another who is found by the court to be incompetent to manage his or her own interests. The conservator acts toward an incompetent as a guardian acts toward a ward.

consideration: In the law of contracts, an inducement sufficient in the eyes of the law to cause a party to make a contract. The inducement must have enough value to be deemed a sufficient inducement and must be thought by a contracting party to confer a perceptible benefit.

consignment: 1. A general term for a shipment of goods or for the goods themselves. **2.** A method of selling, in which an agent sells goods owned by another, receiving payment for the sale either as a percentage of sale or a flat fee per sale or some combination of both.

consistency: In accounting, adherence to the same accounting methods over a period of time, so that statements of operating results and financial position will not be distorted by material changes in accounting methods within a period or from one period to another. Consistency demands that when a substantial change is introduced, its nature and impact must be fully disclosed and explained in the financial statements.

consolidation: In real estate, the merging of two or more properties or debt obligations into a single property or obligation; for example, the merger of several properties into one or the merger of several mortgages on a single property into one mortgage on that property.

constant: An element that does not change, in contrast to other elements that may be variables; for example, an unchanging element in an equation or in a body of data being processed by a computer system.

constant-dollar value: The value of an item as if the dollar had constant value, neither inflating or deflating. This is done by adopting a given year as a base year and figuring the values of items as if the dollars used to buy them purchased as much as they did in the base year. For example, a car purchased this year for $8,000 may be worth

$4,000 in "1970 dollars," if the dollar's purchasing power is now 50% of what it was in 1970.

constant payment mortgage: A mortgage repayment mode with a level periodic payment for the life of the mortgage debt obligation, in which interest repayment is high and principal repayment low in the early years of the mortgage, and proportions reverse in later years; the main home mortgage form used in the United States between the Crash of 1929 and today. This mode of computing mortgage interest has been a major source of tax advantage to home owners, as interest is deductible from income for tax purposes, and the average life of such mortgages has been about half the average life of mortgage terms during the period since the Crash; one of the main motors in the uninterrupted surge in home ownership in the period, and especially since World War II.

construction contract: A formal contract between owner or developer and builder, specifying all terms, conditions, and payments incident to that construction described by the contract, and incorporating such plans, specifications, drawings, and bids as the parties agree to include in the contract.

construction contract awards: An economic indicator used to assess future investment in construction and therefore the impact of that investment on the economy. Since construction contracts indicate the money appropriated or otherwise set aside for payments of awarded contracts, this is a relatively hardy indicator of future economic prospects.

construction loan: A short term loan to a builder, usually from a commercial bank or savings and loan association, with periodic payments during the period of construction and often geared to the progress of the work; therefore the periodic payments are sometimes called progress installments or payments. This form of interim financing is later retired and superseded by longer term financing, in most instances committed by a lender before the project is started or the construction loan secured.

construction manager: An individual or organization hired by an owner or developer to handle every aspect of a construction project, for a fee; contrasts with a general contractor, who is hired to produce a job at a price, which is supposed to include the contractor's profit.

construction permit: See building permit.

constructive: That which will in law be interpreted or construed into being by judicial action, although it is not necessarily evident from the physical facts before the court. Examples include a contract when no document of contract exists; notice where no notice was physically supplied, but notice should have been easily available from examination of accessible public records; or eviction, where a lessor has destroyed by his or her actions the lessee's ability to quietly enjoy the occupancy of leased premises, thus invalidating the lease.

constructive contract: A contract which a court will literally construct out of the relations between the parties before it, when no written contract actually exists; for example, under some circumstances, a binding agreement springing from oral agreements and subsequent actions stemming from those agreements, without a written contract.

Consumer Price Index (CPI): A national monthly index generated by the United States Bureau of Labor Statistics, which compares a weighted average of prices with the same weighted average for a previous year selected as a base year. It is a basic measure of increases in the cost of living, and was formerly called the "cost of living index." It serves as a measuring basis for many cost adjustments throughout the economy; for example, many leases contain clauses providing for rental adjustments based upon Consumer Price Index changes, as do many labor contracts.

consumer protection laws: A general term for a substantial number of United States statutes protecting consumers in the marketplace, extending as far back as the Pure Food and Drug Act of 1906, and including such major statutes as the Food, Drug, and Cosmetic Act of 1960; and the Truth in Lending Act in 1969. Consumer protection laws are administered by several major agencies including the Federal Trade Commission and the Food and Drug Administration.

contemporary architecture: A very wide term, encompassing many architectural styles popular in the twentieth century, all having in common substantial departures in design and conception from the traditional architectural schools of their regions, though often incorporating substantial traditional concepts and materials. Also called modern style.

contiguous: Close to, though not necessarily adjoining, adjacent, or abutting.

contingency: A possibility, which may or may not occur, but for which preparation can be made, as when contracting parties agree to alternative courses of action depending upon the occurrence of future events, such as condemnation of a property or death of a partner.

contingent fee: A fee, payment of which depends on the occurrence of a specified event, such as commissions resulting from a real estate sale.

contingent interest: An interest, estate, or right which does not now exist, but will come into being if some now-perceivable event occurs, such as the inheritance of an estate from one now alive after the death of an heir also now alive.

contingent liability: A liability which does not now exist, but will come into being if some now-perceived event occurs; contingent liabilities are potential, not probable. When considered probable, they become contingent but real, and are treated as real in accounting statements.

continuance: The postponement of a scheduled court case.

continuation: The updating of an abstract of title; usually covering the period between the beginning of a process of sale with a binder or escrow deposit and taking the title search up to the date of the closing.

continued bonds: Bonds that are not redeemed when mature, but instead are carried on as interest-bearing obligations, although not necessarily at the same rate of interest.

contour map: A map showing the shape or contour of the land, using curved map lines to indicate elevated sections of the map; sometimes in the form of stamped or molded plastic, with the contours showing in relief.

contract: 1. A legal agreement in which two or more parties, for adequate consideration, make and accept promises to do or not to do specified things. Also the written record of that agreement, agreed to and signed by the parties. **2.** To make a legal agreement with one or more parties, for adequate consideration, to do or not to do certain things.

contract for deed: See land contract.

contract of sale: A formal agreement between buyer and seller, in which the seller agrees to supply specified goods or services and the buyer agrees to pay for those goods or services at agreed upon prices. In real estate, the sale is consummated at the closing, although title is formally passed by deed or lease somewhat later, after some post-closing details are completed. In an installment sale, title may pass long after the contract of sale is consummated, although purchaser may by contract take possession of the property while installment payments are being made.

contractor: One who contracts to do a job for another, operating independently, although often under very specific terms of agreement covering such matters as materials to be used, quality of work to be performed, schedules, and deadlines. A contractor may contract an entire job as general contractor or may contract with a general contractor to do part of a job as subcontractor.

contract rent: The amount of actual rent specified in a lease; contrasts with economic or market rent, which is an estimate of the rent that might have been commanded by the property in the rental market.

contributed capital: The money invested in a firm by its owners, including both money invested in capital stock and money they later put into the firm for operating purposes.

contribution: 1. A share payment made to accomplish a purpose, as in a contribution to capital or to payment of any joint obligation. 2. For tax purposes, any gift which is defined by law and regulations as tax-free.

contributory negligence: Negligence by a party claiming damages at law or in the course of pursuing an insurance claim, which contributed to the situation causing the damages and sometimes to the severity of those damages; a finding of contributory negligence therefore can partially or wholly invalidate the claim of the claimant.

controlling interest: That percentage of ownership of the common stock of a company which enables one or more stockholders to secure effective control over the operations of the company. The percentage necessary for control varies from 51% of some closely held companies to less than 20% of some very large and widely held companies.

conventional mortgage: A private mortgage loan, rather than one made by a government organization; also sometimes implies a constant level rather than a variable rate mortgage; occasionally used to distinguish a first from a second or subsequent mortgage.

conversion: 1. The unauthorized taking of another's property, whether by physical taking or by an action which in law can be construed as unauthorized taking. 2. Transformation of one thing into another. Examples include transformation of an old house that has become a slum property into a prestigious and expensive row house; an apartment building into a cooperative or condominium; raw materials into more finished materials, such as coal into coke or textile fibers into yard goods; or one instrument of value into another, such as paper money into gold or bonds into common stock.

conveyance: The transfer of legal title to land, and the document transferring that title. The term has developed a much wider meaning as well, and is now used to describe any transfer of title to real or personal property.

conveyance tax: See transfer tax.

cooperating broker: A real estate broker who works with another broker who is directly credited with making a sale; the selling broker is paid by the seller of the property, and in turn pays the cooperating broker some portion of the fee or commissions received from the seller.

cooperative apartment: A form of apartment ownership, in which a tenant in a multiple occupancy building owns a share in the building, holds an open-end lease on the apartment occupied, and shares on a pro rata basis with other tenants the total cost of running the building. The tenants are stockholders in the building, in contrast to condominium owners, who own their portions of their dwellings.

coordinates: The two points necessary to specify the location of a point on a rectangular graph, such as the longitude and latitude readings on a map.

coping: The top of a wall, usually made of a different material than the main body of the wall and often curved.

corner lot: A lot fronting on the corner or angle formed by two streets, usually with access to both; often more valuable than lots of equal size fronting on only one street.

cornice: The top molding of a wall or building, serving as both decoration and a practical means of covering the seam between wall and ceiling or roof.

corporate income tax: A tax levied by government on corporate profits. Profits are normally stated by corporations as pre-tax, or net-before-taxes. Corporate income taxes are graduated according to taxable income, as are personal income taxes.

corporate resolution: A resolution passed by a corporation's board of directors authorizing an action, such as the sale or purchase of real property or the creation of corporate debt through such instruments as bonds and loans.

corporation: A business entity created under law, which functions in all ways as an individual under law and is regarded as an individual in the eyes of the law. Corporations may be formed by a single individual or by an unlimited number of individuals jointing together as stockholders. In the main, the liability of stockholders for the actions of the corporation is limited to the resources of the corporation, so that in the event of bankruptcy stockholders may lose only the value of their ownership interests; in contrast the individual proprietor and partners' liability is personal and unlimited.

corporeal: Composed of matter and tangible to human perceptions, such as land, buildings, automobiles, and other items of real and personal property.

corpus: A physical body; a body of value, as in the corpus or body of an estate. The corpus of an estate can earn money or can be used for other purposes; but the body of value itself remains as a physical perceivable entity.

correction deed: A deed correcting and thereby reforming a deed previously issued for the same real property.

correlation: In appraisal, the step that compares and adjusts the income, market data, and cost approaches to arrive at a final appraised valuation figure for a property.

corridor: **1.** A passage within a structure, often with several rooms opening onto it. **2.** A strip of land, allowing access to a desirable area.

co-signer: See co-maker.

cost: **1.** The price to be paid for anything, whatever medium of exchange is used for payment. **2.** In economics, the amounts committed to pay for the factors of production, including all expenses necessary for production. **3.** To determine what something will cost, applying all necessary expense factors, as in "to cost out" an item.

cost approach: See appraisal.

cost basis: In accounting, the valuation of assets based upon their original cost minus any depreciaiton and without allowance for the addition of intangible factors, such as good will or developing antique value.

cost effectiveness: An evaluation of whether or not to do something based on the cost-benefit relationship resulting from the move.

cost of living: The level of expenditure necessary to maintain a current standard of living for families and individuals, as measured against previously necessary levels of expenditure. The Consumer Price Index, formerly called the Cost of Living Index, is a major United States cost of living indicator.

cost of living index: See Consumer Price Index.

cost-plus contract: A contract in which the parties agree that the contractor will submit bills for payment based on costs actually incurred plus either a fixed fee or a percentage of those costs.

cost-plus pricing: The pricing of goods or services on the basis of costs plus an estimated necessary profit margin. This pricing technique is usually a budgeting planning device, rather than a means of reaching final marketplace prices, which must reflect the realities of competition and other market factors, including government regulation and public attitudes.

cotenancy: A general term describing several forms of joint ownership interest, including community property, joint tenancy, tenancy by the entirety, and tenancy in common.

cottage: A small house; often a summer house.

counteroffer: An offer made in response to another's offer, functioning as a rejection of the first offer and changing the roles of offerer and offeree at that moment in the process of negotiation.

county: An administrative division of a state, performing a wide variety of governmental functions.

county road: A public road for which a county is primarily responsible, even though the funds to maintain it may come wholly or partly from other governmental bodies.

coupon bonds: Negotiable bonds payable to their bearer, carrying interest certificates or coupons which are clipped when mature and presented to the issuer of the bonds for payment. Coupon bonds need not be endorsed, either at passage of title in them or at the presentation of clipped coupons for payment.

court: 1. A small or short yard, alley, or street, that is wholly or largely enclosed. **2.** A meeting place at which legal issues are heard and decided.

covenant: 1. A written agreement between two or more parties, embodied in one or more contract clauses; in this sense, synonymous with contract, and so used when referring to express, written contracts and their parts. **2.** A specific promise or agreement between two or more parties, which is embodied in a real estate contract; so often encountered, and therefore of such general nature, as to be part of many such real estate contracts, and to be given in law a name of its own. Examples include a convenant against incumbrances, which functions as a warranty by one who conveys land that there are no incumbrances on the land other than any stated in the contract between the parties; a convenant of seisin, in which the conveyor asserts possession of salable title; and a covenant of warranty or quiet enjoyment, in which the conveyor warrants title unobstructed by the claims of third parties.

covenant running with the land: A convenant that passes with title to real property, and therefore from successive owner to owner, such as an agreement to limit or restrict the kinds of uses to which the property may be put by its future owners.

cover: In insurance, for an insurer to assume certain kinds or risks and potential liabilities when issuing an insurance policy, such as specified fire and casualty costs in a homeowner's insurance policy.

coverage: See cover.

CPA: See certified public accountant.

CPI: See Consumer Price Index.

CPM: See Certified Property Manager.

crawl space: The narrow space between the ground floor of a house and the ground, in the absence of a basement.

creative financing: In real estate, the imaginative and unconventional financing of sales or projects, as when a very tight mortgage market forces buyers and sellers to reach outside the banking system for needed financing, including the granting of mortgages wholly or in part by the sellers themselves; or the manipulation of purchase arrangements, borrowed funds, and tax advantages by a developer or promoter so as to generate project financing with little or no use of the manipulator's own funds.

credit: 1. The ability to secure goods and services now with a promise to pay later. Credit comes in many forms and from many sources, including both moneylenders and producers. It may be granted on the basis of a simple promise to pay, as in most routine commercial transactions between buyers and sellers, or may be granted only if completely covered by collateral, as with most home mortgages. **2.** In accounting, an entry on the right side of an account, recording the reduction or elimination of an asset or expense, or the addition to or creation of a liability, net worth, or revenue item. In double-entry bookkeeping, each credit is accompanied by a debit entry to a balancing account, so that the books always reflect the current relationship between assets and liabilities.

credit approval: The granting of credit to a purchaser or borrower by a seller or lender; for example, approval of credit for an appliance purchase by a retail store manager or approval of an individual line of credit by a bank branch manager.

credit balance: In general, the excess of credits over debits in any account, as in banking, where the excess of credits over debits in a depositor's account indicates that the depositor has funds currently on deposit. When an account shows a debit balance, the depositor either has an overdraft in the account or is using an overdraft privilege or line of credit.

credit bureau: A private organization that maintains files containing credit information and often a good deal of personal data on those who have previously used or sought credit, for the use of commercial customers seeking to determine the creditworthiness of customers asking for credit; those listed in the files of credit bureaus are by law granted the right to examine their own files.

credit instrument: A document evidencing debt, including all paper instruments other than paper money and coins. In a certain sense, even paper money and coins issued by a government solely on the basis of its full faith and credit, as in the United States, are credit instruments. The most widely used of all credit instruments is the check, accounting for well over 90% of all commercial transactions in the United States.

credit insurance: Insurance against uncollectibles, in which the insurer shares the risks developed by the extension of credit to customers.

credit investigation: Any investigation of the potential creditworthiness of one seeking credit entered into by a lender, seller, or one acting for a lender or seller, including the use of credit bureaus and direct checking of such matters as bank references supplied by the potential creditor.

credit investigator: One who is employed by a lender to gather information about the creditworthiness of a potential borrower. Credit investigators may be employees of a lending institution or of a private organization serving lending institutions.

credit line: An overdraft privilege granted by a lending institution, allowing a customer to borrow sums within a stated range without treating each loan as a new loan, requiring separate approvals and documents from the lender. Credit lines are often stated in fixed sums, such as $50,000 credit line at the bank, but are in fact somewhat variable, depending on the borrower's bank balances, business and personal status, interest rates, and general economic conditions.

creditor: On to whom money is due. In the widest sense, one who has the right to collect anything of value from anyone for any reason, including the right to collect from another as a result of a legal proceeding.

credit rating: An assessment of the creditworthiness of a business or individual made by private organizations, such as Dun and Bradstreet, specializing in the gathering and evaluation of credit information. A credit rating may be expressed on a scale, such as A to D, or may be expressed in evaluative comments.

credit report: A report made by a credit investigator or bureau on the creditworthiness of one seeking credit.

credit risk: The degree of exposure to risk faced by a lender with respect to a specific customer, as in an evaluation of a not-very-creditworthy firm as a "high" credit risk.

credit standing: See credit rating.

credit terms: The specific arrangements for repayment defined in a credit sales contract, including such matters as the length of time allowed for payment, the rate of interest, penalties for slow payment, and actions in the case of nonpayment.

credit union: A cooperative that lends its members money out of funds deposited by its membership, usually at somewhat lower interest rates than those available from commercial lenders. Widespread in the United States, credit unions are often formed by such organizations as fraternal societies and trade unions.

creditworthiness: An estimate made by a lender as to how likely a potential borrower will be to pay back a requested loan. Lenders will base estimates on such factors as available collateral, the character of the credit applicant, the capital available to that applicant, presumed capacity to repay based upon such factors as current income and future prospects, and general economic conditions as of the time of application for credit.

creek: A small stream or inlet.

cropper: See sharecropping.

cubic content: The volume within an enclosure or structure, measured in cubic feet; an estimating tool, in terms of such matters as building and heating costs.

cul de sac: A dead-end street, alley, or other passageway; in residential areas, often a street with a turning area at its end, allowing access to homes but precluding through traffic.

culvert: A drain or sewer built under a road, protecting it by carrying runoff or sewage under rather than directly over it.

curb line: On a road, the line between the vehicular and pedestrian rights of way.

currency: All paper money and coins acceptable as legal tender, but not including negotiable paper, such as checks, even if it is freely transferrable from bearer to bearer. Currency is often used synonymously with paper money, but the term does include coins.

current assets: Those assets that are held in cash or are relatively easy to convert into cash, including such items as collectibles, short term investments, and inventory. They are normally convertible into cash within one year, but for accounting purposes some assets that take longer than a year to convert may still be classified as current.

current expense: A normal operating expense chargeable to an accounting period, as contrasted to extraordinary and nonrecurring expenses.

current income: Income attributable to an accounting period, normally as distinguished from cash receipts, which may not be treated as income in the acounting period in which they are received.

current liabilities: Any debt which is due and payable within a specified short period, usually one year, including both short term debts and longer term debts maturing and payable within the period.

curtain wall: A non-load-bearing outer building wall, which functions as an enclosure rather than as a structural support, such as many of the glass outer walls of office buildings.

curtesy: In the common law, a freehold estate, held by a man for the rest of his life, in the property owned by his deceased wife during her lifetime, if they had a child born alive; this interest survives now in some states as a part interest in a deceased wife's property under circumstances specified by statute and court decisions.

curtilage: The enclosed space surrounding a dwelling; also in the absence of a fence, occasionally used to indicate that body of land closely surrounding a dwelling and its nearby outbuildings, if any.

custody: The care and keeping of anything; if property, immediate and personal possession short of the complete control of ownership, accompanied by responsibility for protection and preservation of the property.

cutoff date: Any date at which something is stopped, as in a cutoff date for extension of credit or a cutoff date for accounting purposes, which sets the end of an accounting period.

cutover land: Land which has lost its timber relatively recently due to logging. Much American land has been denuded of its early timber, and in many areas more than once; land carrying a regrown forest is not thought of or described as cutover.

cutthroat competition: Ruthless competition between businesses, using a substantial number of unfair and often illegal competitive practices, and especially the device of temporary price-cutting to drive competitors out of business; sometimes practiced by large, better capitalized companies to drive out weaker, marginal companies, and by new competitors in a field to establish a sales position.

D

damages: Compensation due for loss or injury, gained by legal process. Such compensation may be merely nominal, as when one alleging slander receives a small sum of money damages and a public apology and vindication; may be bare money compensation for physical damages suffered, as when one receives only enough to cover the current or replacement cost of real or personal property; or may represent compensation for a wide range of losses or injuries beyond, such as extra damages mandated by statute, in some jurisdictions in cases involving fraud, trespass, or negligence, as well as punitive or special damages awarded at law in cases involving violence, fraud, and other aggravating circumstances. Compensation for real property taken or adversely affected by a state's use of its power of eminent domain is sometimes called land damages.

damper: A movable plate in a furnace or fireplace flue, used for adjusting the air draft.

dampproofing: The moisture-proofing of a wall, by treating it with liquid-resistant material.

data: 1. Generally, a synonym for information. In electronic data processing, information that is ready or easily made ready for input into a computer system. **2.** In research of any kind, the raw material of the study.

data base: 1. Any body of information that can be used as raw material for studies, products, or specific information. **2.** In electronic data processing, a body of information in a computer memory that can be reached into by computer, or *accessed*, for information.

date of issue: The date on which an instrument of obligation, such as an insurance policy, or bond or other debt instrument, becomes operative. The instrument bears that date rather than the date on which the instrument is executed, or any other date.

datum: In real estate, a reference point, such as a point, line, surface, or map reference.

daybook: A journal of original entry for business transactions, in which a chronological record of transactions is maintained for later entry into an accounting system. Once widely used, the daybook has in the main been replaced by the journal. It survives, however, in the records kept by people conducting business away from their offices, such as outside sellers.

days of grace: See grace period.

DC: See direct current.

deal: In general, an agreement. Deals range from contracts with full legal force to verbal agreements with little or no legal force, intended to lead to contracts. Deals may lead to development of a single contract or of a number of legal instruments which together embody the agreements reached.

dealer: Any person or organization buying or selling goods and services who takes title to whatever is bought and passes title on whatever is sold, as distinct from brokers and agents, who represent and deal with buyers and sellers, but do not take or pass title. Dealers are sometimes also brokers and agents, as in the real estate and securities industries, where many dealers buy and sell for themselves through their own accounts while, acting as brokers, they also transact business for their clients. In real estate taxation, a dealer's taxable gain on a realty transaction is treated as ordinary income, while an investor's gain can qualify for capital gains treatment.

dealer property: Property that is part of a dealer's inventory, being held with intent to resell, rather than as long term investment or for personal use.

debenture: Any long term debt instrument issued by a company or institution, secured only by the general assets of the issuer. Debentures are usually issued as bonds, primarily by corporations and governments. They are therefore only as good as their issuer's ability to meet the debt obligations they create.

debenture bonds: Unsecured debt obligations issued by governments and corporations backed only by their promise to pay, and only as good as the repayment ability of their issuers.

debit: In accounting, an entry on the left side of an account, recording addition or creation of an asset or expense, or the subtraction or elimination of a liability, net worth, or revenue item.

debt: A fixed sum owed by one to another, payable now, and collectible at law by the creditor. In a somewhat wider sense, all debts owed by one to all others, as in a "national debt." The term is also loosely used to describe any obligation, however unenforceable, as in the "moral debt," or "debt to society."

debt ceiling: See debt limit.

debt limit: The maximum lawful debt which may be incurred by any government. Debt limits are set by law, and for sovereign states may be revised by law, as in the instance of the United States, which has often raised its own debt limit. Most states need state constitutional amendments to raise their own debt limits, but in fact are at least as much influenced by bond market considerations as by statutory constraints. Most municipalities need state approval for debt limit changes.

debtor: One who is legally responsible for the payment of debt, however that debt was incurred. One liable for payment of a judgment is just as much a debtor as one responsible for repayment of a loan.

debt service: The amounts a debtor must pay a creditor to keep a debt currently paid up, including due and payable interest payments and principal repayments. Debt service often also refers to the total of all such payments due on all debts by a single debtor in a specified period.

decedent: A dead person.

decibel: A sound measurement unit, indicating volume and intensity; increasingly used to measure noise levels and noise pollution.

deck: Any attached open porch, of any size, located anywhere on a building, and used primarily for recreational purposes.

declaration of condominium: The basic legal document required of a condominium developer, which must be filed as required by state law containing specified information. Although the required content of the filing varies, in the several states, it normally includes a master deed or master lease, along with a description of the land, the title, the condominium to be developed, and the uses to which it will be put, and a body of maps, bylaws, and legal miscellany. This document is sometimes called a master deed or master lease.

declaration of homestead: See homestead.

declaration of restriction: A document describing all restrictions on a group of properties under development, in which the developer lists all such matters applying commonly to those properties, such as restrictions on land use and building code requirements; occurs either as an attachment to the developer's filed plan or as a separately filed document.

declaration of trust: An action or document by which one holding title to property or to an estate states that it is being held in trust, and that he or she is holding it as trustee rather than as owner.

declaratory judgment: A judgment declaring the rights of the parties before the court, rather than requiring execution of the court's judgment.

declining balance method of depreciation: A method of figuring depreciation by applying a fixed percentage to each year's balance remaining after the previous year's depreciation has been subtracted; a way of accelerating depreciation taken for tax or operating purposes, as the percentage applied is larger than straight line depreciation provides. For example, a building purchased for $100,000, with an anticipated life of 20 years for depreciation purposes, will depreciate at the rate of $5,000 per year for 20 years on a straight line basis. But the same building, depreciated at 200%, or double the straight line rate, and using a declining balance method of figuring that depreciation, will depreciate $10,000, or 10% of $100,000 the first year; and so on, yielding far greater depreciation and consequent tax deductions far sooner. Another method of accelerating depreciation using a declining balance approach is the sum-of-the-years'-digits method, in which the digits representing each year an asset will depreciate are added together, and the resulting sum is divided into the number of years to arrive at the percentage of depreciation to be applied each year; for example, the same asset depreciating over 10 years will yield 55 digits, which divided into 10 years, yields a first year depreciation of 18.18% or $18,180, rather than the $5,000 yielded by straight line depreciation. The use of these forms of accelerated depreciation is limited by taxing authorities and court decisions.

decree: The judgment of a court of equity, ordering execution of the provisions of that judgment.

dedication: The transfer of title to or easement upon privately owned land to the state or public, by act of its owner rather than by state taking, as by exercise of eminent domain. The owner may transfer the land by action of applicable statute, as when a developer gives roads and other common areas to the state by recording state ownership on an officially filed subdivision map; by express written or oral statement; or by implication, as when an easement informally granted becomes permanent on passage of the statutory period.

deductible: 1. In the insurance industry, the amount of the insured's loss which will be borne by the insured before the insurance company's risk starts. For example, a "$200 deductible" provision in an automobile collision insurance policy means that the first $200 damage to the insured's automobile will be borne by the insured, with insurance company liability starting after that $200 deductible. **2.** In taxation, any expense item which serves as a subtraction from taxable income.

deduction: See deductible.

deed: A document legally conveying current title in real property from one to another. The document must be signed, sealed, witnessed, delivered, and conveyable; must name grantor and grantee; and must describe the property conveyed. There need be no consideration for conveyance of a deed, as it may be a gift. Title passes on valid conveyance of the deed, which is normally, but not necessarily then recorded; after passage of title, the deed is no longer significant or needed, except as evidence of passage of title.

deed of reconveyance: See deed of trust.

deed of release: A deed used to end an encumbrance upon property resulting from a debt for which the property has been collateral; encountered when a deed of trust has been the mortgage form used.

deed of trust: A deed passing title to property from an owner to a trustee, who holds that property as collateral for a mortgage loan advanced by another. Should default on the mortgage occur, the trustee is empowered to sell the property, paying from the proceeds the mortgage loan amount to the lender and any balance to the former owner. On repayment of the mortgage loan, the trustee conveys the property back to its previous owner, using a deed of reconveyance.

de facto: Literally, "in fact." Often used to describe the realities of a situation, as distinct from its appearance or legalities. For example, a de facto government may be in actual possession of state power, but may not have been accorded legal, or *de jure*, status.

defalcation: The misappropriation or other illegal use of funds by one in a position of fiduciary trust. The term is normally used in relation to corporate or government officials who have so abused their trust.

default: Failure to do a legally required act, and subsequent liability for the resulting consequences. For example, failure to make payment of a mortgage loan may make a debtor liable for immediate payment of the entire loan amount, with resulting foreclosure; or a bond default may force a corporation or city into bankruptcy. Failure to defend an action at law may result in a judgment by default, in favor of the plaintiff.

default judgment: See default.

defeasance: A condition which, if met, defeats the legal effect of an instrument. In real property law, it occurs as a collateral deed, made at the same time as another conveyance, setting forth conditions which if met, cause the complete undoing of that other conveyance; for example, the completion of payment of a mortgage loan, which undoes the transfer of title to a trustee or mortgage lender, restoring it to its previous owner, by operation of a defeasance clause in the mortgage loan agreement.

defeasance clause: See defeasance.

defeasible fee: See fee simple conditional.

defective title: See cloud on title.

defendant: One named by a plaintiff as the object of a lawsuit.

deferral: Any item of expense or revenue that should be carried forward for accounting purposes so that it is attributed to the period in which the benefits stemming from the expense are received or the revenue is earned.

deferred charge: A charge that by its nature should be spread, all or in part, over future accounting periods rather than be treated as a current operating expense. For example, research and development costs are often properly spread over future years, with little or no charges expensed into the current period.

deferred income: See deferred revenue.

deferred maintenance: Property maintenance functions which have not been performed in a timely way, resulting in physical deterioration; a condition adversely affecting price on sale of property.

deferred payment method: A mode of payment on sale of an asset that attempts to defer tax payment on gains until the cost basis to the seller of the property sold has been reached by the buyer's installment payments; used when the buyer's initial payment is more than that allowed by installment income tax rules, and promissory notes for the balance have no fair market value. For tax purposes, the deferred payment method is effectively a kind of installment sale, but that is difficult to prove to the satisfaction of taxing authorities.

deferred revenue: Advance payment received but not actually yet earned, and therefore for accounting purposes held for attribution to the period in which it is earned.

deferred tax: A tax that will result from current income and transactions at some later date beyond the current taxing period; for example, money earned in a current year and accrued in a profit-sharing plan, which will be taxable only when the money in that plan is paid out.

deficiency: 1. An amount claimed by a taxing authority over what a taxpayer has actually paid. **2.** In accounting, the amount by which liabilities exceed assets, which normally must be balanced by capital contributions to avoid insolvency.

deficiency judgment: A judgment against a debtor's personal assets, beyond that which is owed on a defaulted debt instrument. For example, a judgment against a defaulting mortgage borrower, when a foreclosed mortgage loan has failed to yield enough proceeds to pay off the balance of the loan and associated costs, is a deficiency judgment; sometimes, however, such a judgment is blocked by the loan being nonrecourse, meaning that the lender is unable by the terms of the loan to come against other assets of the borrower, or is blocked by statute.

deficiency letter: A formal notice from a taxing authority, notifying a taxpayer of alleged taxes due, usually in addition to taxes already paid.

deficit: The amount of deficiency, or excess of liabilities over assets, at a specified time, as at the end of an accounting period. In a much wider sense, the term is used as a synonym for "loss," and is often used to describe a process rather than a fixed sum at a specific time, as in "We are running at a deficit."

de jure: That which is legal and right according to law. For example, a government that is recognized as legitimate according to the past laws of a country, as interpreted by its legal institutions, is *de jure*, as distinct from a government that simply has power and exercises it, which is *de facto*. In the modern world, the distinction as to questions of state power is somewhat blurred.

delinquent tax: A tax that is overdue, unpaid, and usually accompanied by penalties for late payment.

delivery: The legal transfer of a right or interest in real or personal property. The transfer may be by means of physical delivery or by means of an instrument of conveyance, such as a bill of sale or deed; it may be absolute or conditional, actual or constructive; and it must be accompanied by intent to transfer on the part of the transferor.

demand: **1.** In law, the claiming of a specific right, asserted to be an absolute right under law, as in the demand for withdrawal of a demand deposit. **2.** In economics, the total of wants for a product, service, or body of products and services.

demand certificate of deposit: See certificate of deposit.

demand loan: A loan that has no fixed date of termination, but may be terminated at any time by either lender or borrower.

demise: In law, a conveyance of a real property interest for a specified period or for life; used commonly as a synonym for lease.

demolition loss: A loss in the value of real property due to the demolition of structures on it. For tax purposes, it is treated as a current loss if on purchase there was no intent to demolish and demolition occurs after purchase; if intent to demolish was present on purchase, then for tax purposes the demolition is treated as if it had added value to the property on purchase, and must be added to the basis of the property owner rather than taken as a current loss.

demonstration home: See model.

denomination: The face value of ownership, debt, and currency certificates. While debt instruments and currency are issued in face value certificates, stocks are normally issued in multiple share certificates, such as a certificate for 100 shares; the denomination of a $10 bill being $10.00, and of each share whatever is the par value of the single share.

density: The number of people, structures, or units per defined area, such as the number of people per building, dwelling unit, or block in a city. In suburbs, the number of single family homes or condominium units per acre allowable in various areas is set by local law in a practice called density zoning.

density zoning: See density.

Department of Housing and Urban Development (HUD): A Federal department responsible for the development and administration of programs aimed at improving the quality and quantity of the nation's housing, with special attention to the needs of the poor and disadvantaged. It has administrative control over the Federal Housing Administration (FHA), the Government National Mortgage Administration (GNMA), and the Office of Interstate Land Sales Registration, and handles a wide range of Federal housing, housing loans, and housing grant matters.

department store: A substantial retailer, carrying a considerable quantity of goods and organized into several subsidiary cost centers, accounted for separately and often separately staffed and managed.

depletable: Capable of being used up, usually referring to natural resources, such as coal, oil, metal ores, and standing timber.

depleted cost: For accounting purposes, the cost that is left after accrued depletion has been subtracted.

depletion: The concept that natural resources can be and are used up over a period of time, and that tax policy and accounting practice must take into account that exhaustion of resources. Also refers to the amount of resources so used up.

depletion allowance: 1. In taxation, the amounts of the deductions from taxes allowed their owners for the using up of natural resources, such as oil, coal, metals and timber. Depletion allowances, when occurring, are set by law. **2.** In accounting, the value reductions set for depletion of specified natural resources.

deposit: 1. A sum given to another as evidence of good faith; for example, a sum given to a real estate seller to bind a contract, which is to become part of the purchase price if the sale is consummated, to be returned to the buyer if the sale is not consummated, or to become liquidated damages if the sale is consummated but the buyer defaults. **2.** A sum given to another as security for performance of an agreement, such as a sum supplied to a utility company by a customer as security for services to be rendered. **3.** A body of materials in nature, such as a body of ore under the ground or a body of gravel accreted on the bottom or bank of a stream due to stream action. **4.** An amount placed into a bank account, which is then drawn upon for business or personal use or held for the accretion of interest, and which provides a base for the bank's ability to create credit and make loans.

deposition: Testimony, given pursuant to a pending legal action by order of the court or by applicable law, that is taken out of court, written down, and attested, for use as evidence by the parties during that court action.

depository: 1. A person, institution, or place to store, anything of value. Also spelled depositary, when referring to a person or institution entrusted. **2.** A bank authorized to receive and hold government, trust, or other bank funds.

depreciable cost: The basis upon which an asset's depreciation will be taken, often the money cost of the asset to its current owner.

depreciation: The lessening in value of an asset due to age, use, and obsolescence. Depreciation is an accounting estimate, essential for appraisal and tax accounting purposes. For appraisal purposes, it functions as a major element in evaluating the current value of real property. For tax purposes, although its significance is similar to that of depletion, it results from use rather than using up. A building may be fully depreciated for tax and accounting purposes and still be whole, usable, appraised at as high a value as it ever was, and ready to go through another whole depreciation period under new ownership, while a stand of timber may shrink year by year as it is used up or depleted. Some of the main methods of calculating depreciation are the straight line, sum-of-the-years'-digits, and replacement methods.

depreciation reserve: Those valuation amounts set aside for accounting purposes to reflect the depreciation that has accumulated on an asset. Depreciation reserves are accounting estimates, rather than actual reserves.

descent: Inherited succession, through which property can be acquired from the estate of one who is deceased, whether by the terms of a will or by operation of common law or statute.

description: That part of a document conveying real property, such as a deed, lease, or mortgage, which legally identifies the property being conveyed, in some instances by complete physical description and history of title, in others by such brief identifiers as street addresses and map references.

determinable fee: See fee simple conditional.

developer: One engaged as an entrepreneur in the development of real estate projects, usually consisting of many related structures or units, such as groups of houses in subdivisions, office parks, and condominiums.

development: A group of related structures, usually on contiguous land, such as a housing subdivision; while often used to describe large numbers of such structures, such as Levittown, the term can describe a much smaller group of units. Also refers to the process of preparing and building such related groups of structures.

development expense: 1. Any expense incurred in new product introduction. **2.** Any expense related to advertising and promotion. **3.** A cost directly or indirectly related to the exploration and exploitation of natural resources.

development loan: An interim loan to a developer, for use in preparation of raw land for building; often staged as land preparation proceeds and often part of overall construction loans, which may include the funding of the raw land development process.

development rights: A wide term, generally describing all those rights, short of ownership, sold by owners to those wishing to use their property for profit-making purposes, such as developers seeking to build or lease dwellings, or drillers seeking to extract minerals.

devise: A gift of real property by the terms of a will, consisting of land or any other kind of realty.

devolution: The passage of a right or interest to another by operation of law, such as the passage of property to its inheritors.

dictum: A judge's comments, of some interest and possible future significance, but having no direct bearing on the disposition of a case currently before that judge.

diminishing balance method: See declining balance method of depreciation.

direct current (DC): Electrical current that flows only one way within a circuit; in contrast with alternating current (AC), which constantly reverses the direction of its flow within a circuit; the two kinds of current are incompatible.

direct tax: A tax specifically directed to a taxpayer and paid by that taxpayer, such as an income tax, in contrast to a tax on goods or services, which can be passed along to the ultimate consumer of those goods, such as a sales tax.

disaster loan: A loan made by government to private parties to lessen the impact of such natural disasters as floods, riots, and volcanic eruptions.

disbursement: The immediate actual payment of money, by check or cash. Disbursements are cash out, rather than expenditures, and affect cash flow, not profit and loss.

disclaimer; 1. A denial of responsibility made in advance of any possible claim of responsibility or culpability, as in an accountant's disclaimer of responsibility for the figures underlying an unaudited annual report, or a seller's attempted disclaimer of responsibility for the quality of goods sold "as is." **2.** In law, rejection of a proffered right, property, or previously asserted claim.

disclosure: 1. The revealing of facts which may be relevant to interested and involved parties, such as the existence of possibly adverse interests on the part of a fiduciary. An example is a statement of relationship to a buyer made by a real estate broker to a represented seller, as required by the fiduciary relationship between seller and broker. **2.** The legally required process of revealing facts about people and organizations, as in the disclosure requirements surrounding the issue of stocks for public sale, those required of lenders by the Truth in Lending Law, and those required of politicians by campaign spending laws.

discount: 1. Generally, any specific subtraction from a sum due prior to payment. **2.** To make a specific subtraction from a sum before payment. In a wider sense, to evaluate skeptically assertions made by others. **3.** A reduction in price paid, usually but not always in advance of payment, as in a 2% reduction in stated price for payment received within 30 days of billing, or for quantity purchased. **4.** A reduction in the net proceeds of monies loaned, almost always in advance of payment of loan proceeds by lenders to borrowers, as in the subtraction of stated interest of 8% from the proceeds of a $100 loan. The amount of the loan is $100, the proceeds to the borrower are $92, and the borrower pays back $100. **5.** The amount by which a security is selling below its face value, as in a $1,000 bond being sold for $950, with a resulting discount of 5%. **6.** To make advance allowance for anticipated trends and events, as in discounting the impact of projected political events. In this sense, the term is often used in describing securities price fluctuations as stemming from anticipated events.

discounted cash flow: The evaluation of cash spent now on capital expenditures in terms of both the cash spent now and an assumed compound interest rate on that cash over the anticipated life of the asset acquired.

discount rate: 1. The rate of interest charged by a bank when discounting bank and commercial paper. Discount rates depend on a number of variables, including the kind of instrument being discounted and the market's assessment of the quality of the issue and issuer. **2.** The rate of interest set by Federal Reserve banks on loans to member banks. This rate varies with both economic conditions and government money policy. Raising this discount rate makes money more expensive to borrow, and is thought to be deflationary; lowering it makes money less expensive to borrow and is thought to be inflationary.

discovery: A legal procedure aimed at finding evidence in the possession of another party to an action, who is by law obliged to disclose all relevant facts and documents to other parties seeking such facts and documents.

discrimination: Actions favoring one group over another, often prohibited by law and public policy, as in the many kinds of racial, sexual, religious, political, ethnic, trade, and other economic and social discriminations. The Constitution, several Federal, state, and local laws, and a series of major court decisions prohibit public and private discrimination in the sale and rental of realty, and in associated financial and insurance matters.

dishonor: To refuse to pay the amount due on an instrument presented for payment, as in a bank's refusal to pay a check that has been stopped by its issuer or the nonpayment of any money market instrument by its issuer when due.

disintermediation: The flow of money to those savings vehicles yielding the highest interest, as in the flow of personal savings from savings accounts to government obligations when interest rates are higher on government obligations.

display advertising: Advertising in print media, such as newspapers, periodicals, billboards, and point of purchase materials, that uses prepared graphics to develop visual impact.

disposal field: A drainage field for a septic system; usually composed of gravel and tiles.

dispossession: A removal from real estate by means of legal action. The most usual dispossession proceeding is that of landlord against tenant, as for nonpayment of rent.

dispossess notice: A formal notification of dispossession served on a tenant by process of law.

dissolve: To terminate or cancel. Business organizations of all kinds can be dissolved by legislative, judicial or voluntary action, although some matters may remain open in proprietorships and partnerships. Contracts can be dissolved, as can legal proceedings and restrictions.

distraint: The seizure of property to satisfy a claim, as in the seizure of a taxpayer's property to satisfy a tax lien, or a landlord's right to seize property belonging to a defaulting tenant, when so authorized by a court.

distressed property: Property which is uneconomic for its current owner. For example, a leasable structure which is losing money because of insufficient occupancy; a rent-controlled apartment building which is occupied, but loses money due to high taxes and operating costs; or a development project that has become so expensive as to make it clear that its developer will lose money.

distress sale: A sale of property at less than normal prices by a seller who needs to sell and is willing to forego profit or take a loss in order to speed the sale; for example, a home sale by one who has purchased a home in another part of the country and is faced with the possibly ruinous prospect of carrying two homes at once.

district: An administrative area identified by its stated purpose, such as a sewer or school district.

division wall: See party wall.

document: 1. Any material carrying inscribed material which can be used in evidence, including such materials as paper, prints, canvas, stones, wood, and leather; and such inscriptions as letters, numbers, drawings, and photographs. **2.** To substantiate through the use of relevant documents.

documentary stamp taxes: See stamp taxes.

doing business: Act of conducting business within the geographical bounds of a regulating authority, and therefore becoming subject to the regulatory powers of that authority. The term is used to define several situations, but is most often encountered in taxation, as when a business is adjudged to be doing business for tax purposes in a jurisdiction, and may therefore be taxable within that jurisdiction.

dollar bond: A bond wholly denominated in United States dollars, in which interest and principal are paid in those dollars. Any bond may be so denominated.

domain: The ownership of land and absolute right to dispose of that land, subject only to the overriding right of the state to ownership of that land, expressed as the right of eminent domain.

domestic: **1.** Of a home or domicile. In business, the term usually refers to the original and legal domicile of transactions and legal entities. **2.** A worker employed in the home of another and doing work related to the place of work as a home. For example, someone employed by a family to clean their home is a domestic worker, while someone doing clerical work for a self-employed person working at home is not.

domestic corporation: A corporation chartered in a state and therefore described as domestic to that state.

domestic worker: See domestic.

domicile: That place which in law is regarded as the main place of residence of an individual or business entity. Corporations are domiciled where chartered, but for some regulatory and other legal purposes may be considered domiciled in other locations.

dominant estate: See easement.

dominant tenement: See easement.

donation: A gift, but not necessarily an irrevocable gift.

donee: One who receives a gift, becomes a beneficiary of trust, or receives a power.

donor: One who makes a gift, creates a trust, or confers a power.

door: Any aperture providing means of access; also the hinged or sliding panel covering the aperture providing that access.

dormer: A gable projecting from the sloped roof of a structure; also the vertical window set in that gable.

dormer window: See dormer.

double declining balance method of depreciation: See declining balance method of depreciation.

double digit inflation: A rate of inflation of 10% or more per year.

double entry: A bookkeeping system in which every transaction results in corresponding debit and credit entries into the system. All credits equal all debits at all times, and the net balance of credits and debits is always zero; the standard bookkeeping system used throughout the business world.

double glazing: Two panes of glass with a layer of air between them; used in thermal windows.

double hung window: A window with two vertical sliding sashes, each in its own track, with the sashes meeting midway in the window aperture; usually contains a lock where the sashes meet.

double pitched roof: A roof with two sloping sides that join at or near the center of the roof.

double taxation: A term widely used to describe alleged double taxation of corporate earnings, once through corporate income tax and again through taxation of corporate dividends paid out of after-tax earnings to stockholders.

dowel: A wooden pin used to join two other pieces of wood.

dower: At common law, the life estate right in real estate possessed by a widow on death of her husband intestate, consisting of one third of that real estate; now replaced by statutory rights in most states but still in effect in some.

down payment: A first payment made by a buyer to a seller when making a purchase. The seller may pass title and possession to the buyer on receipt of that first payment, taking deferred payment of the balance of the purchase price, or the seller may pass only possession, holding title until payment has been completed. Sometimes, the first payment is called a down payment, but is merely a returnable indication of the buyer's earnest intent to buy, as in a binder placed on a house, returnable for several possible reasons if the purchase is not consummated.

downspout: A pipe or other drain to carry rainwater away from a roof.

downzoning: A change in the zoning law affecting a given area, changing from more active to less active use, such as from multi-family to single residence use, or from half acre per residence use to full acre per residence use; often used by communities seeking to minimize business and population growth, but sometimes subject to legal attack as an illegally restrictive practice.

draft: A bill of exchange, called a draft in domestic commercial and securities transactions, in which a buyer pays a seller for goods received with a call upon the buyer's bank for the agreed-upon sum. The buyer, or drawer, makes a draft, instructing the bank, or drawee, to pay the sum to the seller, or payee.

drainage: The means by which the water flows off a body of land, whether natural or artificial.

drainage district: An administrative area, responsible for maintaining the area's drainage systems and wetlands, and capable of issuing debt obligations for those purposes.

drawee: The person or company upon which demand for payment of a draft is made, usually a bank responding to the draft of one of its clients.

drawer: A person or company making a draft, usually upon its bank, for payment of a sum to anyone.

drawing account: In some sales compensation plans, in which salespeople are paid wholly or largely on a commission basis, a continuing account the salesperson holds with the company, from which periodic salary advances are subtracted and into which commissions are paid, with periodic payment of commissions earned above salary advances.

dredging: The removal of material from the bed under a body of water; the material so removed is sometimes used for embankment and land fill purposes.

driveway: A private roadway providing access for vehicles to structures on privately owned land.

dry hole: A well drilled in pursuit of oil or natural gas that produces neither.

dry rot: A disease of timber, which causes the timber to decay and turn to powder.

drywall construction: Describing an interior wall using no wet materials, such as plaster or mortar, in its construction; made of such materials as wood or sheeted wallboard.

dual agency: The representation of both parties to a contract by a single agent. In real estate, a practice prohibited by law unless both parties consent in writing to dual representation; even with such consent, the dual agent may find it very difficult to withstand later charges of conflict of interest.

duct: A tube used for transporting gases or liquids, such as air in a heating or cooling system, or a conduit used as a passageway for cables or wires.

due date: The date on which any debt becomes payable, as in the maturity date of a bond or note.

due on encumbrance clause: A provision calling for full immediate payment of a senior debt obligation, such as a first mortgage, should the mortgagee further encumber the mortgaged property, as with a second mortgage.

due on sale clause: A provision calling for full immediate payment of a mortgage should the mortgagee sell the mortgaged property. Also called a nonassumption clause, this provision makes it possible for a lender to terminate or continue a mortgage loan with a new owner of the mortgaged property; the mortgage does not then pass with the property.

due process of law: The right to enjoy equal protection and equal responsibility with all others under the law, including the right to be heard, to defend oneself, and to have one's day in court; and the right to be governed by laws and heard by courts that are not arbitrary, capricious, or discriminatory.

dummy: In business, one who substitutes for another in a business situation, such as a dummy stockholder, who holds a stock actually belonging to another, to shield the identity of the real owner; or a dummy corporation, holding property really belonging to another.

dummy purchaser: See straw man.

duplex: 1. An apartment on two floors. **2.** A single dwelling housing two separate dwelling units.

Dutch Colonial: A house style originating in the areas of original Dutch settlement in the New World, often built of stone or brick rather than wood, and featuring gambrel roofs and large porches.

Dutch door: A door with top and bottom opening independently.

dwelling: A structure used or usable as a human residence. A dwelling can be part of a larger structure, as is an apartment, condominium, or cooperative apartment; can be attached to other structures, as is a row house; or can be a separate structure, as is a one-family house.

dwelling unit: A single housing unit, containing one or more rooms, cooking facilities, and capable of being used as a permanent residence; defined with slight variations by local laws.

E

earmarking: The segregation and use of specific funds for specific purposes, as in the use of specific Federal, state, and local tax proceeds for purposes specified by law, or the planned but non-binding setting up of specific funds for stated corporate purposes.

earnest money: A partial payment given as evidence of good faith. The term as popularly used can apply to money paid as a returnable or non-returnable binder on a purchase, to a down payment, or to any partial payment in connection with a contract.

earning power: In real estate, the extent to which a property or investment shows medium and long term ability to generate profits; no comparative yield sums are applied to this very general term.

earning statement: See income statement.

easement: A right which a landowner possesses in relation to neighboring property, without profit, but with advantage. The right itself is called, in law, the dominant estate or tenement; the land over which that right is exercised is the servient estate or tenement. An easement may be appurtenant, or passing with the land of its possessor; for example, a right of way or a shared driveway. It may be personal, and limited to its possessor; then it is an easement in gross. It may be private, and limited to a single neighboring landholder, or public, as when a public path has passed across private land for enough years to satisfy statutory requirements, with no attempt on the part of the landowner to exercise ownership rights. It may be prescriptive, as when land has openly been adversely used by another for enough time to satisfy statutory requirements. It may stem from necessity, with a court implying easement to meet practical needs; or it may be negative, as when a high rise building, which would block neighboring access to light and air, is prohibited by legal action.

easement appurtenant: See easement.

easement by necessity: See easement.

easement in gross: See easement.

easy money: An economic condition in which a nation's money supply is expanding, and credit is easy to obtain. In the United States, a period of easy money results in large part from Federal manipulation of the amount and cost of money available for commercial bank reserves and, therefore, for bank credit available to potential borrowers. In addition to Federal credit control, other factors, such as the condition of the international money market also affect available money supplies.

eaves: That part of a roof extending over the exterior walls for more than a few inches.

ECOA: See Equal Credit Opportunity Act.

ecological impact: See environmental impact statement.

ecology: The relationship of living beings to their environment; also the study of the intertwining of life and environment.

economic: 1. Relating in any way to the economy. 2. Relating in any way to the study of economics. 3. The most efficient and least costly way of handling an economic matter.

economic depreciation: See economic obsolescence.

economic life: See service life.

economic obsolescence: A loss of value having the same effect as physical depreciation for valuation purposes, but not capable of being treated as depreciation for tax purposes. It can be caused by such external economic factors as loss of privacy or access; by the presence of new and adverse factors in the local environment, such as industrial fumes or a chemical dump; or by neighborhood deterioration. Also known as economic depreciation.

economic rent: An estimate of the amount of rent that might be commanded by a property in the current rental market, at fair market value. Always an estimate; contrasts with contract rent, which is the actual rent amount specified in a lease. Also called market rent.

ecosystem: An environment, with all major living and inanimate portions intertwined; often used as synonymous with environment, and applied broadly to such diverse environments as a whole planet, a region, and a mud puddle.

edifice complex: A term of derogation applied to those who cause large physical structures, such as office buildings, highways, and malls, to be built with private or public funds under their control, when those structures are largely unnecessary and often both economically wasteful and destructive to the organizations and individuals building them; for example, the construction of a very large headquarters building by a corporation in deep financial difficulty, which shortly afterward goes bankrupt, in part due to the financial drain caused by that office building.

EDP: See electronic data processing.

effective age: The age assigned to a building for appraisal purposes, which often differs from the actual age of the building, as unusual physical deterioration may lower anticipated age, and renewal and remodeling may raise anticipated age, for appraisal purposes.

effective date: The date on which an agreement goes into effect, as specified by contract, purchase order, insurance policy, or other specifying document.

effective rate: **1.** The real, as distinct from the quoted, rates of interest paid on borrowings, as in a bank's quoted 8% interest rate that is a real 12% rate on a personal loan. **2.** The real, as distinct from the quoted, yield on investments, figuring the yield as a percentage of market value, rather than as a percentage of face value.

efficiency unit: A small permanent living unit or apartment, distinguished from transient accommodations by its possession of a cooking area and a bathroom; often a single room, sometimes called a studio apartment, but may have two or three rooms.

effluent: **1.** An outflowing stream. **2.** Any flow, whether stream or seepage, out of a waste disposal system, such as a sewage or industrial waste system.

egress: A way of leaving; an exit. Contrasts with ingress, which is a way of entering; an entrance.

ejectment: An action at law taken by an owner to expel another from his or her real property; for example, to expel a trespasser or a previous tenant in occupancy after expiration of a lease.

electronic data processing (EDP): The recording and processing of data by electronic means, using computers and computer-related machines, materials, and techniques. EDP is by far the widest use to which computers are put.

eleemosynary: Connected in some way with charity and charitable organizations.

eleemosynary corporation: A not-for-profit corporation organized for charitable purposes.

elevation: **1.** A drawing of the outside of a structure; either a side or front view. **2.** Height, as measured from any other height; where no other reference point is specified, height above sea level.

embezzlement: The fraudulent taking of valuables by one acting in a fiduciary capacity for their owner. The valuables taken may be in any form, including cash and all other kinds of property; the embezzler may be in any position of fiduciary trust, including employees such as bank tellers, company treasurers, public officials, agents, and representatives.

emblement: A crop grown as a result of personal labor and attention, which in law is the personal property of its grower, and which continues to belong to its grower even after tenancy of the land on which it is grown is terminated. A landlord is legally required to allow removal of such growing crops on termination of tenancy, and to allow re-entry for purposes of removal if harvest time occurs after termination of tenancy.

eminent domain: The right of government to take property from private holders at any time, with or without payment, temporarily or permanently, for public purposes. The right is absolute; the question of payment depends on factors that must often be adjudicated. In times of peace, such taking mainly arises around such public projects as roads and dams and almost always involves payment to the private holders; in times of war and other national crises, such taking may be uncompensated.

Employee Retirement Security Act (ERISA): A Federal law that attempts to protect employee retirement benefit rights under existing and future private benefit plans, providing safeguards regarding adequate plan fundings, administration, and structure, as well as dealing with certain Federal tax aspects of such benefit plans. It also provides the legal basis for the development of Individual Retirement Accounts.

empty nester: One whose children have matured and left the family home, and who continues to occupy that home.

encroachment: 1. The physical intrusion of some element of the real property of one onto the property of another private owner or upon publicly owned property; for example, a garage roof or tree that overhangs but does not close a public road, or a fence built partly on another's property. **2.** An additional element of easement, adding to the extent of that easement, as in attempted expansion of an existing right of way.

encumbrance: A lien, right, claim, burden, charge, or liability on property, which does not necessarily serve to block passage of title to that property, but which usually lessens the value that property would have if unencumbered. The term is usually used in relation to real property, but is sometimes used in relation to personal property as well.

end loan: A loan to a building purchaser, completing the chain of loans financing a structure or group of structures, such as a mortgage loan to the buyer of a new single family home in a development, or to a new condominium unit buyer.

endorse: 1. To sign a document, such as a check, bill of exchange, or other negotiable instrument, and thereby make passage of title possible. **2.** To publicly approve of someone or something, as in recommendation of a product.

endorsee: One to whom an endorsement and delivery are made.

endorsement: The actual signature of the owner of a document, making that document negotiable and passage of title possible. That signature must be on the document or otherwise attached to the document. Where the endorsement is to a specific entity, both signature and the delivery of the signed instrument to the one specified is required for the transaction to be completed; where the endorsement is in blank, as on a bearer bond, only delivery is needed. Also spelled indorsement.

endorser: See endorse.

energy: The power released by a change in physical state, as in the change from water to steam. The power so released can be unusable by humans, as in a thunderstorm, or usable, as in a power plant that generates the energy to heat a city by burning fossil fuel.

energy conservation: The saving of increasingly scarce and costly energy by application of a wide number of techniques aimed at reducing energy losses, switching to more available and sometimes less expensive sources of energy, and developing new energy sources; for example, the use of insulation to cut fuel waste and the development of solar energy to replace fossil fuels.

energy policy: The policies, plans, and actions of government regarding the use, conservation, pricing, finding, and developing of energy for public and private purposes.

Energy Research and Development Administration (ERDA): A Federal agency responsible for research and development activities in energy and energy-related matters, such as energy conservation and the development of alternative sources of energy.

energy source: Anything that can be used to produce energy; in practice usually referring to those sources that can now be used to produce energy for human purposes. Thunderstorms, therefore, are sometimes described as potential energy sources, but hardly ever as energy sources.

enjoin: See injunction.

entail: Any restriction imposed by prior testators upon the free disposition of that estate by subsequent owners; quite commonly encountered in families seeking to provide an unbroken line of family inheritance, particularly as family-owned real property is passed by will for several generations.

entrance: An aperture providing access to a defined area, such as a parcel of real property, any defined portion of that parcel, or any structure or portion of a structure on it. Also refers to use of that aperture to effect access.

environmental impact statement: A detailed report on the impact a proposed action will have on the environment it affects, as required by applicable Federal, state, and local laws and regulations; includes a full description of the action, its anticipated environmental effects, possible alternatives, and associated resource allocations.

Environmental Protection Agency (EPA): An agency of the United States Government, charged with monitoring, protection, and standard-setting functions in such areas as air, water, noise, pesticide, and radiation pollution, as well as sewage, industrial waste, and other liquid and solid waste disposal; the EPA administers a wide range of educational, regulatory, and technical assistance programs in such areas.

EPA: See Environmental Protection Agency.

Equal Credit Opportunity Act (ECOA): A Federal statute forbidding discrimination against borrowers by lenders on the basis of marital status, sex, race, color, religion, age, ethnic origin, or for any other substantial reason; requires lenders to inform borrowers of their statutory rights, of whatever action has been taken by the lender on the loan application, and if requested by lender, the reasons for the action taken.

equalization: The process of adjusting assessments, and therefore property taxes, to reflect fair comparisons with similar properties in the same or other taxing districts; the work of state, county, and local equalization boards.

equalization board: See equalization.

equitable conversion: In law, the treatment of real property which has been sold but not closed, and on which title has not yet legally passed, as if its title had already passed to its buyer, with its seller holding title only as security against the buyer's promise to pay the purchase price at closing. The seller's interest in the real property thereby becomes personal property, a money interest, and capable of being passed on to the seller's heirs should the seller die before the closing occurs. Equity or fairness is then done both seller and buyer, and the real property transaction is then completed.

equitable lien: A lien created by court action, where no lien would otherwise exist, as when a court implies the existence of a lien on property from the intent of parties to a contract.

equity: 1. The money value of that which is owned, arrived at by subtracting all that is owed from the value of the ownership to arrive at a net ownership value figure. Some examples are: the value of real property minus all mortgages and other borrowings; the market value of stocks in a margin account minus the borrowings in the account; and the value of all outstanding common and preferred stock in a corporation. In some instances, as in determining the value of stock in a margin account, the ownership value can be easily determined at any time, as both market value and borrowings are firm figures. But often, as in attempting to determine a homeowner's equity in a mortgaged home, equity is only an estimate because the market value of the home is only an estimate until the home is sold. **2.** The concept of fairness and justice applied to that portion of the English common law relating to the rights and duties of individuals. Once administered through a separate system of courts, called chancery courts, cases involving matters of equity are now handled within the regular court system.

equity financing: A stock issue, in which a corporation sells a piece of its ownership to others to raise money, as distinct from raising money by borrowing.

equity of redemption: The right of a property owner whose property has been forfeited for non-payment of mortgage debt, to reclaim that forfeited property by paying debt, interest, and associated costs; must be exercised before the property is sold to satisfy the mortgage.

equity participation: 1. The share an investor or investing organization takes of an investment; for example, of a real estate investment or a new securities issue. **2.** The share taken by a party to a joint venture, business organization, or any other pool of shared assets.

ERDA: See Energy Research and Development Administration.

ERISA: See Employee Retirement Security Act.

erosion: The gradual loss of land, and often of subsurface materials, by the action of the elements and waterways.

escalation: A contractual provision allowing or mandating cost increases on items covered by the contract, on the occurrence of stated events. For example, many commercial leases provide for rent increases in the event of increased taxes or labor costs; some mortgages tie interest rates to one or more money market rates; and many construction contracts provide additional payments to contractors in the event of increased costs.

escalator clause: The specific clause in a contract allowing or mandating escalation under certain circumstances.

escape clause: A contractual provision allowing one or both parties to avoid contractual obligations under prescribed circumstances, as for non-performance of contractually defined duties by another party.

escheat: The taking of property by the national government when there is no other legal inheritor, on the theory that the state is the residual owner of all property within its boundaries.

escrow: The holding by a third party of something of value which is the subject of a contract or proceeding between two other parties, until that contract or proceeding has been consummated; the third party is an escrow agent. Escrow agents may be individuals, attorneys, brokers, escrow companies, banks, title companies, or any other persons or organizations agreed upon by the parties to the contract. In some states, real estate sales are conducted through such escrow agents, rather than directly by the parties to the transaction, with the parties depositing all documents and checks with the escrow agent, who ultimately consummates the entire transaction.

escrow account: A bank account holding funds in escrow, with the bank or the depositor acting as escrow agent for one or more depositors. Such accounts are maintained by mortgage lenders, who in many instances hold the funds of mortgage borrowers in escrow for the payment of property taxes and other property-related fees and charges, as well as by banks, attorneys, and fiduciaries for a wide variety of other purposes.

escrow agent: See escrow.

estate: **1.** Any and all individual ownerships or interests and the total of all ownerships and interests in real or personal property, including absolute, conditional, and contingent interests. In economic and legal senses, the term describes anything owned on which a monetary value can ultimately be placed. **2.** The sum of all such individual ownerships and interests remaining after death.

estate accounting: Accounting practice and procedures dealing with matters connected with the administration of estates, as specified by law and administered by the courts.

estate income: Income derived from property held by estates.

estate tax: An excise tax upon the entire estate of a deceased, levied by the Federal Government and the states. The tax is in form a progressive transfer tax on all valuable property of the deceased, including life insurance proceeds, jointly owned property, and intangible interests on which an evaluation can be placed by taxing authorities.

estoppel: In law, actions or assertions that are barred because of previous actions or assertions, such as the commission of a previous fraud or illegal act; misstatement or concealment of facts causing another to take action to his or her own detriment; or creation of a document which recites facts which may not thereafter be denied, such as those found in a valid deed, contract, or loan instrument.

estoppel by deed: See estoppel.

estuary: A body of water in which river meets sea, with fresh and salt water mixing, and a sea tide coming some distance into the mouth of the river.

eviction: The legal removal of a tenant from occupied realty. That removal is usually accomplished by a legal proceeding and judgment, although in some circumstances it is accomplished by the landlord's re-entry, if legal; but mere dispossession of a tenant by a landlord is not in itself a legal eviction.

evidence of insurability: Proof that one seeking insurance is free of conditions unacceptable to an insurer; for example, the results of a medical examination showing an insurance applicant to be free of physical problems that would cause an insurer to decline to issue the life insurance policy sought.

exception: 1. In real estate, something specifically excluded from property passing to another by lease or deed, which otherwise would have been part of the property conveyed. **2.** In insurance, synonymous with exclusion.

exchange: A conveyance of property for property, rather than of property for money, although money, which is called *boot* in this kind of transaction, may also be involved. This is sometimes called a tax-free exchange, as no tax is paid on gains that would otherwise have been taxable in a money-for-property transaction; in fact, it is a tax-deferred, rather than tax-free transaction, with tax on all the taxable gain in a property due when a taxable transfer or ownership takes place. Business and investment properties that are substantially similar in kind and in form of ownership can usually be exchanged, except that leaseholds of thirty years or more may be exchanged for freehold interests. Personal residences and property held primarily for resale, as by dealers, are excluded from this favorable tax-deferred treatment.

excise tax: A tax on two quite different kinds of activities: sales of goods and intangible privileges. It is usually described as a single kind of tax on the privilege of selling those goods and exercising those privileges. Excise taxes are levied, either as a percentage of the selling price or a fixed amount per item sold, on a wide variety of goods, including such necessities as gasoline and such luxuries as handbags. They are also levied on a wide variety of privileges, such as franchises and licenses.

exclusion: Anything specifically excluded from a set of contractual obligations or insurance policy coverages.

exclusionary zoning: Zoning laws designed to exclude others from an existing community, such as four acre zoning recently downzoned to limit the number of people able to move into a community by enlarging permissible building lot sizes; often used to describe zoning designed to discriminate on the basis of age, sex, race, color, ethnic origin, and other discriminations prohibited by law and court decision.

exclusive agent: One who is the only agent representing another on a specific matter or kind of matter, such as a real estate broker who is the only agent authorized to represent the seller on sale of a house. In real estate, an exclusive agent is entitled to a seller's fee if the property is sold by another broker, but not if the property is sold by the owner.

exclusive right to sell: The right of a real estate agent to be the only seller of a property, and to receive a seller's fee whoever sells the property during the period of exclusive listing, a right conveyed by the owner of the property in writing and for a specified period.

execution: 1. The performance of an act, such as the carrying out of a legal judgment, the signing of a document, or the performance of a contractual obligation. **2.** The seizure of property by an officer of the court pursuant to a legal judgment.

executor: One who is appointed by the maker of a will to carry out the provisions of that will as nearly as possible consonant with the wishes of the maker, and who undertakes to do so after the decease of the maker.

executory contract: A contract which lacks some required performance by one of its parties, and is therefore not yet completed; in real estate, title may not pass until the contract is complete.

executory interest: A future interest in real or personal property, currently stated, and coming into being on the occurrence of specified future events, such as the grant of an interest in land to one named in a will and her or his heirs; the heirs' interest is executory.

exemplary damages: Damages awarded to a plaintiff beyond those directly provable as having been caused by the actions of the defendant; usually awarded for such matters as defamation and other damages to character and reputation, sometimes as specified by statute.

exhibit: **1.** A document or any other tangible item produced and made part of the body of evidence developed during the course of a legal proceeding. **2.** A document or section of a document presented as part of the supporting or illustrative data in a book or report. The distinctions between exhibits, footnotes, notes, and other supporting material are imprecise.

expansion attic: An unfinished attic capable of later being converted into one or more finished rooms.

expansion joint: A joint allowing for expansion of those things joined, to compensate for swelling and contraction due to heat and humidity.

expense: **1.** A cost incurred in the course of doing business and attributable to the business done. **2.** A present operating cost. **3.** Outlays attributed to accounting periods, as determined by accounting systems and conventions used and by company objectives and financial management techniques.

experience rating: The settling of insurance premium rates to reflect past experience of losses and consequent payments due to claims originating in the individuals or groups so rated.

expiration: The ending of a term specified by contract, such as the end of a periodical subscription term or an insurance coverage period.

ex post facto law: A law retroactively providing penalties for actions previously legal, or which changes the nature of the penalties assessed for previously illegal actions; an unconstitutional practice.

exposure: **1.** The siting of a structure or portion of a structure as regards direction and the elements; for example, a north-facing room may be described as having a northern exposure. **2.** The amount that is at risk by an insurer, on an insurance policy, usually measured by the maximum amount of insurance that may have to be paid in claims on that policy under conditions of maximum possible liability. **3.** A very general measure of the risks involved in taking any course of action, and in business with special emphasis on money risks.

express warranty: A warranty specifically stated by a seller to a buyer, in writing or orally, and binding upon the seller if provable by the buyer.

expropriation: The taking of private property by government, usually under a government's power of eminent domain, with or without compensation, as in the governmental takeover and subsequent nationalization of the property of a foreign or domestic company operating within its borders.

extended bonds: Bonds that come to maturity and on which the face value is not paid but held by the issuer, with interest payments instead continued and the original backing of the bonds unchanged. Issuers desiring to extend their bonds must offer to do so and have that offer accepted by their bondholders.

extended coverage: Property insurance coverage which is expanded beyond normal bounds to include risks beyond basic property coverage, as in the extension of basic coverage beyond fire and theft to include floods and earthquakes.

extender provision: See carryover provision.

extension: 1. An agreement to lengthen any agreed-upon term, such as the term of a loan, lease, bond, or option period. **2.** An addition to an existing structure.

extensive cultivation: The farming of large tracts of land with relative small amounts of labor and machinery, and often with little regard for the continuing health of the land in singleminded pursuit of the highest possible short-term cash yield; increasingly an outmoded way of using the land as world population grows and land costs rise.

exterior finish: The finish of the outside walls of a structure, such as paint, brick, or wood shingles.

extractive industry: An industry that takes its materials from nature, as in the mining of coal, iron, and gold, and the drilling and taking of oil and natural gas.

extractive rights lease: See oil and gas lease.

extraordinary depreciation: Depreciation far beyond that ordinarily to be expected, caused by such unusual matters as protracted cold or precipitation, extraordinary use factors, and unanticipated obsolescence, but not including such property loss matters as fire, flood, and theft.

extraordinary expenses: A very unusual and often entirely unanticipated expense, which must be taken into account separately for financial statement purposes, rather than being placed in with and to some extent therefore distorting normal expenses.

exurb: A primarily country area located just beyond the suburbs of a city, and thought to be relatively inaccessible to city commuters; a community description that often changes rather quickly as metropolitan areas and commuting ranges expand.

F

facade: The face or front wall of a building; often used to describe a front wall that is especially designed or ornamented.

face brick: Any decorative brick used for outside walls or ornamental interior brickwork.

face value: The amount stamped, printed, or otherwise affixed on an instrument of value, indicating its stated value when issued or at maturity. Coins, currency, notes, bonds, stocks, insurance policies, and other such instruments have such face values, with bonds and insurance policies carrying stated values as of their maturity dates, and stocks carrying par values that often have no real relation to their market values.

factory: Any building or portion of a building used for the production of goods.

factory built house: A house literally built in sections in a factory, and then moved to a building site for assembly; a kind of prefabricated house.

fair access to insurance: The concept that minority groups are entitled by law and public policy to equal access to insurance, embodied in the reinsurance plans administered by the Department of Housing and Urban Development (HUD), which are called Fair Access to Insurance Requirements, or FAIR plans.

fair credit and information reporting practices: A body of practices developed under the statutory authority provided by the Fair Credit Reporting Act and the Freedom of Information Act, providing those listed in public and private dossiers the ability to examine those parts of their files that have no effect on national security matters, and to dispute any portion of those dossiers they consider untrue, unfair, or legally actionable.

Fair Credit Reporting Act: A Federal statute that defines fair credit checking and reporting practices and provides a basis for regulating those practices, as well as providing recourse for aggrieved consumers.

fair employment practices: A body of practices, defined by a substantial number of Federal, state, and local laws and regulations, aimed at prohibiting discrimination in employment on the basis of race, color, religion, political belief, age, sex, national origin, or any other basis defined in law.

fair housing: The concept that the Constitution and public policy forbid discrimination in housing on the basis of race, color, age, sex, ethnic or national origin, or any similar or closely related reason, as embodied in a series of Constitutional, statutory, regulatory, executive department, and judicial actions, starting with the Civil Rights Act of 1866. Also called open housing.

fair market value: The trading price of anything, at which a willing and informed seller and buyer will or would trade, and without either party possessing extraordinary trading leverage. The term is used widely in setting values for tax assessment and judicial purposes.

FAIR plans: See fair access to insurance.

fair return: A theory and series of formulas developed by regulatory bodies and the courts to determine what rates of profit should be allowed to companies in highly regulated industries such as telephone companies, power-supplying utilities, and railroads.

fallow land: Land that has been plowed, but left unseeded for a growing season.

Fannie Mae: See Federal National Mortgage Association.

FAR: See floor area ratio.

farm: 1. To work the land or work on the land to produce crops and animals, for sale or personal consumption. **2.** A business producing crops and animals from the land for sale and exchange, with business size ranging from the very small farm operation, farmed part-time, in which some family members work at other occupations, to massive farm enterprises known as agribusinesses.

Farm Credit Administration (FCA): A Federal agency charged with the responsibility for administering a wide range of credit alternatives for American farmers, organized into a cooperative farm credit system that includes Federal land banks, Federal land bank associations, intermediate credit banks, production credit associations, and banks for cooperatives.

Farmers Home Administration: An agency of the Department of Agriculture, which loans money on favorable terms to farmers who might otherwise find affordable credit difficult or impossible to secure. Loans are available for a wide variety of purposes, including home and land ownership, operating expenses, and special projects.

farmland: Land that is primarily used for agricultural purposes; often land purchased by speculative investors anticipating use of the land purchased for development.

farm surplus: Farm production which is unsalable at current market prices to available markets, and which is held or destroyed, often pursuant to government policy and accompanied by government support payments to farmers.

FCA: See Farm Credit Administration.

FCIC: See Federal Crop Insurance Corporation.

FDIC: See Federal Deposit Insurance Corporation.

FEA: See Federal Energy Administration.

feasibility study: A formal investigation of all relevant aspects of a proposed project, including such matters as costs and the possibilities of practical accomplishment.

Federal: 1. Relating to some aspect of the national government of the United States. 2. A house style developed in the late 18th and early 19th centuries, featuring such Neoclassical elements as columned porticos, straight lines, and severe simplicity, but lightened by the use of much white paint and ornamental ironwork; the White House is an outstanding example of the Federal style.

Federal Crop Insurance Corporation (FCIC): A Federal agency, part of the Department of Agriculture, responsible for a national system of federally funded insurance against crop losses due to natural and unavoidable causes, such as weather and insects, rather than such avoidable causes as market conditions and uncompetitive work practices.

Federal Deposit Insurance Corporation (FDIC): An independent Federal agency that insures individual deposits up to certain limits in all national banks and in all state banks that are part of the Federal Reserve System, as well as in those other banks which apply for such insurance. The FCIC has substantial regulatory and supervisory powers as well.

Federal Energy Administration (FEA): An independent Federal agency, responsible for developing a coherent policy regarding United States energy resources and conservation, encouraging development of existing and new energy resources and conservation techniques. The FEA also functions as an information resource for energy users and developers.

Federal Home Loan Bank System: A federally organized and administered banking system, consisting of twelve regional Federal Home Loan Banks that supply credit reserves to all savings and loan associations, which must by law be members of the system, and to other lending institutions, including savings banks and insurance companies, engaged in home mortgage lending.

Federal Home Loan Mortgage Corporation (Freddie Mac or FHLMC): A Federal agency that trades in home mortgages, providing a means by which Federal funds are channelled into the secondary home mortgage market, in an attempt to expand and help stabilize that market and make mortgage money available to those seeking it.

Federal Housing Administration (FHA): A Federal agency, part of the Department of Housing and Urban Development, responsible for a wide variety of mortgage and loan insurance functions covering all the forms of residential housing. It acts primarily as an insurer of loans made by private lenders, rather than as a lender itself, and sets standards which must be met before loans will be insured, in such areas as lending practices, documents, procedures, building design, and construction.

Federal land banks: Part of the farm credit system administered by the Farm Credit Administration, consisting of twelve Federal land banks, that make long-term mortgage loans at favorable rates and for a wide variety of purposes to the members of some hundreds of land bank associations throughout the country.

Federal National Mortgage Association (Fannie Mae, or FNMA): A privately owned, federally originated and regulated corporation which buys, sells, and otherwise deals in mortgages, helping to provide liquidity in the secondary market for home mortgages and therefore greater availability of mortgage money for borrowers; originally a Federal agency dealing only in government insured or guaranteed mortgages, but now dealing in these and conventional mortgages. The corporation finances its activities through the issuance of federally guaranteed debt instruments, and in net effect is a mixed public-private financing form.

Federal Reserve Bank: One of the twelve central Federal banks, each operating in one of the twelve Federal Reserve Districts in the United States.

Federal Reserve Board of Governors: The chief policy-making body of the Federal Reserve System, composed of seven Presidentially-appointed, Senate-approved members, each serving seven years, and with terms expiring at different times to assure continuity within the Board. It is an independent body, with major power to influence the direction of the United States through its control of money and credit policies, tools which it openly and consciously uses to influence national and international economic trends.

Federal Reserve credit: The total of all Federal Reserve Bank credit outstanding, including government securities, loans to commercial banks, and checks outstanding; the base of the credit system of the United States, and a key government instrument of money and credit manipulation in pursuit of national purposes. As that credit outstanding increases, so does commercial bank lending power, at a multiple of that increase, fueling both economic activity and the tendency toward inflation; as it decreases, lending ability decreases and economic activity tends to diminish.

Federal Reserve System: The United States Federal banking system, operating as a central money and credit control organization and as a system of twelve regional banks implementing the policies of the central Board of Governors. One of the world's major banking systems, it has substantial impact on national and international economic events and trends.

Federal savings and loan association: A savings and loan association whose main business is home mortgage lending, and which is chartered and regulated by the Federal Home Loan Bank Board.

Federal Trade Commission (FTC): An independent Federal agency, responsible for enforcing and interpreting anti-trust laws and a wide range of other laws relating to unfair competition, consumer protection, deceptive practices, and other matters affecting free and fair competition. The FTC is the main Federal trade regulatory body and has an extremely wide mandate.

Feds: A popular term for Federal officers, applies loosely to all Federal law enforcement officers.

fee: 1. A charge for a professional service, whether rendered by a private practitioner or an employee of government. The term is also often broadly used as synonymous with payment. **2.** A hereditary ownership estate or ownership interest stemming from inheritance; used mainly in relation to real property, but applying also to all such interests, including personal property. It is an absolute, unconditional ownership of land or other estate, which belongs to its holder during his or her lifetime and then passes to the holder's inheritors; synonymous with fee simple and fee simple absolute.

fee simple: See fee.

fee simple absolute: See fee.

fee simple conditional: An ownership interest that would be absolute if not in some fashion limited, as by the occurrence of a stated event, such as departure from specified land uses or passage to other than a fixed line of heirs. Several other terms are used synonymously in the law, including fee simple defeasible, fee simple determinable, base fee, conditional fee, qualified fee, determinable fee, and defeasible fee; no real current differences exist between these terms.

fee simple defeasible: See fee simple conditional.

fee simple determinable: See fee simple conditional.

fee tail: An absolute ownership interest or freehold estate in which the right of inheritance is limited to a fixed line of succession, consisting of the direct "issue of the body," or blood relations. Property so limited is described as being *in entail*.

felony: A serious, usually major crime, such as murder, arson, rape, and robbery involving substantial sums; but except where defined by statute, no longer definitively separated from the term misdemeanor.

FHA: See Federal Housing Administration.

FHLMC: See Federal Home Loan Mortgage Corporation.

fidelity bond: A policy insuring employers against losses caused by employee dishonesty, actionable negligence, and non-performance of obligations; also called a blanket bond.

fiduciary: One who has a relationship of trust, including one holding specific and legal status as a trustee of any kind. A fiduciary may be an executor or administrator of an estate, as well as anyone holding any position of trust, as does a banker, lawyer, or company treasurer.

fiduciary accounting: A body of accounting practice relating to property being held by legally recognized fiduciaries, such as executors, administrators, and trustees.

fiduciary capacity: A relationship in which trust of an agent acting in money and property matters is central to the relationship between the parties. The fiduciary has a position of trust, either defined as such by the very nature of that position, as with trustees and executors, or capable of being so construed by law, as with lawyers, banks, and corporate financial officers.

file: 1. In real estate, to publicly record a document; also the public record so created. **2.** A group of related records, whether held as information on paper in a file cabinet or in computer storage.

finance: 1. To raise and supply money for any purpose, as in securing of funds needed by an enterprise by borrowing, by selling shares, or from personal resources. **2.** The entire field of money, credit, and capital, including theories, practices, and institutions.

finance company: A company mainly in the business of making loans to individuals, businesses, or both, such as personal finance companies, specializing in loans to individuals; and sales finance companies, specializing in the buying and collecting of business accounts receivable.

financial accounting: A body of accounting practice concerned with matters relating to the financial side of a business, including income, expenditures, assets, and liabilities.

financial expense: A business expense directly attributable to financing, as are mortgage and bond interest payments.

financial statement: Any formal statement that indicates the current financial position of a company or individual, such as a balance sheet, profit and loss statement, flow of funds statement, or any other summary document helping to illuminate that financial position, and including any supporting material.

financier: One who finances a business operated by others; usually one whose main business is the use of substantial sums of money to finance large businesses run by others, whether those sums are loaned or are venture capital.

financing fee: A fee charged by lender to borrower or by broker to borrower, for the securing or granting of a real-estate-connected loan, usually for a mortgage loan. The fee is paid at the beginning of the transaction, and is normally stated as a percentage of the total loan, each percent being one "point." The amount of the fee is determined by money market conditions and is a matter of negotiation between the parties; in some periods, no such fee is obtainable by lenders, while in others they may demand and get as much as 3 to 5%. Also called an origination fee or placement fee.

financing statement: A notice filed with an appropriate public recordkeeping authority by a lender who has accepted personal property as security for a loan, specifying the parties and the security; often used by those selling fixtures under conditional sales contracts which may be attached to and become part of real property, to establish their prior liens on those fixtures in case of default.

finder: One who brings the parties to a financial transaction together, whose role in so doing is recognized by those parties, and who is in some way compensated by them for that role.

finder's fee: A fee paid to a finder by one or more of the parties to a financial transaction. Such fees are usually highly negotiable as between parties and finders and are often paid as a matter of practice rather than of contract.

finish flooring: The topmost level of flooring, on which people walk, usually made of some finished, rather than rough, material; but where material such as wall-to-wall carpeting is placed over that flooring, as in some inexpensive new construction, the flooring may be described as finished, but actually be of such subflooring materials as composition board or plywood.

fire brick: A building block made of fire resistant materials.

fire insurance: A form of property insurance, providing protection against losses resulting from fires, often including extended coverage against other hazards, such as smoke or windstorm.

fireproof: Made of materials which will not burn even under conditions of intense surrounding heat. If a container, such as a safe, is of such tight and strong construction as to resist the heat and pressure conditions at the hottest parts of most fires, it is considered fireproof.

fire resistant: Made of materials that resist combustion and pressure, but short of fireproof.

fire wall: A wall made of fireproof or fire resistant materials, designed to stop or impede the spread of fire within a structure.

firm: 1. Any business organization, including corporations, partnerships, and sole proprietorships. **2.** Non-negotiable, as applied to any aspect of a contemplated transaction by one of the parties involved. The term is most often encountered in price matters, where a potential seller quotes a fixed and non-negotiable price.

firm commitment: See commitment.

firm price: A price that is non-negotiable or minimally negotiable; normally found in a seller's market, in which demand is considerably in excess of supply.

first mortgage: A mortgage senior to all other mortgages, in that it is the first loan to be secured by the property mortgaged, and therefore is the first to be paid in the event of sale of the property.

first mortgage bond: A bond wholly secured by a first mortgage on part or all of the property of its issuer, as well as by the issuer's promise to pay. Some bonds that are only partly secured by first mortgages, and otherwise secured by such collateral as second mortgages and their issuer's promise to pay, are sometimes called first mortgage bonds, usually with qualifying phrases added, but are in fact junior bonds, and therefore of lesser quality.

fiscal year: 1. For tax purposes, a 12 month period ending with the last day of any month other than December, in contrast to a calendar year, which ends only on the last day of December. **2.** For accounting purposes, any year-long period, including any 12 months, 52 weeks, or other set of accounting periods running consecutively and adding up to a year.

fixed assets: Assets that are part of the operating capital of a business, such as land, buildings, machinery, and associated tangible production-related items.

fixed charges: Periodic and continuing financial overhead charges that must be paid, and that have no direct relationship to the level of activity of a business, including such charges as rent, interest, and depreciation.

fixed costs: Periodic and continuing operating costs which are not directly and immediately affected by the level of operations, though they may be in the long term. Fixed costs include general administration and indirect labor and materials costs; also called fixed overhead.

fixed lease: See gross lease.

fixed overhead: See fixed costs.

fixed price contract: A contract stating a firm price, in contrast to a contract stating a conditional price. For example, a contract to buy a house states a fixed price and is consummated at that price, while a government contract or any construction contract may have a number of possible price-increasing conditions built into its terms, such as materials costs and labor rate increases.

fixture: Something that has been attached to land or a building and has therefore, in law, become part of that to which it is attached, such as a fence, sink, or built-in cabinet.

flashing: Strips or sheets of metal, such as copper or tin, used in constructions to help prevent leakage in vulnerable areas, such as around chimneys, drainpipes, and dormers.

flat: A dwelling unit all on one level, such as an apartment on all or part of one floor of a multi-family dwelling.

flat lease: See gross lease.

flexible rate mortgage: See flexible rates.

flexible rates: Rates of interest that vary with stated conditions; for example, the flexible rate mortgage, in which the rate of interest varies as other stated factors vary, such as the prime mortgage lending rate or the Consumer Price Index (CPI). Flexible rates can vary with the changes occurring in any stated period; for mortgage loans, rates tend to be re-evaluated at two, three, and five year intervals. Also called variable rates and renegotiable rates.

floater: A form of property insurance covering transportable property, including both personal and business property, and moving with the property insured. Floaters usually cover specific items at their appraised values, and are widely used to cover such valuables as jewels, art objects, money instruments, and equipment, often for all or almost all risks and sometimes worldwide.

floating interest rate: An interest rate that is not fixed, but moves with other money market factors, especially with changes in the prime rate. As a practical matter, most businesses with bank lines of credit have de facto floating interest rates.

flood insurance: Insurance coverage for flood damage; usually written by private insurers, but subsidized by the Federal Government.

floor: 1. A horizontal surface within an enclosure, used for moving about on, such as the floor of a room. **2.** A story in a multi-story building. **3.** A bottom, as in a minimum price requirement set by a seller in an auction.

floor area ratio (FAR): The ratio arrived at by dividing the total floor area of a structure by the total area of the parcel of land on which it stands; a key element in many urban area zoning laws, aimed at limiting building and population densities.

floor loan: The minimum of two or more possible loan amounts in a loan previously agreed upon by lender and borrower. For example, when a permanent mortgage loan to a builder is based upon both completion of construction and the occurrence of other stated events, such as achievement of a specified level of occupancy or cash flow, the lender will loan the minimum or floor amount; when other conditions are met, the balance of the loan will be completed; should the conditions be met by the time construction has been completed, the entire loan will be completed at that time. Also called a floor to ceiling loan.

floor plan: A set of detailed architectural drawings, showing all interior designs and sizes, room by room and floor by floor.

floor to ceiling loan: See floor loan.

flowthrough: See passthrough.

flue: A tube, pipe, or any other such passageway through which smoke and other gases are expelled, as from a furnace or fireplace.

FNMA: See Federal National Mortgage Association.

footcandle: A measure of illumination; one footcandle is the amount of illumination received by a surface one foot away from a single candle.

footing: The support at the base of a structure, serving as anchor and stabilizer, such as the concrete base of a wall or column.

forbearance: A lender's decision not to take action currently against a borrower in default; usually a decision based on some evidence of the borrower's intent and ability to cure the default by payment of amounts due and to keep up timely future payments.

forced loan: A loan which is made by the lender due to the pressure of circumstances, rather than by choice, as in the payment of a customer's overdraft or the extension of an unpaid loan when due.

forced sale: A sale that is made by the seller due to the pressure of circumstances, rather than by choice, as in the involuntary sale of foreclosed property by law or the voluntary sale of goods at a loss to raise cash to save a business.

force majeure clause: A contractual provision shielding the parties from penalties of nonperformance due to circumstances beyond their control, such as acts of God, war, insurrection, fire, flood, and earthquake.

foreclosure: A legal proceeding, in which a defaulted-against mortgage holder, bondholder, or other party entitled to take the property from its owner, takes legal possession of that property, and causes it to be sold at public auction. Depending on the jurisdiction, the sale may be authorized by judicial proceeding or by the terms of the debt instrument in default. Foreclosure sale proceeds are used first to pay all debts and costs due, with the balance going to the former property owner; if less is realized than is due, the former property owner is liable for the balance due, except where a debt instrument holder has previously agreed to treat the debt as non-recourse, limiting liability only to the property itself.

foreclosure sale: See foreclosure.

foreign corporation: A corporation whose main domicile is in a jurisdiction other than the one in which a question is being considered. For example, a corporation domiciled in Delaware is a foreign corporation to a court in any other state; a corporation domiciled in Germany is foreign to any United States court.

forfeiture: The loss of money or a right because of failure to fulfill obligations or the performance of illegal acts, as in forfeiture of a bond for nonperformance of a contract.

forgery: A false writing, made with intent to defraud. Also the written instrument so falsified.

forms: 1. Enclosures used to shape or mold their contents; for example, wooden structures into which concrete is poured when building a sidewalk, and which are removed after the concrete hardens, leaving the sidewalk fully formed and in place. **2.** Blank documents, such as those used for many kinds of legal matters, including many leases.

foundation: 1. The base and main support of a structure, in many instances built below ground level. **2.** A tax-free, non-profit private organization that receives and distributes funds for charitable and other benevolent purposes.

frame: To put together the skeleton of a building, including the main beams and apertures on which the walls of the building will be placed; also the skeleton so put together.

frame house: A house that has a wooden skeleton and also usually wooden siding.

framing: See frame.

franchise: 1. An agreement between a business organization—the franchisor—and a retailing organization—the franchisee—providing the franchisee the right to deal in the franchisor's goods and services. Usually the franchisor provides such supporting mechanisms as financing, marketing, materials procurement, and management help in return for a share of the franchisee's revenues or profits. **2.** The right to perform stated functions, granted by government to a private organization or individual, in such areas of quasi-public and essentially monopolistic operations as power supply, lighting, telephone service, and public transportation.

franchised dealer: A dealer holding a franchise agreement with a producer, usually for a specific length of time and subject to certain terms and conditions involving minimum acceptable volumes of business done by the franchisee and acceptable modes of business behavior.

franchisee: See franchise.

franchise tax: A tax on a corporation's right to do business within a taxing jurisdiction.

franchisor: See franchise.

fraudulent conversion: The possession and illegal appropriation of money or property belonging to another for purposes of personal gain.

fraudulent conveyance: The illegal transfer of property owned by one to another, to avoid a legally due payment or performance of an obligation; for example, the transfer of corporate property to a family member to avoid payment to the corporation's creditors in the face of impending bankruptcy.

Freddie Mac: See Federal Home Loan Mortgage Corporation.

freehold: An estate in real property or that which is affixed to real property, either in fee, which in law means in perpetuity, or for life. One so holding is a freeholder.

freeholder: See freehold.

free standing: A structure unconnected above ground with other structures.

friend of the court: See amicus curiae.

frontage: That portion of a piece of real property bordering a body of water or public road; often a significant element in assessing the value of a given property, as more relative frontage tends to enhance value.

front end load: Sales and other administrative costs charted against some kinds of investment contracts at the start of a contract period; for example, an investor in a mutual fund may buy a five year plan, want to sell it out after one year, and find that half the payments made during that year have gone to pay front end costs and cannot be retrieved.

front foot: One foot of property bordering a body of water or public road; under some circumstances, such as in a resort or central city business area, the main measure of a property's value, which is often stated in dollars per front foot.

front load commissions: See front end load.

front money: The cash used to start an enterprise, such as a real estate development project, as distinct from credit secured from institutional lenders; often the assets of the individuals or organizations starting the enterprise. Also called seed money.

frozen asset: An asset that has been set aside and held by a legal body, and will not be returned to its owner until that legal body relinquishes it; for example, property held by a court pending the resolution of legal action or the property of aliens that is held by a government during and after a war.

FTC: See Federal Trade Commission.

full coverage: Insurance coverage that pays the full amount of any loss incurred on that which is insured, in contrast to deductible coverage, which pays only losses over a specified amount.

full disclosure: See disclosure.

full faith and credit: Describing a promise to pay a contracted debt. If unsupported by collateral, the promise describes a general debt, supported only by the worth of the organization or individual making it.

functional obsolescence: In real estate, a loss in the value of a structure due to the existence of physical factors that make the structure substantially less usable or desirable than newer structures. Examples include high-ceilinged rooms that require more fuel to heat; high-cost and inefficient heating and cooling systems; or factory floors and ceilings unable to sustain the weight of trucks and cranes.

funding: 1. In the widest sense, the securing of money for any purpose, as in the funding of college study through a combination of grants and loans. **2.** The creation of a pool of reserve funds to pay for future obligations, as in the development of pension funds to pay for future pensions. **3.** The conversion of short term debts into funded debts, by the creation of long term debt instruments.

furnace: Any heating unit that burns fuel to supply heat, from a woodburner to a major installation heating a large building.

furring: Strips of material, usually of metal or wood, used to level subsurfaces so that the material next applied will lie flat; for example, strips used to level subflooring before the finished flooring is laid down.

further assurance: A convenant providing that seller will cure title of any defect after passage of a deed between seller and buyer, in order to supply clear title.

future advances: Under the terms of a mortgage loan, those monies to be advanced some time after the consummation of the loan agreement, such as progress payments advanced to a builder as construction work on a project moves through stage after stage toward completion, those payments being mandated by the terms of the mortgage on performance by the builder. Under mandatory advances circumstances, the lender's mortgage lien continues to have priority over all other liens, including those incurred after the mortgage itself was executed. However, where an open mortgage exists, in which a lender has the option of making further advances or refusing to do so, liens occurring after the making of the mortgage may take priority, and further advances may not be senior debt obligations.

future interest: An existing property interest which can only be taken and used at some future time, such as executory, remainder, and reversionary interests.

G

gable: That portion of an outside wall under the V-shape formed by the two sides of a sloped roof.

gallery: 1. A kind of balcony, roofed and open on one side, inside or outside a building; for example, an outside walkway, or the highest balcony in a theatre. **2.** A room used primarily for visual arts displays.

gambling: Risk taking with small factual bases, as in the instance of the entrepreneur who moves into a new business on the basis of predicting a new consumer buying pattern, or the investor who speculates on the basis of a "hunch."

gambrel roof: A double pitched roof, with each side sloping less sharply at the top than at the bottom.

gap financing: Interim financing needed to bridge the gap between the financing secured and the total financing needed to complete a construction project; usually the difference between a floor loan commitment and the total loan amount to be granted on the meeting of specified conditions by the builder or developer. Also called bridge financing.

garage: A building in which vehicles are stored or serviced.

garden apartments: An apartment development in a parklike setting, usually two or three stories high and on landscaped property; commonly found in suburban areas.

garnishee: One who has by legal process been warned not to part with property or wages belonging to another who is defending a lawsuit, so that the court may direct payment to the plaintiff in that lawsuit if warranted; for example, an employer directed by court order to withhold a portion of an employee's wages for possible satisfaction of judgment.

Gaussian distribution: See normal distribution.

gazebo: A light, airy, garden structure, situated whenever possible where it will catch a summer breeze and provide a satisfying view.

general contractor: A contractor who takes responsibility for construction of a whole project, by formal agreement with owner or developer, and who hires others as sub-contractors to perform specific elements of the project. Also called a prime contractor.

general lien: A lien against all the property of a debtor, rather than against only a specific property; for example, a tax or judicial lien.

general mortgage bonds: Bonds backed by a general mortgage on all company property already subject wholly or partially to existing first mortgages.

general obligation bond: A municipal bond backed by the general promise to pay of its governmental issuer, rather than by specified revenues or assets.

general partner: One who shares in all profits and has unlimited liability, in contrast to a limited partner, who has sharply defined shares of profits and limited liability.

gentlemen's agreement: An agreement in which the parties sign no document and produce no other evidence of the agreement they have reached. Such agreements are often tacit, very often extra-legal; they have no legal force, and rely only on custom and the verbal assurance of the parties involved.

geodetic system: The United States Coast and Geodetic Survey System, which covers the country with a network of benchmarks, each indicating longitude and latitude.

Georgian: A house style originating in England in the late 18th century and widely used in the United States during the late 18th and much of the 19th centuries, featuring large, high-ceilinged rooms; tall chimneys; considerable use of Greek and Roman columns; and outside ornamentation.

ghetto: A slum in which poor people live, who are often of the same ethnic background; originally a name for the Jewish quarters of many European cities.

gift deed: A deed made for so small a consideration as to be considered a gift; a legally valid deed, except where it can be shown to have been made to evade creditors, a question that arises when such a deed is made within a family in economic difficulty.

gift taxes: Federal and state taxes on the value of property given to others, the gifts being taxable to the recipient and graduated according to the value of the property given.

GI loan: Slang for a Veteran's Administration (VA) mortgage loan.

gingerbread: Overdone and elaborate architectural ornamentation.

Ginnie Mae: See Government National Mortgage Association.

Ginnie Mae passthroughs: See Government National Mortgage Association.

girder: A strong beam supporting a heavy load; usually used to describe beams, often of steel but sometimes of wood, used in major structures, such as large buildings and bridges.

glass block: A large glass cube, usually hollow, used as a building block, but seldom used for any load-bearing functions.

glut: A market condition in which supply far exceeds demand at current consumption and price levels. Glut is traditionally encountered in agricultural commodity areas, given the wide variance of crop yields from year to year due to factors beyond farmers' control.

GMC: See guaranteed mortgage certificate.

GNMA: See Government National Mortgage Association.

going concern: A business that is in operation and is expected to continue operations, in contrast to a business that either has not yet started operations or is not expected to continue doing business.

going rate: Popular term for the customary rate for services or price for goods; generally refers to an approximation or acceptable range of rates, rather than to a fixed sum.

good faith: Evidencing honest intent, however executed.

good faith payment: See earnest money.

goodwill: The value of a business beyond the total of its tangible assets; normally determinable only in purchase or sale of the business and defined by the price that is paid for the business. It is sometimes, but relatively rarely, treated as an intangible asset and taken into books of account on that basis.

gouging: The taking of unfair and unjust advantage of buyers by sellers in a seller's market, with resulting unusually high profits for those sellers; for example, the selling of milk at very high prices by retailers during a milk strike.

Government National Mortgage Association (Ginnie Mae or GNMA): A federally owned and financed corporation administered by the Department of Housing and Urban Development, which finances several kinds of mortgages pursuant to national policy, in relatively high risk areas that might otherwise have difficulty in securing financing; for example, inner city public housing and commercial development projects. It does so primarily by subsidizing such mortgages through its secondary mortgage market operations, and also issues mortgage-backed, federally insured securities called *Ginnie Mae passthroughs*, which expand the mortgage money market substantially.

grace period: A period beyond the due date of a debt obligation, in which the creditor allows payment of the debt without penalty to the debtor. Sometimes called days of grace.

grade: See gradient.

graded lease: See graduated lease.

gradient: The slope of land, as compared to the horizontal, usually measured in degrees and expressed in percentages; for example, a road that rises 10 feet per hundred feet of length in a given area has a 10% gradient in that area. Grade is often used as a synonym.

graduated lease: A lease with rental payments that start at one level and move up either by fixed amounts at stated intervals or according to other specified determinants; for example, a lease to a new business owner that starts at $100 per month and moves up over the term of the lease by 10% per year, as reflected in the monthly payments. Also called a graded lease and a stepup lease.

grandfather clause: A legal or contractual provision effectively precluding some people from existing activity, or exempting some people from new requirements, by providing that those who have been previously engaged in these activities are the only ones who can continue in them on current contractual or legal bases. Examples include a now-illegal voting law providing that only those whose grandfathers previously voted can now vote, for some time an effective means of denying southern Blacks the right to vote; or a new zoning ordinance that legally exempts those now in place who would be violators of that ordinance if they had built after, rather than before, the ordinance was enacted.

grant: In real estate, any conveyance of real property.

grantee: One to whom real property is conveyed.

grantor: One who conveys real property.

Greek Revival: A house style featuring the columns, colonnades, and straight lines of Classic Greek architecture; widely adopted in the United States in the second quarter of the 19th century.

greenbelt: A land area on which construction is not allowed by local law; often a means of separating incompatible kinds of land use, such as heavy industry and residential areas.

grievance period: A period specified by law in which taxpayers can dispute assessments made by taxing authorities.

gross area: 1. The floor area of a building, measured from outside wall to outside wall, and the walls themselves. **2.** For rentals, floor area measured from the insides of the exterior walls, and not including the walls themselves.

gross income: Total income from all sources before subtracting any applicable deductions or other necessary subtractions, but after any necessary corrections.

gross income multiplier: See gross multiplier.

gross lease: A lease in which the lessee pays a single fixed rental sum and the lessor pays all other charges, such as taxes, insurance, maintenance, and repairs; contrasts with a net lease, in which the lessee pays rent and such other charges. Also called a fixed or flat lease.

gross multiplier: An informal mode of quickly estimating the market value of rental property, multiplying gross rentals by a factor common to similar properties; for example, multiplying the gross rental income of a ten-family building by seven to arrive at a rough estimate of current market values. Useful only for the most casual estimating. Also called gross income multiplier, or gross rent multiplier.

gross negligence: Failure to exercise the slightest bit of care, in clear disregard of consequences to others, and raising a presumption of willful carelessness, but falling short of wrongdoing.

gross rent multiplier: See gross multiplier.

grottalstop: A grotto-like, landscaped highway rest area.

ground: 1. To connect an electricity-carrying line or device to earth. **2.** A first coat of paint on any surface; in the fine arts, the first coat of paint on the surface of a painting; in housepainting, sometimes used as a synonym for primer, the term more often used.

ground cover: Plantings, such as grass and ferns, that cover the ground and prevent erosion.

ground lease: A lease of land only, whether that land is raw or improved; usually a long term lease and often as long as 99 years and renewable. Rental amounts normally include a base amount, with escalators built in over a period of time, and further escalators built in conditional upon the uses to which the land will be put; for example, a 99 year renewable ground lease in a central city business district may set a rental base for the first 20 years, with tax and other cost escalators built in during that period, and include periodic increases during the balance of the 99 year period and beyond as renewed, while also including provisions for a percentage of gross rentals or profits derived from structures built on the site. By separating land ownership from improvement ownership, financing requirements may be lessened, and capital gains taxes on land sale may be avoided. Rentals paid under a ground lease are called ground rent.

ground rent: See ground lease.

groundwater: The water that is naturally in the ground, serving as a source of wells, surface springs, and streams, and of sustenance to growing things, but not including subsurface streams.

guarantee: 1. A legally binding assurance by one of the obligation of another to a third party, as in the assurance of payment of a loan to another. **2.** A legally binding assurance of product quality, issued in writing to the purchaser of that product; in this era of consumer protection, a guarantee can be implied as well as expressed.

guaranteed bond: A bond issued by one business, which is guaranteed wholly or in part by another, as in the instance of a subsidiary, controlled, or affiliated company bond guaranteed by a parent company.

guaranteed loan: A loan to one guaranteed by another, as when repayment of a mortgage loan is personally guaranteed by one other than the borrower.

guaranteed mortgage certificate (GMC): A debt instrument issued by the Federal Home Loan Mortgage Corporation (Freddie Mac or FHLMC), which is a certificate backed by a pool of mortgages it has previously purchased and holds. The Federal Government unconditionally backs these instruments, which are designed to draw private investment funds into the secondary mortgage markets, and thereby stabilize and increase the national mortgage money pool.

guarantor: One who makes a legally binding commitment to guarantee payment or performance due from another.

guardian: One who has legal custody of another by judicial action, such as a minor or an incompetent, who then becomes the guardian's ward. A guardian may convey property owned by a ward. A guardian ad litem is one appointed by a court to represent the interests of a minor only in a specific court action.

guardian ad litem: See guardian.

gutter: A roof channel for carrying off rainwater.

H

habendum clause: That portion of a deed which restates, amplifies, and further defines the precise nature of the interest conveyed in the preceding granting clause, and which starts "to have and to hold," then moving into restatement and beyond.

habitable: In fit condition to be lived in; describing residential property conveyed to another by lease or deed. A lessee may terminate a lease by legal action if rented premises are uninhabitable, either before occupancy or becoming so afterward; a buyer may, under some conditions, legally force a seller to make purchased premises habitable, even after title has passed.

hall: 1. A corridor or area between rooms; an entry area or anteroom is often called an outer hall. **2.** A large public room or arena.

hamlet: A small community; usually treated administratively as a village.

hardhat: One who works in basic industry, particularly in the construction industry; sometimes used as a synonym for blue collar worker.

hard money mortgage: A mortgage loan taking property as security and yielding cash to the borrower, rather than financing a purchase; for example, a remortgage or second money mortgage to yield cash to pay for a college education would be considered a hard money mortgage.

hard sell: A popular description of very persistent, aggressive attempts by a seller to close a sale, usually over the resistance of an unconvinced and therefore highly resistant potential purchaser.

hardware: Those machined pieces, usually of metal, accompanying larger structural elements, such as hinges, locks, knobs, and handles.

hardwood: Any wood coming from a hardwood tree, such as oak, maple, and cherry; refers to the biological group of hardwood trees, not to the hardness of a specific wood.

hazard: The dangers specified in a property insurance policy, against which something insured is covered. For example, a policy covering a retail store and specifying the hazard of fire will cover the store for fire. The same policy, not mentioning or specifically excluding flood as a hazard, will not cover the store for flood.

header: A load-spreading beam or block, which when placed over an aperture, such as a door or window, spreads the weight from above and transfers it to other load-bearing elements and away from the aperture.

hearth: The floor of a fireplace; but in older usage, and in current industrial usage, the fireplace itself.

heater: An area heating unit, such as a window unit that heats a room, rather than a system that heats all or a substantial part of a structure.

hectare: A basic land measure in the metric system, equal to 100 ares or 10,000 square meters; equivalent to 2.471 acres.

heir: One who inherits real or personal property from a deceased person.

heirs and assigns: Words customarily used in the conveyance of real property, normally in the habendum clause, which further clarifies and defines the nature of the grant being made; in the common law, these words were essential to the conveyance of a fee interest in real property, but are no longer really necessary.

hereditament: Any inheritable property.

highest and best use: That use of land which would yield the most financial return, whether or not the land is now being so used; a concept used in land appraisal, often resulting in the imposition of far higher taxes than justified by current uses. For example, a farm in a suburban area may be assessed as if the land were being used for housing, with the resulting taxes forcing the owner to sell the farm.

high rise: A building that is considerably taller than its neighbors; always a relative term. A ten-story building, for example, may be the highest structure on the horizon in a small Midwestern city, and therefore be considered a "high rise"; that same building in mid-Manhattan would, however, be rather small in relation to its neighbors.

high water mark: The highest shore elevation to which water normally rises.

highway trust fund: A Federal fund dedicated to the development and preservation of the national highway system.

hip roof: A four-sided pyramidal roof, with pitched sides rising to a point, as in a church steeple.

historic: In real estate, an area, structure, group of structures, or district that is recognized by law and regulation as worthy of preservation, and in which restrictions are therefore placed on destruction, alteration, and new structure development.

holdback: An amount of money held by agreement and unpaid by a contracting party, such as a developer or a lender, pending accomplishment of stated conditions by the other party, such as satisfactory completion of a job or achievement of a stated level of income on a property.

holder: One who by delivery or endorsement, lawfully possesses the right to be paid the value of a money instrument.

holder in due course: One who legally holds a money instrument which has been received for value in good faith and timely, and without knowledge of any defect in the lawful right to be paid.

hold harmless clause: A contract provision absolving a contracting party from all liability arising from stated circumstances and placing that liability with another of the contracting parties; for example, a leasehold agreement placing all liability for certain kinds of damages to others upon the lessee. Courts may hold such clauses invalid as regards the rights of others so damaged, who may successfully claim against both landlord and lessee.

holding company: A company that is primarily in the business of controlling other companies, fully or in part, usually directly owned subsidiaries.

holding escrow: A contract provision in which an escrow agent takes over responsibility for essentially consummating a real estate transaction, by holding title documents, taking payments, and conveying title when all payments and conditions specified in a contract for deed have been effected; a difficult and little-used mode now rapidly becoming obsolete.

holding period: In taxation, the length of time for which an asset must be held in order to qualify for long term capital gains treatment.

holdover tenant: A tenant who has occupied property under the terms of a lease, and then continues to occupy after the lease term has ended; usually then going to a month-to-month tenancy with the consent of the landlord.

home improvement loan: A loan secured for purposes of renovation of or addition to a personal residence; essentially a personal loan, rather than an additional encumbrance upon the property, except when cast as an additional mortgage or financed by remortgage. Available from the Federal Housing Administration (FHA) and from private lenders.

homeowners' association: A nonprofit membership organization, whose members are all owners of dwellings in a common unit or defined area, sometimes involuntarily becoming so on purchase of their dewllings under the terms of purchase, and sometimes voluntarily after becoming owners. If membership is involuntary, dues and assessments are legally enforceable obligations and nonpayment becomes an encumbrance upon the property owned. When the dwellings are in a condominium, the association is usually called a condominium owners' association.

homeowner's insurance: Property insurance covering a wide range of hazards intrinsic to home ownership, such as fire, weather, theft, and some kinds of personal liabilities, and available to those owning or renting and occupying one-family dwelling units, including single family homes, condominiums, cooperatives, rental units, and mobile homes.

homestead: 1. Land and a single family residence occupied by a family home; usually exempt from debtor's judgments, for the life of its owner, surviving spouse, and minor children. **2.** A parcel of formerly public land, on which an individual has established residence and which that party, called a homesteader, will own after a period, in conformance with United States homestead laws.

home warranty program: An insurance coverage, providing new owners with limited coverage of specified problems encountered in new or used homes; for example, the National Association of Home Builders program, which offers new home buyers one or two years of coverage for specified workmanship and component problems, and up to ten years of coverage for structural defects. Several private insurance company plans cover used home buyers for specified problems for up to two years; home buyers are also covered by common law and consumer protection laws, to the extent that the sellers' legal responsibilities are matched by financial capacity.

honor: In finance, to pay. For example, a bank honors a check by paying its lawful holder its face amount when it is presented for payment.

hotel: A lodging house mainly in the business of renting rooms or groups of rooms to the public, including such features as cleaning and linen service; the term widely describes transient accommodations of all kinds, including longer term residency apartment hotels, resort and convention facilities, and motels.

household: Any habitation occupied by a group of people living together or by one person living alone.

house trailer: See mobile home.

housing codes: See building codes.

housing starts: The number of new housing units started in a given period; a key economic indicatior.

HUD: See Department of Housing and Urban Development.

hype: Exaggeration aimed at securing a sale or promoting a person or activity; short for hyperbole.

hypothecation: The use of pledged collateral to secure a loan. In law, possession of the pledged collateral stays with the owner of the collateral, though the lender has the right to force sale of the collateral to cover default of the loan. In practice, collateral which cannot be delivered, such as a ship, stays with the borrower; collateral which can be delivered, such as securities and warehouse receipts, usually is physically moved to the lender.

I

I-beam: A structural steel column, in the shape of the letter I.

illiquid: Describing a company or individual not in possession of sufficient cash to meet its cash needs and facing difficulty in raising that cash.

implied: In the law, an intent which is inferred from the circumstances surrounding a situation or transaction, and which becomes the legal equivalent of an expressed intent, as with implied contracts or implied trusts, which under some circumstances become equivalent in the law to written contracts and trusts.

implied contract: See contract.

implied warranty: See warranty.

impound: To physically take possession of and hold on behalf of the law and its agents, as in the taking and holding of actual or potential evidence by a court during legal proceedings.

impound account: An account kept in the hands of a lender, into which the borrower prepays sums to be used by the lender for payment of taxes, fees, insurance, and other specified purposes; a means of guaranteeing that the property will remain clear of encumbrances as long as the loan is in effect.

improved land: Land to which value has been added by such constructions as buildings, culverts, and sewers, and which therefore is no longer raw land.

improvement: A value-adding addition to real property, such as a building, an outbuilding, a fence, a road, or the resurfacing of a road. For tax purposes, that which adds to the value of a property must generally be capitalized, with deductions therefore taken over a period of years; in contrast, maintenance and repair, which do not add to the value of the property, can be deducted as business expenses in the year incurred.

imputed interest: Interest which will be implied by taxing authorities, and applied retroactively to a transaction. The questions arise when seller and buyer fail to set an interest rate or set what taxing authorities regard as too low an interest on a transaction, in an attempt to minimize taxable capital gains on the sale of an asset by stating what would otherwise be interest as sales price.

in bond: See bond.

incentive contract: A contract that specifies extra rewards for better-than-contracted performance.

inchoate: Describing a right or interest which stems from existing circumstances, but will only come into legal being if possible future events occur. Examples include a wife's possible interest in a husband's real property, if he predeceases her; or a mechanic's lien which has not been legally filed and will take effect when filed.

income: 1. Total business or personal revenue received from all sources, usually within a defined period, such as a month, calendar year, or fiscal year. **2.** The total increase in net assets achieved by a business in any accounting period. **3.** In general, any item of determinable value received.

income approach: See appraisal.

income averaging: As provided for in Federal personal income tax law, the ability to lump current income and several previous years' income for figuring income tax rates; when current income is much higher than the average income, lower tax rates apply.

income bond: A bond bearing interest that is only payable out of the profits of its issuer, in contrast to bonds that carry interest as an unconditional debt obligation of the corporation.

income property: Real property used by its owner primarily as a source of income; for example, a farm leased to tenants or rental property.

income statement: An accounting statement, summarizing the income, expenses, and resultant profit or loss of a business organization for any accounting period; usually issued yearly, often quarterly and monthly as well; a profit and loss statement (P & L).

income tax: Any tax based on the income received, usually net, of any defined economic unit, including individuals and both business and non-business organizations. Income taxes are usually graduated, with rates rising according to net income. Federal income taxes were levied during the Civil War, starting in 1861, and stopping after the War; modern Federal income taxes date from 1913; state and local income taxes also developed after 1913.

incompetent: 1. One who is by judicial action declared unable to handle his or her own affairs, for such reasons as insanity or advanced senility. **2.** One who is not legally empowered to make a binding agreement, such as a minor who is unable legally to convey property, or a corporate employee who is not an officer empowered to sign contracts.

incontestable: Firmly binding upon the insurer after a specified period following issuance of the policy; applied to certain policy protections, notably in life and health insurance. For example, a health insurance policy may waive the right to contest a heart condition as pre-existing, and therefore not covered, after one year from policy issuance; that policy protection then becomes incontestable.

incorporated: See incorporation.

incorporation: 1. One of the three major forms of business organization, the others being sole proprietorship and partnership, and the form favored by most medium-sized and large businesses, as it provides for limited ownership liability, easy ownership transfer in the form of stock sale, multiple ownership by stockholders, maximum financing flexibility, and a wide variety of other advantages over the other two ownership forms. **2.** The process of becoming a legal corporation.

incorporation papers: See certificate of incorporation.

incorporeal: Possessing no physical body; for example, such real property rights as easements, profits deriving from the use of property belonging to others, and rentals.

increment: Any increase or growth in steps, usually small, rather than continuous.

incremental: 1. An increase, usually relatively small, tied to existing operations, as in the addition of space for a few new stores to an existing shopping mall, or of a few new residences to an existing residential development. **2.** In accounting, marginal, describing a cost that results from the exercise of choices in production or marketing.

indemnity: 1. The amount of insurance coverage specified in an insurance policy. **2.** A governmental guarantee of immunity from prosecution in certain stated circumstances, normally by legislative action.

indemnity bond: A bond guaranteeing against losses caused by the employee or agent of the idemnifying party, who is the guarantor of that bond.

indenture: 1. A deed owned by two or more parties which states their rights and obligations toward each other regarding the jointly owned property. **2.** An apprenticeship agreement, by which one party is legally bound to serve another for a specified period of time; common in colonial times, but now prohibited by law. **3.** An instrument naming a trustee to act for all holders of a bond issue and stating the amount, form, and conditions involved in the issue.

independent appraisal: An appraisal conducted by an outside appraiser, who is in no way financially interested in the appraisal results.

independent contractor: A contractor who is self-employed, and who contracts to do specific work in his or her own way, rather than as an employee and under the control of the supplier of that work. Independent contractors carry their own insurances, pay their own unemployment insurance taxes, and handle their own withholding statements. The rather fine line between employees and independent contractors is often resolved by taxing authorities and insurance companies in favor of defining those who spend most of their time working out of the premises of others, on the business of those others, as employees.

index: A measure of such factors as cost and performance, like the Consumer Price Index and the Dow Jones stock market indexes.

indexed lease: See indexing.

indexing: 1. The tying of cost and price changes to changes in specified national indexes, such as the tying of rental increases or decreases to changes in the Consumer Price Index. **2.** An investment technique, in a mutual fund or an individual portfolio, that attempts to organize and weight its holdings so that it will perform much as a specific major stock index performs, such as Dow Jones or Standard and Poor's.

indirect liability: A potential liability, that may become a real liability in the future; for example, the co-signer of a note may become liable if the primary borrower defaults on the note.

indirect lighting: Lighting that does not shine directly on the area to be lit, but uses some reflecting or diffusing device to spread and soften the effect of the light on the area.

indirect taxes: Taxes on things, rights, and privileges, such as sales, franchise, and excise taxes, rather than taxes directly on people and organizations, such as income taxes.

individual proprietorship: See sole proprietorship.

indorsement: See endorsement.

industrial bank: A commercial bank primarily oriented toward the extension of consumer credit, in contrast to commercial banks primarily oriented toward business banking. Sometimes called Morris Plan banks, after Arthur Morris, a pioneer in the development of consumer credit financing, they are called industrial banks because they were originally conceived of as appealing to workers in industry.

industrial broker: In real estate, a broker primarily involved in selling industrial and other commercial properties.

industrial park: A planned real estate development, in which most of the property is to be devoted to industrial uses; sometimes an area developed by a community with the aim of attracting industry, and carrying tax and other concessions.

industrial property: Property zoned for industrial uses and usually holding structures and other improvements intended for industrial use. Such property may be used for other purposes as well, but is often difficult to convert to other uses, although in some areas, industrial structures have successfully been converted into such commercial uses as shopping malls and residential housing.

industrial revenue bond: A kind of municipal bond offered to investors, funding tax-advantaged arrangements as inducements for businesses to locate in municipalities. These arrangements are often very advantageous in terms of both taxes and plant construction costs. The bonds themselves are not federally tax-exempt to their purchasers.

industrial waste: The waste products associated with industrial production, such as the chemical byproducts of some industrial processes, which often pose hazards to the environment and must be disposed of at considerable cost.

in entail: See fee tail, entail.

in fee: See fee.

inflation: A rise in the general level of prices within an economy, accompanied by a decrease in the purchasing power of the unit of currency used in that economy. Inflation is often, but not always, accompanied by losses in real purchasing power, as when a cost of living index goes up by 10%, while average wages go up by only 5%, with a resultant 5% loss of purchasing power; in contrast, if average wages went up 15%, the net would be a 5% increase in purchasing power. But under conditions of rapid inflation, adulterations of quality and smaller quantities supplied at similar prices create hidden inflation as well, pulling the real purchasing power of the dollar down considerably more sharply than the standard figures indicate.

information returns: Tax returns which must by law be filed with the taxing authorities, supplying information on payments made to others, for checking purposes, as when an employer files a form telling the Federal Government what wages have been paid and to whom.

infrastructure: The body of organizations, people, and skills that binds together the economic operations of a nation and defines that nation's level of technology and socio-political sophistication. Infrastructure includes such factors as the level of technical skills available; the transportation industry; the telephone, telegraph, and broadcasting systems; the power systems; and the public health and education systems.

ingress: A way of entering; an entrance. Contrasts with egress, which is a way of leaving; an exit.

inheritance: That which is received through a bequest from another; also that which is held and may be passed to another by bequest.

injunction: A writ prohibiting a defendant from doing or continuing to do something which is, or can become, harmful to a plaintiff. An injunction is often issued by a court to restrain a defendant from pursuing a certain course of action while a legal proceeding is being adjudicated. For example, an injunction may be issued to restrain a defendant in a patent or trademark infringement case while the suit is pending, as continued infringement could cause irremediable harm to the plaintiff during the time it takes to complete the suit, even if plaintiff ultimately wins. Injunctions have also been widely used by employers against unions in collective bargaining disputes.

inn: A hotel that stresses the food service aspects of its business, but also offers lodging to the public; increasingly used as synonymous with hotel.

inner city: A city center, including its main central commercial district and the residential areas directly surrounding it; a term not firmly definable and describing areas expansible as metropolitan areas expand.

innocent purchaser: One who buys a right or interest in property for good consideration without actual or constructive knowledge of any defect in the title of the seller.

in personam: A legal action directed against a person, rather than against a thing, which is an action *in rem*.

in rem: A legal action directed against a thing, such as an action against a property or one which directly affects a property, rather than against a person, which is an action *in personam*. An action stemming from a purchase of real property, or from a mortgage or lien, is an action *in rem*.

insolvency: Inability to pay debts as they become due; usually a prelude to bankruptcy.

inspection: An examination aimed at determining whether defined standards have been met. Examples include inspection of a new house by regulatory authorities to determine whether or not building codes have been complied with and appropriate inspection and approval documents issued; or a lender's examination of property pursuant to a mortgage application. Also used to describe any examination of a property by a potential purchaser.

installment: A part payment of a financial obligation, often made periodically, as in part payment for a purchase of a loan.

installment bond: A single bond that matures essentially piece by piece, the principal of which is paid in installments rather than all at once. It has the same net payment effect as a set of serial bonds, which mature one by one over a period of time, differing only in that it is a single bond.

installment buying: A widespread form used for the credit buying of consumer goods in which the buyer pays for goods purchased in a series of payments, usually equally spaced and of equal size, including interest to the seller. Once the main means of credit buying in the United States, installment buying has now been partly replaced by credit card buying, in which the consumer buys with credit extended by a commercial lender, usually a bank, and repays the bank, often on a revolving credit basis.

installment note: A document evidencing existence of an installment payment contract, and specifying the terms of payment.

installment sale: In real estate, a sale in which 30% or less of the gross payment for the property sold is received by the seller in the year of sale, and the seller elects to treat the sale as an installment sale for tax reporting purposes starting with that tax return covering the year of sale. Where taxable gain results from that sale, tax deferral results on those portions of the sales price taken as income in subsequent years, although that taxable gain receives long or short term tax status and treatment as if it had become taxable in the year of sale.

institutional investor: An investing organization, such as a bank, mutual fund, pension fund, foundation, or other repository of substantial funds, that buys and sells debt and equity interests and instruments, such as bonds, stocks, mortgages, mutual funds, and currencies.

institutional lender: An organization, such as a bank, savings and loan association, insurance company, or pension fund, which buys and sells debt instruments and makes loans in such areas as real estate and commercial financing.

instrument: A document, embodying a formal and written legal entity, such as a deed, contract, will, or any of a whole range of financial obligations, such as checks, notes, and securities.

insulation: A material that protects against the elements and the operation of elemental forces, such as asbestos against fire and composition sheathing against electrical shock.

insurable interest: Any interest held by one in another's life or in property of any kind, to the extent of the loss that might be suffered if that life were lost or that property were damaged or destroyed. An insurable interest must usually be shown before insurance will be granted.

insurance: A legal agreement, by which one party, the insurer, agrees to compensate the other, the insured, for losses resulting from the occurrence of specified events and usually up to specified limits. Those insured must have insurable interests. Usually, the insurer is an insurance company, which covers the insured through an insurance policy, on which the insured pays premiums periodically.

insurance policy: A legally enforceable contract, in which an insurance company undertakes to cover the losses of an insured, in return for premium payments.

insured: One with an insurable interest whose potential losses are covered by a legally enforceable insurance policy.

insurer: One, usually an insurance company, undertaking to cover the losses of others by issuing insurance.

intensive cultivation: An attempt to maximize crop yields from land under cultivation, using the best available combinations of techniques, seeds, soil and plant nutrients, and irrigation; used where land is in short supply relative to the farm products needs of the population, in both technically advanced and developing nations.

interest: 1. A legal right to all or part of something of value, as in an insurable interest, a beneficial interest under the terms of a will or trust, or an ownership interest, through ownership of all or part of a business. **2.** A sum of money paid for the use of money, usually expressed as a percentage of money borrowed, as in 10% over the principal of a loan charged for the loan.

interest rate: The interest percentage charged by a lender for a loan, which varies with the kind of loan, the money market, the general economic conditions, and the financial condition of the borrower, and therefore the amount of risk involved in making the loan. Stated and actual rates of interest being charged are often different, but true rates of interest charged retail borrowers must be clearly stated under the provisions of Truth in Lending Laws.

interim: 1. Any period of time between fixed dates, such as the period between now and the first of next year. **2.** Describing a document, instrument, or function which by its nature is temporary, usually intended to be superseded by another, more permanent document, instrument, or function.

interim certificate: A temporary document, effective until a more permanent document is or is not issued, such as a temporary proof of insurance or automobile registration.

interim financing: A short term loan, designed to be replaced by a longer term loan, such as a construction loan running for a term as short as a few months to as long as three years, which is to be replaced by such permanent financing as a long term mortgage, rather than being replaced with other short term financing.

Internal Revenue Code: The body of statutes codifying the tax laws of the Federal Government.

Internal Revenue Service (IRS): That Federal agency responsible for the enforcement of the tax laws of the United States, except as to several excise taxes, and for promulgation of regulations interpreting those laws.

interpleader: A legal action by one claiming to be an innocent and uninvolved holder of property and instruments of value against two or more parties claiming ownership of that which is held, asking the court to require the claimants to litigate between themselves, as when claimants to an escrow account take legal action against an escrow holder who will not pay one as against the other and run the risk of then being forced to pay the other as well.

interstate land sales: Those sales of land made across state lines, and subject to the disclosure rules set forth in the Interstate Land Sales Full Disclosure Act, which requires Federal registration of such land, full disclosure of all material facts concerning the land to prospective buyers before purchase, and a three day cooling off period after purchase, in which buyers can cancel purchases; affects land, rather than land carrying completed structures.

inter vivos: Between living people; usually in law applied to the voluntary transfer of property from one living person to another through the establishment of a trust or the presenting of a gift.

intestate: Having died without having made a valid will; also, the individual who has died without making such a will.

intrastate exemption: An exemption from the necessity of Federal registration of a security offered for sale solely within a state by an issuer resident in or a corporation incorporated in and doing business in that state; but Federal antifraud and state registration requirements, if any, still apply.

intrinsic: That which is inherent in something by the very nature of the thing itself; usually applied to matters of value, as in estimating the underlying value of an industrial plant in terms of what the materials in the plant would bring as scrap, or of a silver plate in terms of what it would bring at current market prices if the plate were melted down.

inventory: To survey and record all things possessed; also the possessions so surveyed themselves. In this sense, a body of real properties, a group of trust properties, a set of ideas, a body of skills and people, or the material goods in the possession of a business may all be inventoried, and be inventory.

inverse condemnation: An action brought by a property owner against government for condemnation in fact, or for damages caused by government actions, as when low-flying aircraft near an airport lower property values or government has been slow in effecting payment when it has in fact long since exercised its power of eminent domain and taken property.

invested capital: The total value of the ownership shares held by the owners of a business.

investment: 1. In the widest sense, any attempt to profit from the use of money or other valuables. Generally, investment is the attempt to use money to make money, but such things as time and love are in popular usage described as having been invested as well, often for anticipated non-monetary rewards. **2.** A store of value.

investment capital: See capital.

investment credit: In Federal taxation, tax credits allowed business for investment in machinery and equipment during a tax year; restricted to tangible personal property and excluding real estate or that which becomes part of real estate by becoming permanently attached to it.

investment property: See income property.

involuntary bankruptcy: See bankruptcy.

involuntary conversion: The replacement of property by cash outside the will of the property owner, as when a property is taken by the state by condemnation, or lost for any insurable reason and replaced by insurance proceeds; the sum received is taxable only to the extent that it exceeds the value of the property it replaces, as long as replacement occurs within the period specified by applicable statute.

irrevocable trust: A trust which is permanent and may not be revoked by its maker; the main form taken by trusts, constituting passage of title to trust property and removal of that property from the estate of the trust's maker.

irrigation: The watering of agricultural land by means of a system of channels and pipes constructed to distribute and regulate the flow of water to the land.

irrigation district: An administrative area controlling the irrigation system of that area, and possessing taxing powers as regards irrigation matters and needs.

IRS: See Internal Revenue Service.

Italianate style: A house style of the 19th century patterned after Italian Renaissance architecture, widely used in the Midwestern equivalents of the New York brownstone, and featuring tall, often paired windows, high ceilings, heavy ornamentation, and a cupola.

J

jalousie: An adjustable slatted blind or shutter.

jamb: The vertical side of an aperture, such as a window or a door.

job shop: A firm that produces to fulfill specific orders, such as a custom builder of furniture.

join: See joinder.

joinder: In law, the joining or uniting of two or more parties or actions into a single legal proceeding.

joint: 1. Sharing common interests or liabilities with one or more others, and thereby uniting with those others in matters concerned with shared interests or liabilities. **2.** The place at which two or more parts, such as metal pipes or wooden pieces, join together.

joint account: A bank account held in common by two or more people or businesses.

joint and several: That which is shared with others and at the same time held individually, as is liability, when another is able to claim against one party or several parties to a contract of debt obligation at the claimant's option.

joint contract: A contractual obligation undertaken in common by two or more parties.

joint endorsement: Endorsement of an instrument by two or more parties, made necessary by that instrument being payable to those parties.

joint mortgage: A mortgage borrowing by two or more mortgagors; they are both legally responsible for full payment of the mortgage.

joint note: A note signed by two or more makers, for which they jointly assume responsibility, each for the full amount of the note should all other makers fail to pay any share of that joint obligation.

joint ownership: The holding of any form of ownership interest by two or more persons, each holding equally and each taking all ownership interests belonging to those owners predeceasing them. A joint ownership interest can be passed only to other joint owners, but the sole surviving joint owner is able to pass ownership interest to others, to the extent that it may be legally passed by a sole owner. Also called joint tenancy.

joint tenancy: See joint ownership.

joint venture: An undertaking for profit entered into by two or more people; usually but not always limited to the accomplishment of a single goal, such as the building of a factory abroad or the financing of a new mine; a general term, rather than a specific form of business organization, as such an undertaking may take any business form.

joist: A horizontal beam supporting a floor or ceiling.

journal: In bookkeeping and accounting, any book originally recording transactions.

journal entry: In bookkeeping and accounting, any written entry recording a transaction in acceptable form and with enough information to be usable in constructing accounting data.

journeyman: A skilled craftsperson who does professionally competent work; in some trades, one who is so certified by a standard-setting group.

judgment: A court decision, complete and binding upon the parties to a matter before a court, subject to appeals directed to higher courts; functions as a lien placed upon the property of the parties, as regards payment directed by the terms of the court's decision.

judgment lien: See judgment.

judicial sale: A sale made pursuant to court order, usually as forced by a foreclosure proceeding.

junior bonds: Bonds which have less claim upon the issuer's assets than do other bonds, and which therefore in a default situation can make claims only after the claims of those other bonds have been satisfied.

junior mortgage: A mortgage, such as a second or third mortgage, which has less claim upon the property mortgaged than do other more senior mortgages, and which therefore in a default situation can make claims only after the claims of those other mortgages have been satisfied.

just compensation: That amount of compensation for the taking of property by government which is fair in the eyes of the court and consonant with due process of law; usually fair market value at the time of the taking.

K

key lot: A lot that is important to one attempting to assemble a parcel of land for development, whether because of its location or the timing of its acquisition.

keystone: The wedge-shaped stone at the top of an arch, locking the other stones of the arch together.

kicker: An extra payment demanded by a lender, above the interest specified in the loan, such as profit participation in the project being financed; sometimes found by courts to be legal payments and sometimes illegal extra interest payments prohibited by state usury laws.

kilo: In the metric system, a prefix meaning 1,000; when attached to another descriptor, meaning 1,000 of whatever is described; for example, 1,000 watts equal 1 kilowatt, 1,000 grams equal 1 kilogram, and 1,000 meters equal 1 kilometer.

kitchenette: A small cooking area in a room or apartment, sometimes separated from other living areas by a small partition.

L

labor: 1. Those who, taken as a group, work for pay and are not primarily supervisors or owners, even though they may have minor supervisory tasks or ownership shares. **2.** Effort performed to produce and distribute goods and services; in this sense, a factor of production, like land and capital. **3.** Very widely, a synonym for work.

labor agreement: A formal and written agreement between management and organized labor; a collective bargaining contract, covering such matters as wages, working conditions, fringe benefits, and grievance procedures.

labor banks: Banks organized and owned by unions and their members. Such banks differ in no way from other banks in functioning or regulation.

labor costs: The total gross wages paid to labor, which includes both direct and indirect costs, but does not include fringe benefits, clerical wages, or executive salaries.

labor-intensive: Describing any kind of business or economic unit that requires a substantial amount of labor relative to the amount of capital employed in it. For example, the garment industry requires far less investment per employee than the nuclear industry. The garment industry is then described as labor-intensive, while the nuclear industry is described as its opposite—capital-intensive.

laches: A delay in asserting a claim, creating circumstances in which a court rules that the delay is a bar to proceeding with a claim which might have been valid had it been timely. Examples include delay for years, causing a defendant to be unable to make a case because of the difficulty of securing proper evidence, or a delay while circumstances causing a complaint proceed to conclusion, such as a construction project alleged to damage a complainant, which is complained of only after completion, when it might have been complained of earlier.

lally column: A steel support column, often filled with concrete.

land: Earth, all but the great bodies of water that are seas; all that is below the surface of that earth and accessible, such as oil, coal, and other extractable substances; all that is permanently attached to that earth, by human or natural acts, such as a building or a meteorite.

land agent: One representing others in land transactions; especially one representing companies and moneyed individuals in large land and subsurface rights transactions.

land banks: See Federal land banks.

land contract: A mode of purchasing land in which seller takes a very small down payment from buyer, holds title while giving the buyer possession, and passes title only when payments have been completed; if buyer defaults, seller keeps title and payments so far received. Also called a contract for deed.

land damages: See damages.

land grant: A grant of land by government to private parties, for the accomplishment of purposes consonant with public policy; for example, the widespread granting of public land to private colleges in the last century, resulting in a number of colleges, such as Cornell University, popularly called land grant colleges.

landlocked: Property which has no means of access to a public way, and is therefore not available for development.

landlord: One who has the right to lease property as proprietor of that property, and does so to a lessee.

landmark: 1. A historic place, as defined by law; often protected against destruction and major alteration, and tax-advantaged to encourage preservation. **2.** A boundary marker.

land office business: A very active level of business, with a large number of transactions; usually, but not always, profitable business.

land patent: An instrument conveying government land to private parties. Also called letters patent and patent.

land poor: Describing those whose major assets are land, but who have insufficient cash to meet their cash flow needs, often because of cash demands caused by land ownership, such as taxes and maintenance.

land reform: Changes in traditional ownership arrangements as to land, usually by government decree, and usually resulting in the expropriation of large, privately owned landholdings, either for redistribution among the formerly landless and small holding or for their retention by the state.

land sale-leaseback: A financing method, in which an owner sells property to an investor, who then leases the property back to the seller, while subordinating the newly acquired ownership interest to the interest of a mortgage lender who finances a development on that land by its former owner. The owner-developer thus secures money for the construction and land financing, without net cash outlay, while the investor receives a relatively high rental fee and sometimes other payments from the developer.

landscape architecture: A branch of architecture devoted to the design of outdoor places, as in the design of a park or of the grounds surrounding a structure.

landscaping: The designed and cultivated open spaces surrounding a structure; part of the total design formed by structure and grounds.

land tax: See property tax.

land trust: A trust holding real property assets only, with title in the name of the trustee. Such trusts are generally formed by a living landowner, who passes title to the trust and simultaneously executes a trust agreement making the landowner beneficiary of the trust and limiting the trustee's powers so as to leave the landowner effectively in complete control of the property for all practical purposes. The device can be used to hide the identity of the true owner of land, as when land is being assembled for a development, and also makes financing arrangements and potential liabilities considerably less onerous, when lenders are willing to deal with the trust alone without reaching through to the people behind it.

land use map: An area map, showing the kinds of uses to which the land in that area is being put.

lapse: To be no longer in effect, applied to an insurance policy on which premiums are unpaid; under most circumstances the policy is cancelled after a specified time for failure to pay premiums.

last will and testament: The legal will of a decedent, superseding all previous testamentary dispositions.

late charge: A penalty charge for late payment of a loan installment; not regarded as additional interest.

latent defect: A defect in property sold, which cannot be perceived by the buyer even after reasonably careful scrutiny of the property purchased, as in the instance of a defective part deep in the motor of a heating system or a title to land which is fatally defective due to circumstances that could not be known by the buyer.

lath: The material serving as a base for plaster, such as composition board or wire mesh.

laundered money: Money that has been illegally obtained and then passed through other economic entities to hide its true origin; for example, money obtained from narcotics sales, which is fed as cash into such high cash turnover businesses as restaurants to reappear later as seemingly legitimate profits.

law: That body of rules governing the actions of people in a community, embodied in statutes, cases, rules, regulations, customs, and mores, and ultimately enforceable by the physical force of a nation or by nations acting in concert.

lawyer: One who is licensed in any state to practice law within that state. To practice law in any other state requires separate licensing, but legal specialties require no special licensing.

layout: The physical plan of a structure or area.

leaching: In septic systems, the separation of liquid from solid wastes by the passage of liquid wastes through such porous materials as gravel and sand.

lead-based: Describing material, such as paint, that contains lead; widely used until medical research showed lead hazardous to human health, but now little used.

leader: A pipe carrying runoff from roof to ground.

lease: An agreement by which one who has the power to rent property, called a lessor or landlord, rents that property to another, called a lessee or tenant. That agreement may be oral or written, although in practice it is normally formal and written; in either case it explicitly specifies the terms of the agreement. Realty and equipment are the main subjects of lease agreements.

leaseback: See sale and leaseback.

leased department: In a department store, a section that is leased to an independent proprietor, with the store supplying space, maintenance, and often financial and distribution services, and the proprietor running the department as a separate store. The relationship between store and proprietor is much like that between a market or bazaar and its lessees.

leasehold: That property interest possessed by a lessee, as defined by the terms of a lease, including such matters as rights, obligations, length of lease, renewal options, and termination conditions.

leasehold improvements: Those improvements on a property made by a lessee, for which the lessee is entitled to compensation in the event of a taking of the property by government.

leasehold mortgage: A mortgage loan which takes a tenant's leasehold interest as security for the loan, rather than an owner's interest; usually occurring as a loan using a lease on income-producing property as collateral, especially when that property is otherwise unencumbered by mortgages which would be senior debt obligations.

leasehold value: The value of a lessee's interest in the remaining portion of a lease, when that lease specifies lower rentals than those paid for comparable leases; in some jurisdictions an element of compensation due lessee under conditions of government taking of the property leased.

lease insurance: An insurance coverage providing lessor protection against default by lessee on a lease agreement.

lease-purchase option: See option.

ledger: A book of final entry used in accounting, into which is placed all information derived from original entry sources, such as journals and payment records; the size and complexity of a business' transactions will determine the number and kind of general and special ledgers needed.

legacy: In law, personal property that is passed by will; in general usage, anything, including both real and personal property, that is passed by will.

legal description: That formal description of real property which is complete enough to identify the property for title search purposes; normally made by an independent engineer or surveyor and made part of real property conveyance documents, such as deeds, leases, and mortgages.

legal duty: A duty stemming from law or contract, and which undone may be found to breach a contract, violate law, or create liability for negligence.

legal entity: Any person or organization existing in law, and therefore capable of engaging in legal transactions, taking legal responsibility, acting, or being acted against in law.

legal interest: The highest rate of interest that may be charged by a lender; usually set by the usury statutes of the state, which have jurisdiction over interest rates.

legal liability: A liability enforceable at law, in contrast to a moral obligation, which although sometimes enforceable by mores and consequent social pressure, is not enforceable at law.

legal notice: That notice which satisfies statutory or judicial requirements; depending upon circumstances, such notice may be direct or implied, oral or written.

legal representative: One whom the law will recognize as representing another, as it does executors, administrators, and in some instances receivers in bankruptcy and some kinds of assignees.

legal residence: Any residence at which a person lives at least part of but not necessarily most of the time and which is chosen by that person as a legal residence; synonymous with domicile.

legal tender: Money that is recognized by government as a lawful medium of exchange and usable for payment of sums owed, and which therefore must be accepted by creditors when offered in payment, unless the sums owed are defined in other than money terms or in terms of other currencies. For example, payment of a debt specifically stated in Japanese yen or German marks must be made in the specified currency if demanded by the creditor; payment in United States dollars at the current exchange rate may legally be refused.

legatee: One who is to receive a legacy by the terms of a will.

lending institution: An organization wholly or largely in the business of lending money to others for profit, such as a bank or savings and loan association.

lessee: See lease.

lessor: See lease.

letter of credit: An instrument issued by banks and other financial institutions, guaranteeing payment of drafts up to a specified limit when made by the person or organization named in the instrument; commonly used in foreign trade transactions as a means of organizing payments between correspondent banks without large transfers of funds between them. In commercial transactions, letters of credit may be irrevocable or revocable at will by the issuing institution up to a stated date; may be guaranteed as to payment by the issuing bank and its correspondent bank or by the issuing bank alone; and may be for a fixed amount or constitute a line of credit when travelling; a traveller's check is such a letter of credit.

letter of intent: A non-binding statement of tentative agreement signed by those who may become parties to a contract; should in no way be misconstrued to be in any way legally binding.

letters patent: See land patent.

letters testamentary: A written instrument issued by a court of proper jurisdiction, authorizing an executor to proceed with execution of a will, and functioning as proof that the will has been through probate.

let the buyer beware: See caveat emptor.

let the seller beware: See caveat venditor.

lettuce factor: A euphemism for the amount of money that must be paid in bribery of public officials in connection with a construction project.

leverage: The impact of borrowed money on investment return. For example, a real estate developer carrying relatively heavy debt obligations, such as large construction loans and mortgages, with consequent very heavy interest payments, is said to be heavily leveraged. In times of high earnings, the developer may make money on the borrowed money, and earnings relative to capital invested are high; in time of low earnings, the developer may make little money or actually lose money on the borrowed money, a "reverse leverage" situation.

levy: 1. Any claim by government upon the property of its citizens, including all taxes and seizures. **2.** An assessment by an organization on its members or stockholders to meet organizational obligations.

liabilities: 1. Amounts owed by debtors to creditors. **2.** All items appearing on the credit side of a double entry accounting system, including all amounts owed.

liability: 1. In the law, one of the widest possible range of current, contingent, future, and possible responsibilities and hazards. **2.** In business, whatever is owed by debtor to creditor. **3.** In accounting, any item appearing on the credit side of a double entry accounting system, including both current owings and future owings incurred but not yet due, and including the net worth items carried.

liability insurance: Insurance covering risks associated with the property and personal liability claims of others against the insured, including risks produced by the operations of owners, tenants, builders, and contracting parties.

liable: Legally responsible, or likely to be so, for satisfying the claim of another, and obliged to respond to that claim by either contesting or settling it.

license: 1. A permit by government to do something which by law requires such a permit, such as a real estate broker's license; granted as a matter of government discretion, rather than as a matter of individual or organizational right, for a limited time and subject to conditions imposed by government. **2.** Permission to use the land of another for a specified purpose, such as hunting; revocable at will, on the death of one so licensed, or on sale of the property. **3.** A permit granted by the owner of a patent or copyright to another to make use, usually commercial use, of patented or copyrighted materials or processes.

licensee: One who obtains a license.

licensor: One who grants a license to another.

lien: A claim chargeable by one against the property of another, usually arising from a debt owed by the property holder to the lien holder. If that debt is unpaid, the claim may be pursued by legal action and the property sold to satisfy the debt. One example of a specific or special lien on a property is a mortgagor's foreclosure of a property for nonpayment, followed by judicial sale of the property. Similarly, a mechanic may hold an automobile for unpaid repair bills, creating a specific mechanic's lien against that property, which is eventually satisfied out of the proceeds of sale of the property. A judgment entered against a defendant causes a judgment lien, which is a general lien against all of the defendant's property. The order in which liens are established determines the priority of their payment.

life estate: An estate granted to one who is not an inheritor under the terms of a will, and which is limited to the life of its holder or some other person, the estate then reverting to its grantor or some other party designated by the grantor.

life tenant: One kind of life estate. See life estate.

light industry: As defined by zoning laws, industry that is relatively quiet and non-polluting, such as small assembly plants and parts distributors; contrasts with heavy industry, such as mining, milling, and shipbuilding.

limited (Ltd.): A British term describing the limited liability to stockholders accompanying the corporate form of business organization; attached to corporate names in Great Britain and throughout much of the English-speaking world, and used synonymously with the United States terms "Incorporated" or "Inc."

limited liability: Any limitation on the liability of those jointly engaged in a business enterprise; the corporate form by its very nature offers limited liability to stockholders, whose liability as regards corporate obligations extends only to the value of their stockholdings.

limited partnership: A partnership form, in widespread use in the real estate industry, in which one or more of the partners, known as limited partners and functioning solely as investors, share liability only to the value of their holdings, take profits within stated limits, and participate only financially in the enterprise; one or more other partners, known as general partners, functioning as entrepreneurs, exercise full control of and share unlimited liability and profit opportunity in regard to the enterprise.

linear measure: A measure of distance, such as a foot or mile, rather than of area, such as a square foot or square mile.

line of credit: See credit line.

lintel: A short, horizontal load-bearing beam, set across the top of an aperture in a structure, such as a door or fireplace, and bearing weight from above.

liquid assets: Assets consisting of cash, notes minus an allowance for uncollectibles, and quickly marketable securities; for net liquid assets, current liabilities are also subtracted.

liquidate: 1. To terminate and dissolve an economic entity through sale of all assets, payment of all obligations, and distribution of the remaining liquid assets to those entitled by law to receive them. **2.** To pay and discharge a debt.

liquidated damages: An amount previously agreed upon by parties to a contract or court action, representing damages that will be paid on breach of contract or judicial decision.

liquidation value: The estimated residual value of a business if it were to be terminated and dissolved, all assets turned into cash and all obligations paid.

liquidator: One appointed by law to liquidate a business; often used as a synonym for receiver.

liquidity: The ability to meet obligations out of liquid assets, rather than through debt creation or fixed asset sales.

lis pendens: A pending action at law; in real property law, a recorded document giving public notice that specified real property is the subject of a pending legal action, and so encumbering the property as to make it incapable of being sold during the course of that action.

listing: In real estate, the placing of a property for sale with a broker or group of brokers, the description of the property so listed, and the property so listed.

littoral: The land and nearby water of a lakeside or seaside coastal area.

littoral rights: The water and water-associated rights possessed by an owner of lakeside or seaside land.

live load: The weight of nonstructural building elements, such as furniture, fixtures, and people; building codes specify safe live load levels.

living trust: See inter vivos.

load-bearing wall: See bearing wall.

loan: Property owned by one which, by mutual consent, is used temporarily by another; also the transaction resulting in that use. In business, that property is usually money, which is by formal agreement passed from owner-lender to temporary user-borrower, to be repaid at specified times and at specified rates of interest.

loan application: A borrower's loan request to a lender, accompanied by any forms and proofs required by the lender; in real estate, often a package of materials, including detailed property, legal compliance, and financial capability descriptions and proofs.

loan commitment: See commitment.

loan ratio: The relationship of an amount loaned to the collateral securing the loan, expressed as a percentage; for example, a mortgage loan of $75,000 on property assessed or appraised at a fair market value of $100,000 creates a 75% loan-to-collateral ratio.

loan shark: A lender, operating illegally, charging usurious rates of interest, and normally indulging in unsavory collection practices.

lobby: 1. A public room or area inside a structure, such as a theatre, hotel, or apartment building. **2.** A group organized to exert direct pressure on the legislative process, attempting to influence legislators and administrators to act as the group would like on specific issues.

loft: An open area or floor in a building, usually a building zoned for business uses. A building that primarily contains such areas is called a loft building.

loft building: See loft.

long term contract: Any contract which will take more than one year to complete, and must be accounted for in more than one accounting year. In collective bargaining, contracts longer than one year have been considered long term, but the definition has been changing as more and more contracts are multi-year contracts, with long term more often used to describe three- and five-year contracts.

long term debt: Debts which must be paid one year or more after signing of the loan agreement, in contrast to short term debts, which must be paid less than one year after the borrowing.

long term lease: A lease that runs for several years, usually five or more; a relative term and not sharply defined as to length.

long term liability: See long term debt.

loss: 1. The difference between income and expenditure, when expenditure is larger; the net of the two is net loss, in contrast to net profit, which is the result when income is larger. **2.** The sudden, usually unexpected destruction of an asset without compensating payment, as in experiencing a fraud that is not adequately covered by insurance. **3.** The substance of an insurance claim from the insurance company's point of view; the amount that must be paid to settle a successful claim.

loss factor: The difference between rentable and usable area in rented premises, expressed as a percentage; for example, a lessee may rent 10,000 square feet, but find 1,000 square feet of the rented area used up by washrooms, corridors, elevator shafts, and other necessary but unusable areas, creating a loss factor of 10%.

louver: A wall opening, such as a window or door, containing movable or fixed slats, capable of being slanted to provide ventilation and desired amounts of light while keeping out undesired elements.

low bid: The lowest bid made among those competing for work on a bidding basis; often, but not always, resulting in securing the work.

low water line: The lowest shore elevation to which water normally sinks.

Ltd.: See limited.

lump sum payment: Repayment of a debt by single payment, rather than by any installment payment mode.

lump sum settlement: Settlement of an insurance claim by single payment, rather than by any installment payment settlement mode.

M

MAI: Professional certification designation, meaning *Member, Appraisal Institute*, a certification granted to qualified persons by the American Society of Real Estate Appraisers.

maintenance: The normal care and repair of a structure and the land on which it stands.

maintenance fee: A fee paid by owners to maintain commonly owned areas and services; for example those fees paid for by condominium and cooperative apartment owners for janitorial maintenance, and normal repair functions.

majority stockholder: One owning a controlling interest in a corporation; though earlier it referred to one owning more than 50% of the corporation's stock, it is now often used to describe those holding much smaller percentages, but in effective control.

maker: One who is the original signer of a promissory note, and therefore assumes prime responsibility for payment of that note.

malfeasance: The commission of an illegal or otherwise wrongful act, the proving of which can lead to successful criminal or civil action against the malefactor.

mall: An open or enclosed pedestrian walking area within a shopping area, as in a suburban shopping development or a city street closed to traffic and creating such an area.

malpractice: Misconduct by a professional of such nature as to be actionable at law, including negligence, illegal actions, immoral intent and action, and breach of fiduciary duty; most often alleged against doctors and lawyers.

malpractice insurance: Insurance against successful malpractice claims arising from professional practice; most often successfully pursued against doctors, but sometimes also against lawyers and other professionals.

management: 1. In the widest sense, the operation and control of any function or organization, including the management of one's own time, a household, or the provisioning of an ocean liner. **2.** The operation and control of business organizations, aiming at attaining the over-all goals of those organizations at minimum cost and maximum profit. Management may participate in over-all goal setting and may in fact exercise many other ownership functions. **3.** Those who are responsible for the operation and control of business organizations.

management accounting: Accounting systems designed to help management perform effectively by reporting financial information quickly, simply, and in forms usable by non-financial management people; usually the function of an internal financial officer, such as a controller, sometimes with the help of outside accountants.

management agreement: An agreement between property owner and property manager, setting forth the terms of the agency created, including all fees, privileges, responsibilities, liabilities, and limitations. The property manager is sometimes called the managing agent.

management audit: A review of management's operations and control mechanisms conducted by independent outside reviewers, aimed at evaluating the quality of management's performance as compared with that of similar organizations, usually those headquartered in the same country.

management by crisis: A technique of management purporting to favor the development of operating crises as a means of most effectively clarifying issues, developing effective management, and moving organizations ahead; normally far more an excuse for poor planning and ineffective management than a coherent management style.

management by exception: A technique of managing that focuses major attention on variations from plans and previous business patterns, in the main assuming that if plans are working out as budgeted, little attention need be paid to them, leaving more time for attention to the unforeseen.

management by objectives (MBO): A technique of managing that focuses on formal goal-setting and on reaching the goals set, featuring frequent planning, evaluation and reevaluation activities on the part of management people; usually accompanied by a good deal of organizational structuring and restructuring, as well as by the presence of a substantial number of internal and external consulting personnel.

management company: A company in the business of managing properties or investments.

management consultant: One who is professionally engaged in advising management as to the most effective ways of achieving management's goals. Most such consultants are independent contractors, whose value to management lies primarily in their independence and broad business experience.

management development: The process of attempting to train working managers to become better managers. Much of such development is self-development; much is relatively informal on-the-job skills training and self-training; some is formal in-company and outside professional training courses.

management fee: See management agreement.

management game: Any problem-solving game using organizational models and case studies to develop alternative solutions to the kinds of problems managers face in real life; a widely used training and professional development technique.

management information system (MIS): A computer-based information system aimed at providing mangement with an ongoing flow of operating and financial data that will help provide the basis for consistently informed decision making.

manager: One who manages; in small businesses one who manages at any level; in larger businesses, one who manages above the first line supervisory or foreman's level.

managing agent: See management agreement.

mandamus: A court order commanding a court of lesser jurisdiction, governmental body, private corporation, other organization, or person to do or not do something, without delay; sometimes specifying the exact action to be taken and sometimes commanding that action in general terms, with the specifics left to the doer.

manning table: A table setting out organizational structure and the standard number and kinds of jobs needed to fill that structure; often a maximum rather than average or minimum projection.

mansard roof: A roof with four sides, each side pitched at two different angles of slope, the upper slope being very gradual and the lower slope being almost vertical.

mantel: 1. A shelf above a fireplace; sometimes part of a load-bearing lintel and sometimes non-load-bearing. **2.** An ornamental facing around a fireplace, of which an upper shelf is part.

margin: 1. The percentage of equity owned by an investor who has purchased stock on margin; that is by a combination of cash and brokers' loans; a 70% margin, for example, means that the equity holder has paid 70¢ on each dollar of stock and the broker has loaned 30¢, with the broker holding a lien on the stock to the extent of the 30¢ per dollar loan. If the market price of the stock goes up, so does the owner's equity; if down, so does the owner's equity, with the 30¢ loan remaining stable in dollar amount but varying in percentage. **2.** A synonym for gross profit.

marginal cost: The cost of adding a cost factor, assuming all other variables remain constant; often a theoretical rather than practical measure.

marginal land: Land which is economically relatively undesirable because of its inability to yield acceptable levels of income; for example, inaccessible and rocky hill farmland, or water-poor desert land.

marginal revenue: The revenue resulting from a single additional sale. If revenue per sale remains constant, each additional unit sold yields as much as each previous unit, but if price decreases as units sold increase, revenue for each additional unit sold is less than a full unit price. For example, 5 units sold at $5 each yields $25. If 6 units are sold at $4.50 each, the yield is $27, which is only $2 more than $25. The marginal revenue is $2.

margin of safety: The extent to which loans secured by collateral, such as those in a margin account, are protected by the value of the collateral above the amount loaned. For example, stock used as collateral is always subject to loss in market value, and the amount accepted as collateral must therefore considerably exceed the amount of the loan. In a wider sense, any allowance for error and shortfall.

marina: A harbor installation servicing relatively small boats, with docking and minor repair facilities; sometimes also providing such amenities as showers, groceries, and restaurants.

market: 1. Any place at which goods and services are publicly traded, such as an open air market in which dozens of fruit and vegetable vendors sell their goods, a retail store, or the New York Stock Exchange. **2.** To sell, as when a company markets its goods. **3.** The demand for an item, as when the market for microcomputers is booming. **4.** A total of all trading activity in a designated area or kind of product, such as the Australian wool market or the world market for manganese.

marketability; 1. The likelihood that a product will be sold; its salability. **2.** The speed at which an asset may be made liquid without the substantial loss of value that would be caused by a distress sale.

marketable title: A title to real estate good enough to be conveyed and without which a valid real estate transaction cannot be legally consummated.

market data approach: See appraisal.

marketing: In the widest sense, the distribution function, including buying, selling, transporting, financing, and collecting. In modern business organizations, however, the term describes a group of selling and sales-related functions, including advertising, promotion, and direct selling.

marketing concept: A business planning approach that stresses the primacy of customer needs and wants, and regards the main function of the business as satisfying those needs and wants.

marketing manager: One who is professionally engaged in developing marketing activities on behalf of a product or group of products.

marketing mix: The set of marketing activities chosen by those responsible for marketing that they believe will most successfully sell their product or products, including the kinds of activities to be pursued, the amounts to be spent on those activities, and the integration of those activities into a coherent marketing plan.

marketing plan: The total plan adopted by marketing management for moving company products to market, including budgets, personnel, advertising, promotion, and direct selling plans.

marketing power: The relative ability of a firm to successfully sell its products in its markets; usually describing firms with relatively strong marketing organizations.

market position: The rank a firm occupies in its market relative to that occupied by other firms selling to the same market, assessed on the basis of such factors as sales volume, reputation and depth of penetration into specific areas. The term sometimes refers only to sales volume.

market potential: The sales possibilities for a product, in both present and future; a key assessment to be made by those developing new products.

market price: The actual selling price of an asset, such as real estate.

market profile: A detailed description of the market or markets for a product, including such materials as demographic data and market survey results.

market rate of interest: The rates of interest currently being charged on loans by lending institutions.

market rent: See economic rent.

market research: Information gathering and analysis bearing on any aspect of marketing, including such areas as consumer and industrial buying patterns and motivations, advertising, promotion, market definition, competition, and new product development.

market value: The price at which an asset or property will sell in its market now; often an estimate, as with real property, and sometimes a determinable amount, as with most securities.

markup: 1. The amount added to the cost of a product to cover additional costs and profits; for example, the amount added to the wholesale cost of a product sold at retail by the retailer, to cover operating expenses, other selling costs, and profit. **2.** A raising of a retail price; literally the marking of a higher price on an item sold at retail, as when a publisher, jobber, or retailer places a $9.95 sticker over the $8.95 price shown on a book. **3.** A higher evaluation of stores of value, such as factory inventories, and securities held by institutions.

masonry: Anything built of the materials with which a mason normally works, such as concrete, brick, and cement.

Massachusetts trust: A firm owned by investors who hold transferable shares representing the value of their investments in the business and who have only limited liability, just as do shareholders in a corporation, but who have no control over management or management policies. The firm is organized as a trust, with shareholders passing the assets of the firm to management, who are called trustees, and retaining only beneficial interest in profits commensurate with their investments.

mass appraising: The appraisal of many related properties in the same period, such as those in a neighborhood or town, as is often done preparatory to reassessment, and sometimes done in preparation for government taking.

master deed: See declaration of condominium.

master lease: 1. A lease between owner and lessor of premises serving both as conveyance between the parties and to set the bounds of all subleases executed by the main lessee. **2.** See declaration of condominium.

master plan: A development plan created by government for an area as small as a township or as large as a major metropolitan area, which attempts to define guidelines for the physical growth of that area, with attention to such long term problems as population density, land uses, pollution, and the quality of life in the area.

master policy: An insurance policy covering an insured operating in several locations at once, and supplemented in some locations by provisions meeting varying statutory requirements.

material costs: The costs of all substances used in the course of doing business, including those materials directly used in production and those used in all other aspects of business.

materiality: Relevance to the matter at hand, as when evidence presented in a legal action relates directly to the matter being adjudicated rather than being irrelevant to the main issues to be decided, or when a matter taken up or omitted on an accounting statement is relevant to proper understanding of company affairs by those who must be informed, such as directors, stockholders, the general public, and regulatory authorities.

maturity: The point at which a financial obligation becomes due and payable, such as the date at which a debt becomes payable, or an insurance policy becomes payable due to occurrence of stated conditions.

maturity date: See due date.

MBO: See management by objectives.

mean: A measure of the central tendency of a set of statistical observations, especially important in analyzing normal distributions. The mean is calculated by totaling the values and dividing the result by the number of observations, so the mean of 3,7,4 and 12 is 26 divided by 4, or 6.5. In popular usage, the mean is often called the average, though that term can also refer to the mode or the median average.

meander line: A boundary line created by a surveyor to indicate the path of a winding watercourse that forms the true boundary of a property.

median: A measure of central tendency of a set of statistical observations; the median is the middle number of a series of numbers arranged in order, so in the series: 1,2,16,44,56, the number 16 is the median. In a normal distribution, the median is theoretically the same as the mean, but when the data is highly variable, references to the median as "the average" can be misleading, since that term popularly refers to the mean.

megalopolis: A huge metropolitan area, such as the "city" that stretches from southern Massachusetts to northern Virginia; sometimes used to describe any very large metropolitan area, such as the New York, Chicago, and Los Angeles metropolitan areas.

melon: A relatively large sum of money to be divided among several people, whether proceeds or profits.

memorandum of agreement: A non-binding statement of intent signed by those who may become parties to a contract; usually a contract of sale in real estate. Although often called a binder agreement, it does not bind, unless it goes beyond its stated purpose and becomes, by nature of its language, signatures, and recordation, capable of becoming in fact a legally enforceable contract.

merchant bank: A bank engaged in a combination of investment banking, securities-related, and commercial banking functions, such as the international Rothschilds and Hambros banks; while active in Europe, they are not a United States banking form, for legal and historic reasons.

merger: 1. In real estate, the combining of two or more ownership interests into one such interest, as when a lessee buys a leased property and in so doing merges the previously held leasehold interest into the newly acquired absolute ownership, or fee interest. **2.** The complete takeover of one business by another, whether accomplished by termination of the legal existence of the firm taken over or by its continued legal existence while under the complete control of the acquiring firm. A firm may maintain its name and be operated as a wholly owned subsidiary for public identification and marketing reasons, yet lose all legal existence in such a takeover.

meridian: A basic surveyor's reference line, consisting of a circle around Earth touching both north and south geophysical Poles.

meter: 1. A basic metric unit of distance measurement, equal to 39.37 inches. **2.** A machine measuring flow quantity, such as those that measure the flow of water, gas, heating oil, and electricity to structures.

metes and bounds description: A mode of land description, which identifies the boundaries of a piece of land by use of distance and angles, starting at one point and following the boundary line around the land until it reaches its starting point.

metropolitan area: An area which includes one or more substantial cities and contiguous suburban areas, such as the Chicago, New York, and Los Angeles areas.

mezzanine: A balcony or partial floor, usually between the first and second floors of a building; in theatres, often the first balcony.

military clause: A lease contract provision, allowing a lessee on active duty in the armed forces to terminate the lease on short notice or without notice in the event of circumstances forcing a change of residence, such as discharge or transfer.

milking: To systematically, intentionally, and usually illegally strip a company of its assets; often prior to a change of ownership, bankruptcy, or dissolution; for example, by selling assets at bargain prices to a company owned by those in control of the company being looted.

millwood: Those finished parts of a structure, otherwise constructed on site, which are factory made and assembled into the structure on site; usually refers to such wooden parts as doors and frames.

mineral right: See subsurface right.

minimum lot area: The minimum legal size of a building lot, as set by local law.

minimum property requirement: The minimum standards required by the Federal Housing Administration for properties it will insure, in terms of soundness of design and construction, site location, and fitness for occupancy.

minority interest: An ownership interest that is less than a controlling interest in a company. In some companies, a minority interest may be anything less than 50% of ownership; but in large companies, where a controlling interest may be as little as 10%, a minority interest may be anything under 10%. As a practical matter even substantial minority interests may be granted some share in policymaking.

MIS: See management information system.

misfeasance: The improper and sometimes civilly or criminally actionable doing of an act which if properly done would be lawful; in practice, the term is often used to describe the doing of an unlawful act, and in that context is synonymous with malfeasance.

misrepresentation: A false statement of fact that is material to a transaction or agreement; such a statement may be explicit or capable of being constructed from actions; and it may be intentional or unintentional.

mistake: In the law of contracts, an innocent error of fact on the part of the parties that is so material as to cause a court to alter or cancel the contract, such as mutual misunderstanding of performance promises or property descriptions; but mistaken reading of contract terms or misunderstandings as to the law affecting the parties are not such mistakes.

miter: Two boards cut and fit together at an angle.

mixed use: Real property that is used for more than one purpose, such as a multi-story building or suburban mall area that is used for both offices and apartments, or even for a school, offices, hotel rooms, apartments, and shops.

mobile home: A residence, which although attachable to land and therefore capable of becoming part of land, like a fixture, is also capable of being detached and moved long distances by road, such as a house trailer; also used more generally to include all trailers used as temporary or permanent homes.

mobile home park: A site used for the medium and long term parking of mobile homes, usually containing such facilities as water hookups and sewage disposal, and providing for the affixing of mobile homes to the land, if desired by their owners. Many such sites are also used for the short term parking of house trailers. Also called trailer parks.

model: 1. A less-than-full-size representation, sometimes tangible, as in a ship or building model; sometimes symbolic, as in a mathmatical model; and sometimes symbolic but cast in technological form, as in a computer model.   2. A full-size demonstration construct, as in a demonstration home or apartment used to help sell homes in a large building development or apartment building.

model home: See model.

Moderne: See Art Deco.

modernize: To bring an existing structure closer to current technological standards; for example, to redesign a kitchen to take advantage of new materials and fixtures which are thought to be more versatile and efficient, or to replace existing window units with recently developed heat-conserving units.

modern style: See contemporary architecture.

modular construction: See prefabrication.

modularity: Describing the quality of being interchangeable; for example, prefabricated housing units that feature interchangeable parts or computer hardware and software that may be used with many kinds of programs and equipment.

modular unit: See module.

module: 1. A self-contained, standard, and often interchangeable unit, such as a prefabricated room or plumbing assembly used in prefabricated homes.   2. A basic proportion, against which other proportions will be developed in a construction, such as the over-all allowable length or width of a projected building.

moisture barrier: Condensation-inhibiting material used to slow the development of moisture in the walls of buildings.

molding: Strips of sometimes decorative material used to conceal the joinder of walls, floors, and ceilings; usually of wood.

money: A medium of exchange, generally accepted as having and holding a specified value against which the values of non-monetary items can be measured and expressed, as when a loaf of bread, which is non-monetary, can be bought for a dollar, which is a standard unit of money.

money market: A worldwide body of markets engaged in trading the short-term debt obligations of governments, financial institutions, and commercial firms, in such forms as commercial paper, bankers' acceptances, and Treasury bills.

money market fund: A kind of mutual fund, trading mainly in the kinds of short term debt obligations found in money markets, such as certificates of deposit, commercial paper, Treasury bills, other United States Government securities, and banker's acceptances.

monopoly: Effective control over a market by a single seller or a group of sellers, with no substantial competition and therefore no major buying choices available to purchasers other than refusal to buy at all—and no choice possible in the instance of monopoly-controlled necessities. United States examples are telephone services, power utilities, and postal services.

month-to-month tenancy: A tenancy in which the leasehold interest of the lessee is limited to one month, and which is renewable monthly, usually informally by landlord's lack of notice of termination, but which may be terminated at will by either party, usually on one month's notice; often effected by occupancy without a formal lease specifying a longer period, or by holdover tenancy after a lease has expired, the monthly period on holdover being specified in the original lease.

monument: An object serving as a survey marker, natural or constructed, such as a market post or pile of rocks.

moot: A legal question that has not yet been settled by judicial interpretation, is too abstract for such settlement, or is no longer relevant, having had its basis removed by operation of other factors.

moratorium: A sanctioned delay. Examples include a government-ordered postponement of debt repayment of a bond previously issued and due for payment; a private lender's agreement not to request payment from a debtor for a limited period; or a town's decision not to issue building permits until further notice.

Morris Plan bank: See industrial bank.

mortgage: A legally enforceable lien on property created by the pledge of that property as security for repayment of a debt or other obligation; also the legal document setting forth that lien, the terms of payment, and all other pertinent matters. In the common law, now largely superseded by state statutes, a mortgage was not a lien, but an actual transfer of property, voided by the mortgagee's performance of all obligations stated in the mortgage instrument. The most common mortgage forms are the constant payment mortgage, which provides for fixed payments for the life of the mortgage with relatively large interest and low principal payments at the start, and relatively low interest and high principal payments at the end of the mortgage loan period; and the balloon mortgage, which provides for low payments, sometimes consisting only of interest due, for the term of the mortgage, and repayment of all or a large remaining portion of principal at the end of the mortgage loan period. In recent years, a considerable variety of flexible rate mortgages have also become available.

mortgage banker: A firm or individual not otherwise in banking and finance that acts as a principal in mortgage loan transactions, and finances mortgage loans out of personal or company capital; a mortgage banker either holds the mortgages as investments, or more frequently, resells the mortgages, which are usually for interim financing purposes, to institutional investors. Also called a mortgage company.

mortgage bond: A kind of bond, secured by real or personal property, in contrast to unsecured bonds.

mortgage broker: A firm or individual in the business of bringing together lender and borrower to effectuate mortgage loans, taking profit from the transaction, but not directly financing mortgages.

mortgage company: See mortgage banker.

mortgagee: One who holds a mortgage on the property of another, being named as mortgage holder in the mortgage instrument.

mortgage foreclosure: See foreclosure.

mortgage insurance: A federally funded program which insures private lenders against losses stemming from some kinds of mortgage and housing loans. Administered by the Department of Housing and Urban Development, the program is intended to encourage lower down payments and interest rates and the availability of loan money to those of relatively modest means.

mortgage life insurance: A form of diminishing term life insurance, for the amount of the balance due on the mortgage, payable on death, or in some instances on the total disabling of the insured mortgage borrower.

mortgage market: The aggregate of activity by those giving and getting mortgage loans in a given area; often referring to a state, as the states regulate mortgage loan rates and terms, but sometimes to the entire country. The term is sometimes used as synonymous with the rate of interest generally charged by lenders in a mortgage market.

mortgage premium: An extra charge, beyond the interest charges, attached to a mortgage transaction by the lender. It is often denominated in "points," that is, a specified percentage of the morgage loan. For example, a bank or other lender might issue a mortgage loan of $20,000 at the going interest rate, plus 2 "points," or 2% of $20,000 for an extra charge of $400, payable on consummation of the mortgage loan.

mortgagor: One who mortgages a property, usually in return for a loan.

motel: See hotel.

Mother Hubbard clause: A mortgage loan contract clause enabling the lender to foreclose on any or all properties mortgaged by borrower with lender, in the event that any one of the mortgages is in default; not legally enforceable in most jurisdictions.

mud room: An entrance area, providing a transition from a yard area to the interior of a dwelling; often used for storage of tools and cleaning equipment.

mullion: A vertical strip separating the panes of glass in a window or door.

multiple dwelling: A residence containing more than two dwelling units, and so recognized by zoning laws.

multiple line insurance company: An insurance company that covers many kinds of property insurance risks, but not usually life, accident and health insurance; most major property insurers are multiple line companies.

multiple listing: The listing of real estate for sale with a number of brokers, often an association of brokers covering a given geographical area, rather than with a single broker.

multi-use building: See mixed use.

municipal: See municipality.

municipal bond: A debt obligation of any unit of government in the United States, other than the Federal Government, including state and all other lesser governmental units. Such debt obligations are, with a few exceptions, exempt from Federal and sometimes from state and local taxes, and therefore are often attractive tax shelters for those of substantial income.

municipal corporation: The basic legal form taken by the municipal form of local government.

municipality: A self-governing local governmental unit of any size, including cities, boroughs, towns, villages, or any other designated unit, but not including such governmental units as counties, states, and nations.

mutual company: A company that distributes profits to its members in direct proportion to the dollar quantity of business they do with the company; there is no stock, but rather equitable holding that varies with the quantity of business, as when mutual savings banks distribute dividends to their depositors and mutual insurance companies distribute dividends to their policy holders.

mutual fund: An investment fund that pools the invested funds of others and invests those funds on their behalf, usually in a specific kind of investment, such as money market instruments, municipal bonds, or common stock.

mutual insurance company: An insurance company that issues no stock, but instead distributes its profits to its policy holders as premium rebates or dividends. Although policy holders become equity holders to the extent of their premium payments, effective control is normally in the hands of trustees and management.

mutual savings bank: A savings bank that issues no stock, but instead distributes its profits to its depositors. Although depositors become equity holders to the extent of their deposits, effective control is normally in the hands of trustees or management.

mutual water company: A water company in which the stockholders are those using the water supplied by the company.

N

NAA: See National Apartment Association.

NAHB: See National Association of Home Builders.

name change: In real estate, a legal change of name that should be noted when transferring property, so that no defect or seeming defect in title will result, as when a name that had been incorrectly changed by immigration authorities on entrance into the United States is later officially corrected, or when a married name is used to convey title in land that had been acquired while using a pre-marital name.

NAR®: See National Association of Realtors®.

NAREB: See National Association of Real Estate Brokers.

NASD: See National Association of Securities Dealers.

national account: Large customers who buy products or services from a seller for use in many locations, often scattered nationwide, and who are handled as special accounts by the seller, often with separate sales representatives, pricing policies, and distribution handling.

National Apartment Association (NAA): A national trade association composed of those in multi-family housing and related businesses, with many local chapters.

National Association of Home Builders (NAHB): A national trade association, composed of those in home building and related businesses, heavily involved in educational, professional development, publishing, and legislative activities.

National Association of Real Estate Brokers (NAREB): A national association of real estate brokers, composed mainly of brokers who are members of minority groups; also called Realtists.

National Association of Realtors® (NAR)®: The largest national real estate trade association, composed of real estate brokers, managers, appraisers, salespeople, investors, and substantial numbers of others involved in the real estate industry; heavily engaged in educational, professional development, publishing, legislative, and ethical standard setting activities through national, state, and local organizations, and also through several affiliated organizations. Formerly known as the National Association of Real Estate Boards.

National Association of Securities Dealers (NASD): A securities dealers trade association, representing United States securities dealers, and holding some enforcement powers granted by the Securities and Exchange Commission, enabling it to regulate over-the-counter operations by dealers.

national bank: A bank chartered by the Federal government to conduct a commercial banking business, in contrast to a state chartered bank.

navigable waters: Streams and bodies of water that may serve useful purposes for the general public, clearly including those waters that form a waterway over which commerce may be pursued, but also in some jurisdictions including waters which may only be usable by the public for such purposes as boating, hunting, and fishing. Waters legally found navigable are public, rather than private, property.

negative cash flow: Cash losses, as when a property costs more in cash to manage than its gross cash receipts in a given period; some real estate investments are thought favorable by investors even when their cash flow is a net minus for relatively long periods, due to a combination of tax advantages and anticipated property appreciation.

negative easement: See amenity.

negative shelter: A tax shelter which has been in effect for so long that the tax shelter aspects of earlier years have reversed, and money formerly sheltered has now become an addition to current income; a result avoided by the use of other, later tax shelter arrangements to shield both current income and money returning to current income from previous tax sheltered investments; also called back end income.

negligence: In law, failure to do what a reasonable person would do under the same circumstances, with consequent actionable damage to another.

negotiable: 1. Legally transferable to another merely by delivery or by endorsement and delivery, the new holder then becoming owner for all legal purposes. **2.** Open for bargaining, rather than being firm as stated; usually referring to prices and terms in a business situation.

negotiable instruments: Instruments, such as checks and promissory notes, which can be legally transferred merely by delivery or by endorsement and delivery, the new holder then becoming owner for all legal purposes.

negotiable price: A price fixed as a result of discussion and agreement between the parties to a purchase contract, rather than fixed by the seller.

negotiation: 1. The act of transferring a negotiable instrument. **2.** The process of collective bargaining. **3.** The process of bargaining in any business situation, as in the development of a trade agreement satisfactory to the contracting parties.

neighborhood: An area within a community sharing common characteristics, such as residential, commercial, or industrial land use, and in residential areas sharing such characteristics as income levels and sometimes ethnic origins.

Neoclassic: An approach, rather than a house style, featuring the columns and straight lines of Greek and Roman architecture, as demonstrated by the Federal and Greek Revival styles.

net: The remainder, after all else has been added and subtracted; in business, always capable of being expressed discretely, almost always as a specific plus or minus number.

net after-tax estate: See net estate.

net assets: See net worth.

net avails: The actual amount a borrower realizes from a discounted note, subtracting the amount of the discount from the amount borrowed.

net bonded debt: The net of bonds issued minus bonds in any way paid minus funds held in the issuing corporation or government as a reserve against repayment.

net cash flow: See cash flow.

net estate: The net of a decedent's estate minus charges and expenses, but before taxes. Sometimes, however, the term is used as an abbreviated reference to net after-tax estate, which is the balance of the estate minus charges, expenses, and taxes.

net income: The income remaining for the equity holders in a business after deduction of all expenses and other deductions from all revenues.

net lease: A lease which rents only land or land and structures, with the lessee paying for all other costs arising from that which is leased, including such costs as taxes and all maintenance; for example, a lease of an entire shopping center from its owner by an operating company.

net listing: A listing arrangement in which a seller receives a fixed amount, with the selling broker receiving all monies received on sale above that net amount; an unethical and in most states an illegal arrangement.

net liquid assets: See liquid assets.

net loss: The net of expenditures and revenues during a given period, when expenditures exceed revenues.

net-net: A final net figure; synonymous with bottom line.

net price: The actual price paid by buyer to seller for a purchased item, after all discounts, adjustments, and negotiations have been completed.

net proceeds: See net avails.

net profits: The net of revenues minus all appropriate costs. The term is often used as a synonym for net income, but in ordinary business usage may refer to either net profits before taxes or net profits after taxes.

net profits after taxes: The net of revenues minus operating expenses and taxes.

net profits before taxes: The net of revenues minus operating expenses but before deductions for taxes.

net sales: The net of gross sales minus all returns, allowances, and other appropriate deductions.

net worth: The value of total ownership interest, the net of total assets minus total liabilities; expressed variously according to the form of business organizations, as stockholders' equity, owner's equity, partner's equity or proprietor's equity. The net worth of an individual includes personal as well as business assets and liabilities, and is the net of all assets minus all liabilities.

New England Colonial: Generally used to describe a building in an early New England architectural style; usually a two-story structure, with a center door and entry hall and shutters flanking all windows in deference to the New England winter.

new town: A substantial planned new residential development, often organized into a new municipality; commonly a suburb of a larger municipality. Sometimes called a satellite city.

New York Stock Exchange (NYSE): By far the largest stock exchange in the United States, and one of the world's largest stock exchanges. Often referred to as "the Exchange" or "the Big Board."

no contest: See nolo contendere.

no deal, no commission clause: A contractual provision in a real estate listing contract stating that a broker's commission will be paid only if title actually passes from seller to buyer; in its absence, the general rule is that a broker's commission is payable if a willing and able buyer who is ready to buy at an offered price has been brought by broker to seller, even if seller ultimately decides not to sell.

nolo contendere: A plea of no contest made by the defendant in a criminal case, which operates for purposes of that specific case as a guilty plea, but which does not constitute an admission of guilt that can be used against the defendant in another case, criminal or civil.

nominal consideration: In the law of contracts, an amount of consideration so small as to be clearly a fiction, usually for the purpose of hiding the true amount of consideration involved, yet at the same time functioning to make it clear that no gift is being made and that the party offering the consideration is, in law, a purchaser rather than one receiving a gift.

nominal partner: Someone who gives every appearance of being a partner in a firm, such as being included on a firm's letterhead, but who in fact has no legal connection with that firm.

nominee: One who is named by another to take defined and limited actions on the other's behalf; in effect, a limited agency, as when one votes the proxy of another or purchases land on behalf of an undisclosed principal.

nonassumption clause: See due on sale clause.

nonbearing wall: A wall which carries no weight but its own, such as an exterior curtain wall or interior partitioning wall.

noncallable bonds: Bonds that mature only at their stated maturity dates and that cannot for any reason be recalled or redeemed by their issuers before maturity.

noncompetition provision: A clause in a commercial lease covering the possibility that either landlord or tenant may cause damaging competition to arise nearby; for example, a landlord may be prohibited from renting to a competing business within a given geographical area or within a development; or a tenant may be prohibited from renting another space within a given area for another similar business that might detract from the business done in the leased space.

nonconforming use: A land use that is permitted by local law even though it does not conform to current zoning laws, because it was in existence before the current zoning laws were in being; for example, a small business located in what is now a wholly residentially zoned area. Such uses are often limited to a period of years, or to the period of ownership of current owners, with alterations, additions, and changes of use sharply limited or prohibited by law.

nonfeasance: Failure to perform a legal, usually contractual duty, but without intent to do so.

noninsurable risk: A risk that insurance companies are unwilling to insure, usually because of the nature of the risk involved. Risks considered noninsurable by some are viewed as insurable by other companies, which charge far higher premium rates. In some instances, companies legally required to insure risks they individually regard as noninsurable will pool such risks, as in an automobile insurance assigned risk pool.

nonmember bank: A commercial bank that is not a member of the Federal Reserve System.

nonnegotiable instrument: An instrument that lacks one or more of the requisites for being negotiable, and that therefore, while being an instrument of value, is not capable of being freely negotiated.

nonoperating company: A company that engages in no operations of its own, being dormant or having converted its assets into leases or investments.

nonoperating revenue: Revenue from all sources other than operations, such as dividends and land rental income for non-real estate companies.

nonperformance: Actionable failure to perform obligations under the terms of a valid contract.

nonprofit corporation: A corporation organized and chartered to be not-for-profit, from which no stockholder, manager, or trustee can legally take profit, and which often is wholly or partially exempt from federal and some state and local taxes due to the nature of its socially and legislatively approved activities, in such areas as education and charitable causes.

nonrecourse loan: A loan by the terms of which a borrower makes only a promise to pay, supported only by any collateral that may be stated in the loan agreement. Should default occur, the creditor has no other recourse or claim against the borrower, and that is so stated in the loan agreement.

nonrecurring charge: A one-time expense, so treated on accounting statements.

nonrenewable resource: See wasting asset.

normal distribution: In statistics, a frequency distribution, also called the Gaussian distribution, that has a characteristic bell shape—high in the middle, sloping sharply on either side, and then trailing off on both sides. According to the central limit theorem, for any kinds of data, the larger the sample, the more likely the distribution will assume this normal—that is symmetrical—shape. In a normal distribution the main measures of central tendency—the mean, the mode and the median—

all have the same value, and the measures of dispersion—the standard deviation and the variance—show the spread of data around that central value. Statisticians use tables based on the theoretical normal distribution to help them predict information about actual populations; applications range widely, from analysis of intelligence test scores to controlling quality of production processes.

notary public: A state-licensed person, legally authorized to perform a variety of document-related functions, including the taking and certification of affidavits, depositions, and oaths; of payment demands and protests of several kinds of financial instruments; and certification of documents. The notary's seal is admissible legal evidence.

note: A negotiable instrument in which the note's maker promises to pay a specified sum, at a specified time or on demand, to the note's payee. The maker may defend against making the promised payment for lack of a valid agreement as between the original maker and payee, but not against other holders in due course.

notes payable: The sum of all notes promised and owed by a business to its creditors, such as banks and suppliers.

notes receivable: The sum of all notes promised and owed by others to a business, such as customers.

notice: Information on a matter which has actually been transmitted pursuant to law or by a legal agency, or has actually been given in writing or orally to a contracting party in compliance with terms set by contract; which has been put on such public records as to legally constitute notice, as it will be constructed by judicial action; or which would have been easily available if one had sought it through normal means, rather than diligently avoided it. Examples include a written notice of loan default required by law or contract from lender to borrower; public posting constituting notice of the opening of bidding or of a completed sale; and constructive notice of the existence of a lien on property, stemming from its public recording.

notice of dishonor: A document which is issued by a notary public at the request of a note holder who has been refused payment of a note by its maker, and which functions as legal evidence that the note has been dishonored, or unpaid.

notice of lis pendens: See lis pendens.

novation: The replacement of an existing contract by a new contract, by agreement of the parties to both the existing and the new contract. The new contract may alter the parties, the terms, or both.

nuisance: Any act or omission which interferes with the enjoyment of life and property of others. A public nuisance interferes with the life and property of many; for example, the operation of a noisy and fume-creating group of machines in a quiet residential neighborhood. A private nuisance interferes with fewer people; for example, the creation of a hazard to health and plants caused by a neighbor's pesticide spraying. The distinction between public and private nuisances is often unclear, as many nuisances tend to harm both individuals and the community at large.

nuisance tax: A very low-yielding tax, which is usually more trouble and sometimes expense to administer and pay than it is worth to the taxing authority; many taxes so considered by those taxed are considered well worth levying by tax authorities.

null and void: Describing that which is legally unenforceable, as when a contract carries a clause which courts will void.

NYSE: See New York Stock Exchange.

O

obligation: 1. Any kind of legally enforceable duty to another. 2. Any kind of money debt to another, for a specific sum and legally enforceable.

obligation bond: A bond executed by a mortgage loan borrower in favor of the mortgage lender, personally pledging the payment of overdue interest, real property taxes, and assessments during the mortgage period.

obsolescence: See economic obsolescence and functional obsolescence.

occupancy permit: An official document certifying that a building may legally be occupied and used.

occupancy rate: The percentage of occupancy of a rental structure, measured in rentable space or units occupied; for example, a building with 10,000 rentable feet that has 8,000 feet rented is 80% occupied, or a building with 10 units that has 7 rented is 70% occupied. Stating occupancy in terms of space is the more accurate of the two methods, and is more generally used.

occupant: One who is in physical possession of real property on a continual basis.

OFCC: See Office of Federal Contract Compliance.

offer: To make a proposal to another, possibly involving, but not limited to buying and selling. For example, in the real estate industry, one may offer or bid to buy a property for sale at a proposed price, or offer to sell at a proposed price. That offer, once made, remains open for a reasonable time unless specifically limited as to time or withdrawn, with acceptance creating conditions of contract, if all other material terms can be agreed upon by the parties. Contracting parties, both in commercial contracts and in collective bargaining, may make and counter with offers.

offer and acceptance: See offer.

offering price: 1. The price set by a potential seller for something that is for sale. **2.** The price at which a new securities issue is brought to market.

office buildings: Buildings functioning mainly, though not necessarily exclusively, to house offices, rather than for other commercial or industrial uses.

Office of Federal Contract Compliance (OFCC): A Federal agency responsible for the execution of national policy forbidding employment discrimination by those doing business with the Federal Government.

office park: A group of office buildings set in a landscaped area, and designed and developed as a single project; usually located in suburban and exurban areas.

officer: One who is by charter and in law designated as a responsible official of an organization, capable of acting for that organization within specified legal limits; usual designations of officers in business include president, secretary, treasurer, controller, and vice president.

offset: 1. A sum balancing or reducing an opposite sum, as when damage claims and counterclaims by the parties to a lawsuit eventually wholly or partly negate each other, or when sums entered on both sides of a single account wholly or partially cancel each other. **2.** A widely used printing process.

offsite: Those areas which are not directly part of a building site, but which generate related costs and carry related improvements, such as sewers, sidewalks, and streets.

oil and gas lease: A lease of subsurface drilling and extraction rights, in return for flat fees, royalties, or both; often accompanied by a lease of all other subsurface rights as well.

omnibus clause: In liability insurance policies, a clause extending coverage to unnamed others beyond the insured, who may be, for all practical and policy purposes, standing in the shoes of the insured for coverage purposes, as when automobile coverage extends to the "guest" driver of an insured car.

on center: The distance from the center of one structural component to the center of another, as from the center of one stud to the next.

on the block: See auction.

open and notorious possession: Possession so public and clearly stated that it serves as constructive notice to all that a claim of possession has taken place; an essential element of constructive notice in instances in which adverse possession is claimed.

open beam construction: An interior design element, featuring the use of heavy interior beams, as in a hunting lodge or ski resort.

open credit: A line of credit, in which a lending institution or seller extends credit to a customer or buyer up to a set limit, so that the credit is available and ready to be used as desired, without specific approval by the creditor each time it is used.

open end contract: An agreement between buyer and seller, setting out most of the terms of their contract, but leaving some terms open, or indefinite. For example, all terms but maximum quantity may be agreed upon; then the buyer has the right to purchase the goods specified, at the terms and price set, in any desired quantity above a stated minimum.

open end mortgage: A mortgage that gives the mortgagee the right to borrow more from the mortgagor on the same mortgage, rather than being forced to undertake additional mortgages if a larger amount is desired.

open house: In real estate selling, the opening of a house for sale to prospective buyers for a specified period without appointment.

open housing: See fair housing.

open listing: The listing of a property for sale with more than one broker simultaneously, without forfeiting the owner's ability to sell the property independently without any broker or brokerage commission.

open market: A market open to all potential buyers and sellers, rather than effectively controlled by statutes or business organizations; often describes a main tendency rather than a pure state, as most markets are in some ways restricted.

open mortgage: See open end mortgage.

open space: Natural areas left undeveloped, either by law or by agreement between local authorities and developers. Examples include a large tract of forest, marshland, or shore left forever wild in the public interest; or a several-acre lawn area within a large housing development.

operating budget: A budget for current income and expenditures, rather than for capital items.

operating company: A company actively engaged in conducting one or more lines of business, in contrast to a nonoperating company, which is dormant or has converted its assets into investments or leases.

operating costs: See operating expenses.

operating expenses: Costs incurred while conducting business and attributable to the conduct of the business, including labor, maintenance, taxes, insurance, utilities, and all other connected operations.

operating ratio: The relationship between items on an operating statement, usually expressing one item as a percentage or multiple of another; for example, operating costs may be expressed as a percentage of gross income, or sales costs as a percentage of net revenue.

operating statement: A financial report on the operations of all or part of a business organization for a given period; for example, a rather detailed statement of income and expenditures or a cash flow statement.

opportunity cost: The best return that might be realized from an investment, taking investment goals into account, expressed as a cost and contrasted with the return that is currently being realized; for example, the ability to invest surplus cash in relatively safe securities yielding 8-10% after taxes, rather than in current operations yielding 4-5% after taxes, with the cost being the difference between the two percentage ranges.

option: 1. The right to buy or sell something at a certain price within a specified time, usually as stated in a written agreement enforceable at law, in which that right has been conveyed in return for some kind of consideration. Examples include an option to buy real property within a specified period; an option to buy rented housing after expiration of or during a stated rental period; or a tradable option to buy a security or commodity. **2.** A choice, such as between alternative contract terms during negotiations, or modes of payment in settlement of a life insurance claim.

optional bond: A bond that may be called in and redeemed by its issuer at some time or times before its final maturity date; a callable bond.

option period: The time during which an option may be exercised, according to the terms of the option.

oral agreement: An agreement between contracting parties, that, in the absence of a written agreement, is legally binding upon the parties; sometimes but rarely enforceable at law, although never against a legally valid written agreement. Contracts for the sale or lease of real property must be in writing and signed by the parties to be legally valid, except that leases of one year or less may be oral agreements. Also called parol contract.

ordinance: In the most general and historic sense, synonymous with law or statute; now primarily used to describe a statute or regulation enacted by a municipal corporation.

ordinary depreciation: Losses in value occurring from normal aging and wear and tear, rather than from extraordinary factors, such as damage due to fire and natural causes.

organization expenses: Expenses connected with the organization of a new business enterprise, such as legal fees, registrations, and deposits.

orientation: The placement of a structure in relation to its environment, referring to such matters as the direction of exposure to sun and wind.

original cost: The purchase price of an asset, as of its acquisition date, without any post-acquisition costs.

original entry: An accounting entry, recording a transaction and entering it into an accounting system for the first time.

origination fee: See financing fee.

outlay: An expenditure, in cash, cash equivalents, or property.

outside audit: See external audit.

overage: Any amount more than is specified in a plan or on a document. The term may be used as either a plus or a minus; profits may exceed stated minimums under a rental agreement, creating overage that in turn triggers additional rental payments, or expenditures may be higher than plan or budget, creating a minus overage.

overbought: The condition of having bought more of something than was economically wise, and of now facing the necessity of selling at less than normal profit or at a loss, as when a retailer buys more merchandise than he or she can sell and is forced to hold a sale to move that merchandise; sometimes applied to a whole market, as when a company stock is bid up by speculators and has nowhere to go but down.

overbuilt: Describing an area which has more units of a kind than the market can readily absorb, as when a suburban shopping area has experienced a relatively large amount of building and has empty commercial establishments.

overdraft: The amount by which a call on established credit exceeds the credit available; usually the amount by which a check exceeds the balance in the bank account on which it is drawn.

overdraft privilege: See credit line.

overdue: Any obligation that has passed beyond the date it was due to be fulfilled; usually refers to a debt obligation that has become due and payable, but has not yet been paid, but can also refer to some other kind of timed contractual obligations, such as completion of a construction contract.

overextension: Spending or borrowing far beyond prudent limits, as when so much has been spent on plant expansion beyond sales prospects as to endanger company credit relationships; or an investor has bought far more stock on margin than that investor's net worth indicates prudent; or so much has been borrowed, reborrowed, and expended that current borrowings are far too great for prudent bankers to justify.

overhang: The projection of a roof over exterior walls.

overhead: All costs that cannot be directly attributed to the output of goods and services; therefore all costs other than direct labor and materials.

overimprovement: A construction which is too costly to allow the most profitable use of property; for example, the construction of a million dollar residence on a smallish plot surrounded by homes selling in the $75-100,000 range, the nature of the neighborhood then reducing the fair market value of the million dollar home.

overinsurance: Property insurance of considerably greater value than the property insured, with resultant higher than necessary premium payments and sometimes unrealistic claims.

overlying mortgage: A mortgage that is subordinate to other mortgages, and therefore a junior mortgage.

override: A bonus paid to executives and managers, usually computed as some portion of revenue, profits, or compensation paid others, and most commonly as a percentage paid sales management for achieving specified sales goals or as a percentage of the commissions paid their selling staff.

oversold: Describing a stock or a market which is thought to have been sold more than is economically justified, and therefore to have declined in price to an unrealistic level.

oversubscription: Purchase by the public of more securities than the amount of a securities issue, resulting from simultaneous sale of the issue by a number of sellers; usually handled by pro rata cutting of buyers' purchases.

over-the-counter market: The market for securities not listed on any United States stock exchange, which are traded nationally and internationally directly between buyers and sellers, usually through dealers.

overpass: An elevated road over another roadway of any kind.

overvaluation: 1. The placing of a higher than reasonable valuation figure upon property; often the subject of property tax disputes. 2. Governmental support of a national currency at exchange rates higher than those which would occur if that currency were allowed to float freely, to reach its value against all other world currencies as economic and world currency market conditions would determine.

owner: One who has legal title to property.

owner's equity: See net worth.

ownership: See owner.

P

package: A container, whether something physically holding goods or a document holding a group of ideas or agreements.

package mortgage: A mortgage that includes some items of personal property, such as kitchen and laundry equipment in a house mortgage, that mortgage then becoming a loan on house, land, and personal property, all treated as realty.

package policy: An insurance policy that is actually a group of coverages that might be written in several different policies, but are written as one omnibus policy.

paid-in capital: The total capital put into a corporation by its stockholders, including cash, property, services, and any other item of value that can be evaluated, and including both initial capital and any later contributions to capital.

paid-in insurance: An insurance policy on which all premiums have been paid in advance of maturity date, and on which no other premiums will be due.

paid-in surplus: The net of all capital put into a corporation by its stockholders minus the par value of the corporation's stock, including the difference between the par value of stock and the price at which it is sold to the public, plus all additional capital.

P & L: See income statement.

panel heating: A heating mode using heating elements, such as coils, built into and therefore concealed by internal wall, floor, or ceiling sections.

paper: A general term referring to such loans as those evidenced by mortgage instruments, commercial paper, and Treasury bills, as well as the instruments themselves, which are in most instances tradable in secondary markets.

paper money: Money issued by a government in paper, rather than in coins, which may or may not be convertible to precious metals. United States paper money is not so convertible, and is backed only by the full faith and credit of the federal government.

paper profit: A so far unrealized gain; usually used to describe increases in the value of securities since bought by their current owner. In one sense, the profits are real—securities used as collateral are valued at current market prices rather than prior purchase prices.

par: Full stated value, as indicated on the face of an instrument. Therefore, a stock's par value is its face value, and a check cleared at par is a check cleared at its full stated value, without discount or premium.

parapet: A wall built at the edge of a roof or other exterior building surface, such as safety wall built on the top edges of a flat roof.

parcel: Any specific piece of land.

parity clause: A provision that when a mortgage secures more than one loan, all loans secured will have equal claims upon it, should default on any of the notes cause foreclosure.

parol: In the law, a synonym for oral.

parol contract: See oral agreement.

parol evidence: A legal term for oral evidence.

parol evidence rule: In the law of evidence, the general rule that evidence contained in a written instrument will supersede conflicting oral evidence, while not precluding clarifying oral evidence; subject to considerable exceptions and qualifications, as when oral evidence goes to the question of fraud in the making of an instrument, or to the intentions of parties to make a contract.

parquet floor: A finished floor composed of patterned hardwood blocks, often in geometric designs.

partially blind pool partnership: In real estate investment, a limited parnership in which some but not all of the assets to be acquired by the partnership are known to the investor at the time of purchase of the limited partnership interest.

partial release provision: A mortgage clause providing for release from mortgage lien of specified lots from the property mortgaged, on payment from the borrower to the lender of stated sums; usually found in a mortgage on land to be developed and sold off in lots to others, so that on sale of a lot, the developer can pass unencumbered title. Also called release clause.

participation: See equity participation.

participation loan: A loan made by one bank in which another bank shares part of the risk and return, as when a large loan is made by several banks acting together, or when a large bank joins a smaller bank in taking a risk.

participation mortgage: A mortgage in which the lender takes sums beyond interest and other charges stated in the mortgage loan, in the form of some kind of revenue or profit participation on the occurrence of stated events; for example, a percentage of gross profit over a certain level.

partition: 1. The division of commonly owned or tenanted land, or of any commonly owned or held real or personal property, into separately owned units, as on dissolution of a partnership. **2.** An interior wall.

partner: One who has joined with others in some form of legal partnership.

partner's equity: See net worth.

partnership: The association of two or more people for the purpose of doing business together for profit. The main form is that of the general partnership, carrying with it unlimited liability, as well as the ability to bind and be bound by the commitments of individual partners, and needing no formal written agreements between the parties to be recognized in law as valid.

party: One who makes a contract; also a plaintiff or defendant in a legal proceeding.

party wall: A wall between two separately owned structures, serving as an exterior wall for both, and at or very close to the boundary line between the two properties they are on. Although the wall sometimes falls largely or wholly on one side of a property line, both owners share responsibility for maintenance and have a right to use the wall; it cannot be damaged by either's removal of or alteration of the wall without consent of both owners.

passive investor: An investor carrying only a financial interest in an enterprise; a rather imprecise term, as it may include both those subject only to limited liability, such as limited partners in real estate enterprises, and those subject to unlimited liability, such as general partners in some other commercial enterprises.

passthrough: An investment concept, recognized and permitted by tax law, which provides for the flow of funds received directly through a legal form to investors, such as a real estate limited partnership, which for tax accounting purposes passes income and expenses through the partnership form to limited partners. Certain mortgage-backed Federal securities pass debt repayments directly through pooled mortgage funds to investors. Also called flowthrough.

past due: See overdue.

patent: See land patent.

pavilion: A partly open roofed structure; usually for recreational and ornamental purposes, as at an amusement park.

payee: That person or organization to whom a debt instrument, such as a note, check, or money order, is made payable.

payment: A sum paid another in settlement of an obligation, or pursuant to an agreement, whether complete or partial; also the act of paying.

payment bond: A surety bond purchased from a bonding company by a contractor, which guarantees payment of the contractor's labor and materials obligations in connection with a specific job, so protecting the owners or developers from the mechanic's liens of subcontractors, while assuring the subcontractors of payment.

payment terms: The way in which payment is to be accomplished, as specified in the agreement between payor and payee; for example, repaying of a loan in installments or cash on delivery in payment for a purchase.

payor: One who is responsible for payment, and is so named on a debt instrument, such as a note, check, or money order.

pecuniary: That which relates to money, the word most often being used as a synonym for money, as in pecuniary benefit, meaning money benefit, or pecuniary exchange, meaning exchanging money or goods for money.

penalty: 1. In the law of contracts, a sum set by contract to act as liquidated damages on breach of contract; if a court finds the sum set unreasonable, it will set aside the contract provision, and will itself assess reasonable damages. 2. Any punishment imposed by statute or judicial action.

peninsula: A body of land, usually relatively narrow, surrounded by water on three sides and connected to a larger body of land on the fourth.

pension fund: A store of value built up out of the retirement funds of one or more persons and the income from those funds, which may range in size from a few thousand to billions of dollars; in real estate, a prime source of institutional funding for substantial projects.

penthouse: A relatively small structure on top of a substantial building, used for apartments, commercial occupancy, or equipment storage, but usually for one or more luxury apartments, often with more landscaping than is normally possible in the design of city apartments.

percentage depletion: A Federal income tax allowance for the depletion or using up of resources in the extractive industries, such as oil, gas, coal, metals, and minerals, allowing income tax deductions based on a specified percentage of gross income, with no direct relation to the cost of the property being so depleted. Percentages allowed vary with the kind of resource.

percentage lease: A business lease providing for computation of rentals to be paid wholly or partially as a percentage of gross business income; very often used in franchise agreements, and sometimes in retail rental agreements.

percentile: A 100-unit system of ranking items in a frequency distribution, often used in testing, with the percentile indicating the number of people at or below the point specified; for example, a score in the 91st percentile means that only 9 percent of those tested scored better. Related ranking systems are the decile, which uses a 10-unit ranking system, and the quartile, which uses 4 units.

percolation test: A soil test designed to determine the liquid-absorption qualities of an area, in terms of soil drainage and septic area construction needs.

performance bond: A bond guaranteeing that work will be performed to specific quality and time specifications, and providing for forfeit if those specifications are not met.

period cost: A cost that is attributable to a time period, rather than to a product; usually fixed costs, such as real estate costs and interest.

periodic tenancy: A tenancy existing from period to period, in the absence of timely notice of termination, usually without oral or written lease, as when a year-to-year, month-to-month, or week-to-week tenancy exists, based upon rental payments yearly, monthly, or weekly; the payment of rent for the period, and absence of termination notice, act as extension of the tenancy for another period.

period income: Income attributable to a time period, and spread out for accounting purposes over the time properly attributable to it; for example, future interest on bonds already purchased.

peristyle: A series of columns around a structure or a structure-related open space, such as a courtyard.

permanent financing: In real estate, long term financing, as contrasted to short or medium term financing; usually amortized over a period of ten years or more, although interest rates may be reevaluated and adjusted more frequently, as provided by the loan agreement.

permanent loan: See takeout loan.

permit: 1. An official authorization; for example, a building or occupancy permit, or any other official license. **2.** Any authorization, express or implied, oral or written, public or private.

perpetual bond: A bond that is an open-ended promise to pay interest indefinitely, and that has no maturity date; or a bond that has such a long life that it is effectively perpetual.

personal check: A check drawn by an individual upon a checking account either in that individual's own name or one that is shared with one or more other individuals.

personal holding company: A tax avoidance device, now little used because of tax law provisions attacking it, consisting of a corporation formed by a high income individual to circumvent high individual tax rates by holding income in undistributed corporate earnings after paying the lower corporate taxes.

personal income: Gross individual income from all sources, including all income derived from work or property ownership, after expenses and before taxes.

personal loan: A loan made to an individual by a lending institution, such as a bank, credit union or finance company, carrying unlimited obligation to repay, with or without collateral; includes both specific sums loaned and lines of credit.

personal property: All property owned, other than ownership interests in realty and relatively immovable structures attached to realty; includes both tangibles, such as vehicles, books and toothbrushes, and intangibles, such as securities, copyrights, and insurance policies, as well as less-than-ownership interests in land, such as leaseholds.

personal property tax: See property tax.

personal service: Legally valid service of such legal process as a subpoena by personal delivery to the person for whom it is intended.

personalty: See personal property.

petition in bankruptcy: A document filed by a debtor or creditors in a court of bankruptcy, asking the court to place the creditor in a legal state of bankruptcy.

pier: 1. Any heavy supporting component of a structure, such as a foundation pillar of concrete and steel driven into the ground under a building; an aboveground or underground bridge or railway support; or a load-bearing support between windows in an outside wall. **2.** A structure built out over water to provide access to vessels.

piggyback mortgage: A mortgage loan made by two lenders using only one mortgage, and creating a senior and a junior lien using the same mortgage instrument; for example, an $85,000 loan on a property appraised at $100,000 on which a bank advances $75,000 and a private lender $10,000, with the private lender carrying mortgage insurance on the $10,000.

pilaster: A column set into or attached to a wall, serving largely ornamental, but sometimes support purposes.

pile: A kind of pier, driven into the ground and serving as a structural support.

pitch: 1. A rate of slope, as in the slope or pitch of a roof. **2.** Any tarry substance.

placement: In real estate selling, a synonym for listing; sometimes used as a synonym for sale.

placement fee: See financing fee.

planned community: A large group of residences, built according to a master plan and often by the same builder, usually including the kinds of community spaces and maintenance services found in a small hamlet or village and sometimes including small independent businesses serving the community.

planned unit development (PUD): A development, usually residential, which features much higher building density than allowed by local zoning laws, with the developer trading the creation of significant amenities for the higher density allowed; each such unit is developed in negotiation with local zoning authorities, and functions as a negotiated rezoning or specific variance from local zoning laws.

planning commission: A government agency, responsible for initiating and developing medium and long term plans for the areas in which it has jurisdiction; may operate on any level of government.

plans and specifications: A body of detailed drawings and building instructions, providing the specifics of a construction project, and often made part of the contract for development of a project.

plant: In the widest sense, all fixed assets, including land, buildings, and equipment; but more often used to describe buildings or both land and buildings.

plaster: A viscous mixture used to cover walls and ceilings; applied as a paste, then hardening as it dries.

plat: A municipal map, showing all or part of the municipality divided into properties and groups of properties, such as districts, divisions, subdivisions, and individual lots, including streets and other rights of way; used for planning and application purposes by developers and builders.

plat book: A book containing plats and other relevant plans and public documents for a given area, and kept in a place of public record.

pledge: The passing of collateral from borrower to lender as security for a loan, with the borrower keeping title but giving actual possession over to the lender, as when an object of value is pawned or securities are held by a bank as collateral on a loan.

plot: Any defined piece of land, but in real estate usually a piece of real property defined on public records.

plot plan: A detailed drawing of a plot, showing the location and scale of all improvements.

pocket listing: A listing of a property for sale which is given by the property owner to a broker or other seller and is intended for entry into a multiple listing, but which is instead held as if it were exclusive to the seller, sometimes even kept from other sellers in the same organization; an unethical practice.

point: 1. A percentage point, as when a lending institution demands an extra "point," or 1%, of a mortgage, in a lump sum at the start of the payback period before granting that mortgage. Often called an origination fee. **2.** In United States securities trading, a dollar. When a stock starts a trading day at 100 and goes up to 102 by the end of that trading day, it is up 2 points for the day. In the stock markets of other countries, a point is the normal currency unit used for describing trades.

police power: The power of a sovereign government to make and enforce laws and regulations, and to take actions affecting the life and property of those within its borders; in the United States subject to constitutional and common law guarantees protecting the rights and freedoms of private persons, and including taxing, land use, licensing, environmental control, and in some circumstances confiscatory powers.

policy: 1. A general attitude toward a particular kind of matter, indicating what positions to take and actions to pursue when confronted with that sort of matter. In organizations, policies may be written or unwritten, and are normally generated by boards of directors and top management. **2.** A document evidencing an insurance contract, known as an insurance policy.

policy holder: The owner of an insurance contract; often but not always the insured, as when one spouse owns and pays premiums on an insurance policy on the life of the other.

pollution: The contamination of the environment by humans, often with poisonous or hazardous waste products, but also with normally harmless substances in excess of what the environment can break down and absorb by natural processes.

porch: A floored structure attached to the outside of a house; may be a floor only, be roofed, or be entirely enclosed.

portico: An open-sided, roofed area before the entrance to a structure, with the roof supported by columns.

positive cash flow: See cash flow.

possession: In real property law, the actual or constructive occupancy or control of real estate, which may or may not also be legal, and which may be adverse.

postdate: To date a document later than the actual date it is executed; most often done on a check so that it cannot be cashed until the date specified, as banks cannot cash postdated checks until they become due.

power of attorney: Written authorization by one to another to act as an agent capable of making binding decisions regarding assets owned by the authorizer; may be limited to certain assets or for a limited time, or may be unlimited and revocable only by specific act of the authorizer.

power of sale: A mortgagor's or trustee's right, as specified in a mortgage or deed of trust, to sell mortgaged property at public auction to satisfy the debt when mortgage payments have not been kept up and the mortgage is thereby in default; the mortgagor or trustee satisfies as much as possible of the debt from the auction proceeds, with any remainder going to the mortgagee.

preclosing: A preliminary meeting, to prepare for a subsequent closing, in which many details can be worked out between the parties and their representatives; often used in substantial and complicated commercial transactions.

predate: To date a document earlier than the actual date it is executed; an act which may invalidate a contract, and which may in some instances lead to violation of law, as in the instance of checks predated to place deductions in a closed tax year for tax evasion purposes.

pre-emption **1.** The power of government to buy anything for sale ahead of its citizens, at a reasonable valuation. **2.** The power of a government at war to seize property belonging to neutrals and to conduct a forced sale of that property to its own citizens; just short of confiscation without compensation. **3.** The power of any individual or institution to buy ahead of others as a matter of right.

prefabrication: The manufacture and assembly of parts into finished pieces that otherwise would be assembled on building sites, as when a building is put together out of factory-built, mass-produced rooms constructed whole and shipped to the site. Also called component construction and modular construction.

preference bonds: Bonds on which interest is payable only out of corporate earnings, after all other expenses, including more senior debt obligations, have been paid.

preferred stock: Stock conferring equity ownership senior to that conferred by common stock, in that it receives dividends in stated amounts before any dividends can be distributed to common stock; sometimes also in that it carries more control over corporate affairs than does common stock. It may be cumulative, receiving dividends owing from previous unmade distributions, or non-cumulative, losing past unmade distributions; it may be participating, sharing to some extent in profits beyond specified dividends, or non-participating, not so sharing; it may be convertible, or capable of being exchanged for common stock at the owner's option.

preliminary title report: A report issued by a title company or professional title abstractor, serving as a basis for issuance of a title insurance policy.

premium: 1. Something of value, given by buyer or seller beyond the stated terms of a transaction, such as an extra interest charge on a real estate transaction. **2.** That which is paid for insurance coverage; usually used to describe a single payment made, but sometimes describing all payments due for the life of the policy. **3.** The amount by which the price of a security, debt instrument, or commodity is larger than its face value. **4.** The actual price paid for an option contract.

prepaid expense: An expense incurred currently, but properly attributable to future periods for profit and loss statement purposes, unless profit and loss are figured on a cash basis; for example, rent paid in advance for future occupancy; advance payment of insurance premiums or advance payments against anticipated royalties or commissions.

prepaid legal fees: Legal fees paid by clients to lawyers on a periodic basis, for which clients receive certain legal services by prior agreement during the term covered by the prepaid fees; a standard lawyer-client arrangement known as a "retainer," now expanded to include individual clients and groups of clients purchasing legal services, much as health care is purchased.

prepayment: 1. Payment in advance for goods or services to be supplied in the future, such as rent, insurance premiums, and advances against royalties. 2. Advance payment of obligations which will be due in the future, such as property taxes, mortgages, and debts. When such payment of future obligations operates to reduce future interest payments, there may be prepayment penalties; therefore prepayment is often a privilege specifically covered by contract.

prepayment clause: See prepayment privilege.

prepayment penalty: A money penalty imposed by contract on a debtor prepaying an installment loan, to compensate for the lender's foregone interest.

prepayment privilege: The right of a debtor paying off an installment loan, such as a mortgage or personal loan, to pay all or part of the balance due earlier than the payment schedule specified in the loan, so effecting a total interest reduction, without a money penalty being charged by the lender for prepayment, as partial compensation for that foregone interest.

prescription: The acquisition of a real property right, such as an easement, by adverse possession; in the common law, a very long and indefinite period was required for prescription, but now the time required is the statutory period needed to establish adverse possession, and the terms are synonymous for practical purposes.

prescriptive easement: See easement.

present value: An estimate of the value now of money that will be paid in the future, after taking into account loss of interest that might have been earned if the money had been paid now. In recent years, the impact of inflation has altered this concept to include also an estimate of the impact of inflation on the value of future payments.

preservation area: An area or special zoning district setting aside land and structures to be protected from destruction or significant alteration, such as historic places and wild life refuges.

pretax cash flow: See cash flow.

pretax dollars: In popular usage, sums used to make payments that are tax deductible; for example, an automobile purchased for corporate rather than personal use is a tax deductible business expense, and may be described as having been purchased with pretax dollars.

pretax income: Net income before taxes for a business; personal income before deductions for an individual.

price: 1. The amount of money, goods or services offered or asked in return for goods, services or money that are for sale. Asking prices are prices quoted on that which is for sale; offering prices are bids by potential buyers. **2.** Also, the amount for which something is sold, which is often somewhere between what is asked and what is offered.

price renegotiation: The reopening of a contract in being on the question of price, as provided by the terms of that contract, normally on occurrence of specified cost increases.

price variance: A change in quoted price, usually caused by changes in cost factors, especially in periods of rapid inflation.

prima facie: Something which will be presumed to be true unless there is evidence to contradict that presumption, as when evidence presented in a case at law builds a case that will stand, unless successfully rebutted.

prime: 1. Of very high quality; for example, beef, some bonds, and some commercial paper. 2. Sometimes used as a contraction of the term prime rate.

prime contractor: See general contractor.

prime mortgage rate: The lowest general interest rate charged on mortgage loans by lenders in a given period, extended to those thought to be excellent credit risks.

primer: A coat of paint or other such substance, meant to act as an undercoat for a final or top coat.

prime rate: The lowest interest rates charged by commercial banks to their most favored borrowers, usually extended only to large, well-established, and low risk corporations. As the prime rate changes, all other interest rates in the private sector of the economy tend to follow suit.

prime tenant: 1. A centrally important tenant in a structure, such as one occupying a large amount of space or lending significant prestige that will attract other tenants; sometimes a tenant after whom a structure or group of structures will be named. Also called an anchor tenant. **2.** A tenant renting directly, in contrast to a subleasing tenant.

principal: 1. The amount of a loan or note, on which interest is charged. **2.** An amount invested, on which earnings, such as profits and interest, may accrue. **3.** One of the parties to a transaction. **4.** The holder of a substantial ownership share in an enterprise.

principal distributor: A securities firm carrying primary responsibility for selling securities underwritten by others; sometimes a firm which is both underwriter and main distributor. The term is most often encountered in reference to firms selling real estate limited partnerships and mutual funds.

priority: 1. The order of preference enjoyed by creditors, established either by time of filing of liens, or by prior subordination of interests. **2.** Any ranking in order of preference; for example, giving preference to one job over another because it is deemed more important.

private bank: A bank organized as a partnership or sole proprietorship, rather than as a corporation, and chartered under state banking laws; a very old and widely used form in European banking and in United States investment banking.

private easement: See easement.

private mortgage insurance: Mortgage insurance written by a private, rather than a public insurer.

private nuisance: See nuisance.

private offering: An ownership offering, such as a group of real estate limited partnerships or equities, that is exempt from Federal and state registration in compliance with applicable securities laws.

private property: Property owned by individuals and private organizations, rather than by governments.

probate: The validation of a will by act of a probate court, and more generally the judicial settlement of all matters connected with wills over which a probate court has jurisdiction, including the settling of creditors' claims and the appointment of administrators. Probate courts are also often called surrogate's courts.

proceeds: The amount actually received by a party to a transaction, such as a borrower or a seller.

process: 1. A legal document, summoning a defendant to court. **2.** A legal proceeding, including all the steps in that proceeding, from beginning to end.

productivity of capital: The yield produced by invested capital, as when money invested in securities nets 10% per year or money invested in capital goods yields 9%, but without adjustment for tax factors, which may very significantly alter the real money yield of an investment.

productivity of land: The crop yield of land, usually measured on a per acre basis; varies not only with the quality of the land but also with the quality of labor, machines, techniques and nutrients put into the land.

profit: 1. The net of revenues and costs, which may be expressed as a plus or minus figure. **2.** Any yield on capital or on entrepreneurial effort, such as the value of a small business built by a combination of a little capital and a great deal of time and effort.

profitability: 1. The net earnings of a business organization. **2.** The extent to which operations produce earnings, usually expressed as a percentage of sales.

profit and loss statement (P & L): See income statement.

profit a prendre: The right to take profit from the soil of another, including the soil itself and the products of the land, including surface and subsurface rights.

profiteering: The taking of unconscionable profits through exploitation of a social or national emergency, such as war or epidemic; in normal times very much in the eye of the beholder.

profit margin: The net of revenues and costs, described in percentile terms.

profit squeeze: A situation in which profits are dropping, because costs are rising and, for whatever reasons, prices cannot be raised to offset those higher costs; often occurs while volume continues at previous or even higher levels.

pro forma: Latin for "as a matter of form." In the law, a decision rendered to pave the way for appeal.

pro forma statement: 1. A financial statement, such as a profit and loss projection, that, at least in part, makes assumptions as to future events, and that therefore serves only as a model and prediction, rather than as a financial statement reflecting current realities. **2.** In general usage, a statement made for appearance's or form's sake, such as a seller's claim that every listed property is "really prime."

progressive tax: A tax that increases in percentage as taxables increase. For example, federal income taxes tax income at progressively higher rates as taxable income rises; in contrast, fixed rates of tax, such as many sales taxes, tax all purchases of the same kind at the same rate.

progress payment: See advance.

promissory note: A written promise to pay another or the bearer of the note a specific sum, at some time in the future or on demand.

promoter: One who takes an entrepreneurial role in the conception and development of an enterprise, often taking an investment position as well as bringing other investors into it.

property: That which can in any way be legally owned, by any individual, organization, or by the state, including real and personal property, tangible and intangible property.

property insurance: Insurance of any kind that covers property against loss from any of a large number of natural and man-made causes.

property management: In real estate, the day-to-day management of a specific property belonging to another, including the management of such functions as maintenance, leasing, and financial control.

property report: A detailed property description that must be given by seller to purchaser 48 hours prior to sale and must also be filed by the seller with the Federal Government, when subdivided land is sold interstate, in compliance with the Interstate Land Sales Full Disclosure

Act. Failure to file the report gives purchaser the right to cancel the sale at any time.

property tax: any tax imposed by government on real or personal property. Direct taxes on real property are imposed by the states and those of their political and administrative subdivisions, such as counties, cities, towns, villages, boroughs, and districts, that have been granted taxing power by the states, and are taxes on the value of owned real property rather than taxes that are in any way related to the incomes or other assets of those taxed.

proprietary interest: An ownership interest, as in the interest held by an equity holder in a company or a patent holder who licenses use of the patents by others.

proprietary lease: A cooperative apartment lease, in which the lessee is both tenant of the specific unit and co-owner of the multiple dwelling in which the unit is located, therefore being both lessee and proprietor.

proprietor: 1. An owner of a business or one who has legal title to something, such as a patented process or design. **2.** In general usage, any business owner.

proprietor's equity: See net worth.

proprietorship: See sole proprietorship.

pro rata: Proportional division of amounts, as in the division of overhead costs among several products or of utility charges among users sharing a single meter.

prospect: A possible purchaser of goods for sale, viewed by a seller as one who might reasonably be expected to consider purchasing on the basis of need or desire.

prospectus: 1. In the securities industry, a fully detailed description of every significant aspect of a business offering stock for public sale and of that stock, including financial matters, personnel, products if any, and all other pertinent business data. **2.** Generally, a written description of a proposed enterprise, such as a new book or new company.

protest: A statement in writing and certified by a notary public, declaring that a negotiable instrument has been presented for payment or acceptance and has been rejected.

proxy: A written statement, legally authorizing another to vote stock capable of being voted by the authorizer; a normal arrangement in many publicly held corporations, with management routinely soliciting the proxies of shareholders, but also used by those trying to win control of a corporation away from its current management.

proxy statement: An explanatory written statement required by law to be attached to a proxy solicitation by whomever is soliciting the proxy.

public corporation: 1. A corporation which has issued stock through general sale to the public, and which is therefore at least partially owned by those shareholders. **2.** A corporation set up by government and owned wholly or partially by government.

public domain: See public land.

public easement: See easement.

public grazing lands: Public lands that are used for cattle grazing by ranchers, subject to public regulation of grazing on those lands, In the United States, most western land was at one time public grazing land.

public housing: Housing that is financed, built under the direction of, and operated by government; usually but not always aimed at meeting the housing needs of people of small to moderate income.

public interest: The idea that a community has an interest in those matters that affect all or some of its members, and that government has the right and obligation to intervene on behalf of community interests; for example, the obligation to intervene to prevent or remedy water pollution caused by industrial chemical dumping.

public land: Land, such as national park lands, and public grazing lands, that is owned by government, rather than privately owned; also called public domain.

public nuisance: See nuisance.

public ownership: The ownership of any organization by government, as in a federally owned public utility, such as the Tennessee Valley Authority, or a city-owned transportation line.

public place: Real property which is open to the general public, and to which the general public has the right ot access, including some land which is privately owned, such as some shopping center and transportation terminal property.

public policy: The attitude of government on a specific matter or kind of matter, as expressed by statute and official statement.

public property: Anything owned by any government, including both real property and that which would otherwise be personal property.

public records: Those documents available for public inspection, including such real estate connected records as deeds, plats, and tax records.

public sale: The disposition of property at a sale open to the public, at auction or at fixed prices.

public service commission: The most common name for state agencies charged with the regulation of and rate-setting for public utilities in the best interest of state citizens, while allowing the utilities reasonable profits.

public utility bonds: The debt obligations of such public utilities as gas and electric companies; often secured by mortgages on company plant and equipment, and generally regarded as high quality bonds.

public utility commission: See public service commission.

public utility stocks: Ownership equities in such public utilities as gas and electric companies; due to the protected and regulated position of these companies, usually regarded as high quality, relatively stable stocks.

public works: A wide range of projects funded by government to serve public interests, such as canals, bridges, dams, roads, and power projects.

PUD: See planned unit development.

puffery: The making of false and misleading claims for a product or service by its seller, in both personal sales situations and advertising.

purchase money mortgage: A mortgage accompanying a property sales transaction, given by buyer to seller as all or part of the purchase price.

Q

qualified acceptance: A counter-offer in the form of a conditional acceptance of an offer, acting to cancel the offer and reverse the positions of the parties as to offer and acceptance.

qualified estate: An estate or interest which will end if stated events occur, then reverting back to the grantor or passing to others.

qualified fee: See fee simple conditional.

qualified indorsement: 1. An indorsement that in some way limits the free negotiability of the indorsed instrument, such as "for deposit only." **2.** An indorsement "without recourse," which attempts to remove or limit the liability of the current indorser if the instrument is ultimately unpaid or for some reason not accepted for payment.

qualified prospect: A prospective purchaser of goods or services for sale, who is known by the seller to be able to make or substantially influence a buying decision.

quantum meruit: In law, the assumption that one is entitled to receive fair compensation for materials, labor, and services rendered, even in the absence of an agreement setting forth agreed rates of compensation; the law may then imply such an agreement and order payment.

quarter section: One hundred sixty (160) acres, or one quarter of a standard section, as used in Federal Government land surveys.

Queen Anne style: See Victorian.

quick assets: Assets that are quickly and easily convertible into cash, such as cash and readily marketable securities.

quitclaim: 1. a release given by one to another, giving up only a claim against the other as to a specific matter. **2.** A release giving up claim to title; for example, title to land.

quitclaim deed: A deed given by one to another, passing claim, interest, or title to that other, but not claiming to have clear title to pass. If title is legally capable of being conveyed, the quitclaim deed serves to pass title.

quota: 1. A goal, such as the sales goals set for a sales representative by management. **2.** A limit, such as the maximum amount of a certain kind of import that may be brought into a country in a given period.

quote: A price set by a seller; usually describing bids received on work to be performed under contract.

R

radiant heating: Any heating system that transmits hot air, steam, hot water, or electricity to pipes, which in turn radiate their heat into the space to be heated.

rafter: A load-bearing beam that supports a pitched roof.

ranch: A body of grazing land and structures used as an animal farm, usually for such animals as cattle and sheep; but the term has been expanded to include the raising of many kinds of living beings, including fish, birds, and fur-bearing mammals.

ranch style: Any one story house; originally a relatively large single story structure, often with interior open areas as in the Spanish style, from its Southwestern origins.

ratable: Describing property on which property taxes may be legally placed.

rate: 1. A seller's quoted price. **2.** To evaluate, most often in comparative fashion, as when a customer or evaluating organization judges one product as better constructed than another.

rate of interest: See interest rate.

rate of return: See yield.

raw land: Land in its natural state, such as a field or forest, carrying no structures or other improvements. Also called virgin, undeveloped, or unimproved land.

real estate: Land and anything held in law to be permanently attached to that land, including structures and some kinds of fixtures and equipment; real property, as distinguished from personal property.

real estate bond: A bond secured by a real estate mortgage; a debt obligation of its issuer backed by the issuer's promise to pay and further backed by the underlying value of the mortgaged property.

real estate broker: A state licensed broker, who acts as agent, usually for the seller but sometimes for the buyer in real estate transactions.

real estate fund: A publicly owned real estate limited partnership.

real estate investment trust (REIT): A fund dedicated to real estate investments, and accorded special federal tax treatment; in practice operating much as does a mutual fund.

Real Estate Settlement Procedures Act (RESPA): A Federal disclosure act, requiring that settlement costs and procedures be disclosed in advance of settlement to buyers and sellers of one- to four-family homes, where first mortgage financing is accomplished with federally related monies; including financial institutions holding federally insured deposits and federally guaranteed mortgages.

real estate tax: A kind of property tax, levied on real estate; part of a considerable body of state and local taxes.

realize: To convert something of possible or anticipated value into cash or near-cash equivalents; for example, to sell stock that has gone up in value since purchased, or to sell goods in stock to a consumer.

realized appreciation: The difference between the purchase price paid by the seller of something of value and a later higher selling price; for example, on stock or land sold.

realized depreciation: See recapture of depreciation.

real property: An ownership or other legal interest in real estate, including land, structures and some kinds of fixtures and equipment.

Realtist: See National Association of Real Estate Brokers.

Realtor®: A real estate broker affiliated with the National Association of Realtors®.

reassessment: An official re-evaluation of taxable property for taxing purposes.

rebate: 1. A repayment by a seller to a purchaser of part of an already paid purchase price, in contrast to a discount, which is a deduction from a purchase price before it is paid; for example, a promotional device may involve sending a check to a customer after receipt of the customer's payment in full for goods purchased. **2.** In real estate, the return of sums paid in commissions from commission agent to buyer or seller, which is regarded as unethical and is often illegal as well. **3.** In insurance selling, the illegal practice of discounting insurance by means of covert payment back to an insurance buyer of part of the premiums paid.

recapture clause: A contract provision allowing one of the parties to recover a right or interest granted in the contract, as when a seller can regain title to property after a period if profits to be shared by seller and buyer from the buyer's business conducted on that property do not meet stated minimums, or as a matter of right after a stated period of time.

recapture of depreciation: For Federal tax purposes, that part of the net selling price minus book value which is due to depreciation deductions taken by the seller while the asset was in its hands, and on sale is to be treated as ordinary income by the seller.

receipt: 1. A written acknowledgment that something has been received, capable of being used as legal evidence of such receipt, such as a signed contract or a warehouse receipt for goods delivered. **2.** The act of receiving cash or any other assets, to be recorded on books of account.

receiver: A court-appointed custodian of the assets of a debtor, charged with saving whatever of the debtor's assets can be used to satisfy creditors; limited to the custodial role, as the trustee in bankruptcy is appointed by the court to maintain and restore as much of a going business as is possible.

receivership: In law, the position of an insolvent business, one being managed by a court-appointed receiver, rather than by its previous management.

reclamation: The process of attempting to make land, water and air that have been damaged by human and natural action useful and healthful once again, through such activities as reforestation, water purification, irrigation, and flood control projects.

reclamation district: A special taxing district, fuctioning to turn land wholly or partially under water into dry land; in recent years, the concept has expanded to include other kinds of reclamation projects.

reconciliation: 1. In appraisal, the comparing of valuations arrived at by the use of different evaluative methods, and their final adjustment to reach an appraised valuation. **2.** The process of balancing related accounts in a double entry bookkeeping system, and the document evidencing that such balancing has been completed.

reconveyance: The conveyance back to its original owner of real property that had been conveyed to another, as when a mortgage conveying title to the mortgagor under the common law is paid and title passes back to its original owner, or when a third party holding title under the terms of a trust deed passes title back to its original owner on payment of the debt.

record: 1. A document available for public inspection, including such real estate connected records as deeds, plats, and tax records; also to put such documents in a place set aside for such inspection. **2.** Any written or otherwise stored information, usually in sequential form for multiple items; examples include accounting information stored in books of record and legal proceedings, often referred to in the law as *the record.* **3.** To place information in storage, or in storable form. **4.** In computers, a single kind of information, one of many like it; for example, the record of a listing in a national listing system. **5.** The best, most, worst, or least, as in a record snowfall.

recorder of deeds: A government official responsible for the recording of documents relating to real estate transactions in official books of record. Also called registrar of deeds.

recourse: The extent to which one who has an obligation can be legally held to that obligation. For example, the maker of a personal note has unlimited liability to pay that note, but if the note is "non-recourse," the lender has agreed to accept only the borrower's promise to pay, backed by whatever collateral is specified, if any, and has no ability to compel payment from other borrower resources.

recovery: 1. Something, usually of value, awarded by a court to a plaintiff as a result of a successful action at law. **2.** The collection of all or part of a debt that has been treated as uncollectible. **3.** An upward move to a previous higher level, as when securities prices fluctuate. **4.** The move of a whole economy toward relative prosperity after a recession or depression.

redeemable bond: A bond that may be recovered by its issuer before its maturity date, on payment of its face value and usually an additional premium amount to its holders.

redemption: 1. The recovery of a debt instrument by its maker through repayment of the debt it evidences; for example, the recovery of a note after payment, or the retirement of a bond issue at maturity or at full payment before maturity. **2.** The right to buy back an obligation, by payment of money or performance of an obligation, as provided by law and the specific provisions of applicable contracts.

redemption period: The length of time during which a defaulted mortgage borrower or taxpayer may still pay the balance due and associated interest and costs, and redeem property that has been taken by foreclosure or tax sale, as set by applicable state law.

redemption price: The price at which something may be bought back; for example, the price at which a bond may be retired by its issuer before maturity.

red herring: A preliminary prospectus, offering a new issue of securities for public examination; but without some of the details offered in the final prospectus, which actually offers the securities for public sale.

redlining: The refusal of banks, insurance companies, and other financial sources and insurers to make loans and insure property in some geographic areas and with some kinds of people and businesses, or willingness to do such business only at a very high premium rate. For example, banks may refuse to make normal mortgage loans in some poor, black, or Spanish-speaking inner city areas, citing very high default rates and discriminating against a whole class of risks, rather than differentiating between individual risks; or an insurer may refuse to write fire insurance in the same kind of area.

referee in bankruptcy: An officer appointed by a bankruptcy court, responsible for fact finding, hearing, and preliminary adjudication steps under the supervision of the court, and who, if bankruptcy is declared by the court, functions as temporary administrator of a bankrupt's assets.

referral: A sales lead generated by another, and the act of so generating; may be compensable by finding fee or split commission if a sale results.

referral fee: See referral.

refinancing: The replacement of existing debts with new debts, usually extending the term of debt repayment, whether as a matter of convenience or economic necessity on the part of the borrower; for example, the replacement of an existing mortgage with a larger mortgage, supplying needed cash, more and smaller payments, or both; or the replacement of corporate or government bonds about to mature with new bonds carrying a maturity date years in the future.

reformation: The ability of parties to a written document to correct that document later, in such areas as mechanical error, fraud, or mutual mistake; also the act of doing so.

refund: A return of a payment, all or in part; for example, the return of money paid or the extension of credit for defective merchandise.

refunding: See refinancing.

register: A body of information about a specific kind of thing or transaction, maintained in writing in sequence or in a data base capable of being called forth in sequence. Examples are sequenced accounting entries, usually kept in book or journal form; a list of ships registered as vessels of a particular country; a list of lawyers, accountants, doctors, or dentists practicing in a geographical area; or a corporation's stockholders list.

registrar of deeds: See recorder of deeds.

registration: The process of officially registering securities with the appropriate Federal and State regulatory authorities, involving a series of documents and clearances, so that the securities may be offered for public sale.

registration statement: A document filed by a prospective securities issuer with the appropriate regulatory authorities, which must grant official clearance before those securities are cleared for public sale; such a statement includes substantial financial, other business, and personal information relating to the securities issue, its issuer, and the leading people associated with the issue.

regression: In appraisal, the observation that the value of properties will be diminished by close proximity to other, less valuable properties.

regressive tax: A tax that is proportionately heavier on those of small income than on those of larger income. For example, a sales tax, on which all pay equal amounts of tax per dollar spent, is regressive, contrasting with a progressive tax, in which tax rates rise with income.

rehabilitation: The returning of deteriorated real estate to good condition, without major alterations or major modifications of over-all styles and forms; sometimes including substantial upgrading and the use of materials and processes not originally available.

reinstatement: To restore something to its previous position; for example, to restore an insurance policy, which has lapsed due to nonpayment of premiums, to its previous position of coverage of the insured, when payment of the lapsed premiums is made within the period specified in the policy; or to restore a defaulted loan to a current and paid-up status by payment of amounts owing.

reinsurance: In the insurance industry, the transfer of all or part of a risk from the company originally insuring to another insurer, usually resulting in the sharing of a risk undertaken by one insurer with one or more insurers; a very common practice when underwriting major risks.

REIT: See Real Estate Investment Trust.

related parties: For tax purposes, parties sharing family or financial relationships which by their nature raise questions about the validity of transactions between them resulting in tax deductions or other tax advantaged results, such as a sale at a loss that would otherwise result in a tax deduction.

release: **1.** To give up a legal claim or possible legal claim upon another; for example, the settlement of an insurance claim by agreement between claimant and insurer involves a renunciation of all current and possible future claims against the insured by the claimant arising from the same set of circumstances. **2.** The document that is evidence of the giving up of an existing or potential legal claim.

release clause: See partial release provision.

reliction: A growth in land due to the disappearance or withdrawal of the water which previously covered it, as when a stream changes course or a lake dries up.

relief map: A map showing the shape of the land, using such devices as color, line, and raised map areas; also called a topographic map.

remainder: A future interest in an estate after all prior interests have been satisfied. The person who holds such an interest, under the terms of an estate, is called a remainderman.

remainderman: One who is to receive the remainder of an estate after all prior interests set up by the terms of the estate have been satisfied; for example, a child who takes the remainder of an estate that, on the death of one parent pays income to the other parent for life, with the entire estate and its income going to the child on the second parent's death.

remedy: The means by which a right is protected or a wrong righted; at law, the action taken by a court on conclusion of a case in favor of a plaintiff, as distinct from the case itself.

remittance: A payment, usually on a debt or other financial obligation; sometimes used more widely to describe any sum of money sent by one party to another.

remodeling: Making structural changes so great as to alter the basic plan and shape of an existing structure, as when an old factory building is converted into an apartment house or shopping center, or a kitchen is completely redesigned and fitted.

rendering: A drawing of a proposed or completed construction project, done in realistic style, and often in color; not a detailed set of architectural drawings, even though often done by an architect, but rather an artist's view of the project.

renegotiable rate mortgage (RRM): See flexible rates.

renewal: 1. The extension of a debt, by its replacement with another debt; for example, the replacement of a loan due to be paid to a bank with another loan to be paid later. A loan may be renewed again and again, in practice constituting a line of credit. **2.** The continuation of an insurance contract for an additional period. **3.** The replacement of an old machine, machine part, or any other tangible portion of plant and equipment, with new equipment, in contrast to repair of old equipment. **4.** The continuation of any contract, such as a subscription to a periodical.

renovation: Any substantial work done on an existing structure, including remodeling and rehabilitation.

rent: Payment for the right to use anything tangible, including land, buildings, and equipment, usually for a specified period of time, but sometimes for the use itself, as when a machine is rented for a single use rather than for a period of time.

rentable area: The net of all floor areas within the outside walls of a structure minus vertical shafts and building service areas, with toilet areas and corridors included as rentable area when part of full-floor rentals and excluded in part-floor rentals; also called usable area.

rent control: Governmental restriction on the amount of rent that can be charged, usually setting top rents or maximum increases that may be charged on residential rentals; under some circumstances, as in wartime, commercial rentals may be controlled as well.

rent escalation: See escalation.

rentier: From the French; someone whose income is largely dependent on the proceeds of investments yielding fixed dollar amounts, rather than varying with economic conditions; a highly vulnerable economic position in periods of inflation.

rent roll: A list of tenants, rents payable, and leasehold arrangements.

reopener: A contract provision setting terms and conditions under which a contract will be opened for renegotiation, and specifying which matters will then be eligible for renegotiation; for example, a collective bargaining contract providing for a wage reopening at the beginning of the second and third years of a three year contract, or a government contract, providing for a reopening on the question of costs under specified conditions.

repairs: For tax accounting and deduction purposes, those expenditures which are for repairs attributable to current maintenance needs, and therefore are currently deductible as expenses, rather than such repairs as add to the life or value of the property, which must be capitalized and then depreciated over a number of years, yielding only a small fraction of the deductions generated by current repair deductions.

repayment terms: See credit terms.

replacement contract: See novation.

replacement cost: See reproduction cost.

replacement insurance: An insurance contract providing for payment of the replacement cost of property destroyed, rather than its depreciated value.

replacement method of depreciation: The addition of straight line depreciation and a factor for replacement cost, when replacement cost is estimated to be higher than original cost; for example, when replacement costs are estimated at $5,000 higher than the original cost of, and the depreciable life of the item is 10 years, $500 per year for ten years would be added to the straight line depreciation of the item. Generally not an acceptable mode of depreciation to accountants and taxing authorities.

repledge: To use a borrower's collateral as collateral for a loan to the original lender. For example, a bond that has been pledged as security for a loan may be used by the original lender as collateral for a different loan. Repledging requires some form of consent by the original borrower, who owns the collateral although it has been so pledged.

repossession: The act of reclaiming property that has been purchased on an installment basis, when the buyer fails to meet the payment terms of the loan.

representation: 1. A statement, expressed or implied, claiming something to be true which is material to a contract being made; for example, a claim about the worth or performance of a product that is material to the consummation of a sale, and which, if shown at law to have been false and misleading, may cause a court to invalidate that sale. **2.** Any statement claiming to be fact.

reproduction cost: An estimate of the cost of reproducing a specific kind of fixed asset at current prices; in regard to structure, one of the elements of appraisal. Also called replacement cost.

repudiation: The act of refusing to fulfill an obligation; usually a refusal to pay a debt. As a practical matter, legally enforceable debts cannot be repudiated, as legal process will result, but governments can and do repudiate debts.

repurchase agreement: A legally enforceable contract between buyer and seller that specifies the seller's right to buy back what is being sold on specified prices and terms; a device often used in sale and leaseback agreements.

request for bid: A request from a buyer to seller for a bid on work to be performed, sometimes as sole bidder and sometimes in competition with other bidders.

request for proposal: See request for bid.

resale: The second and subsequent selling of items purchased, with no significant change in their character.

rescission of contract: Cancellation of an existing contract, returning the parties to their pre-contractual status, due to mutual misunderstanding, fraud, or a contract clause which comes into operation under stated conditions, as when a buyer defaults on payments due under the contract; may occur through judicial action or by consent of the parties involved.

reservation: A body of public land, not available for private ownership, such as military and Indian national lands; such land may, however, be leased or used by private parties, as when public land is used for grazing or is the subject of oil and gas leasehold agreements.

reserves: 1. Actual funds held to meet obligations or potential obligations; for example, bank reserves, company reserves, national gold reserves, company reserves held for special purposes, and legally required insurance company reserves held to meet potential claim obligations. **2.** In accounting, a series of accounts set aside for specific reasons, such as reserves against amortization, bad debts, contingencies, depletion, and repairs.

residence: A place where one lives or maintains some kind of abode. One may have many residences, in fact and for legal purposes, but only one domicile, which for legal purposes is recognized as the principal living place.

residential property: Land zoned for residential uses only.

residual: A balance remaining. Examples include amounts remaining in an estate after all costs and specific bequests; the scrap value of an obsolete structure; or the royalties or commissions remaining to be paid in the future, after a transaction has been completed.

residual appraisal: An appraisal method used when the value of either land or structure is known, and a valuation is sought for the other; involves capitalizing the known or projected net income from the one known and subtracting it from the total price or value of the land and structure together to arrive at a valuation of the unknown element.

residuary estate: That portion of an estate that remains, if any, after disposition of all that has been specifically covered by the terms of a will and satisfaction of all debts and expenses in connection with the estate.

resort condominium: A resort adopting a condominium form of ownership for all or part of its facilities, with condominium owners contracting with the resort operator as managing agent of the condominium, and often occupying their owned units for a relatively small portion of each year, while renting them through the resort operator for the balance of the year. Rentals may be handled either as individual unit rentals, and credited to the account of the individual owner after deduction of management fees, or as part of a pool of rentals to be divided by all owners equally after deduction of management fees.

resort property: A property primarily used for resort facilities, such as hotels, boat clubs, and ski lodges.

RESPA: See Real Estate Settlement Procedures Act.

restoration: The return of something old, such as a historic building or artifact, as closely as possible to its original state; also the object so restored.

restriction: Any limitation, public or private, on the way property may be used; for example, public restriction imposed by zoning law, or a private restriction imposed by the terms of a deed, mortgage, or lease.

restrictive covenant: A contract provision limiting free use of property by its owner, usually encountered in real estate contracts; for example, requirements that new home styles in a housing development be approved by a homeowners' committee, or the now-illegal restriction of the sale of homes to whites.

restrictive endorsement: An endorsement on a negotiable instrument that limits or destroys its further free negotiability; for example, "for deposit only to the account of . . ." is a common restrictive endorsement on the back of a check.

retainage: That portion of periodic or progress payments due to contractors and subcontractors pursuant to construction contracts which is held back by those from whom payments are due, such as owners and prime contractors, until the entire contract has been accepted as completed.

retainer: A fee paid for professional services to be rendered over a period of time, rather than for specific services rendered; for example, a law firm may be paid by a client on a yearly fee basis, which will cover certain kinds of services rendered and will usually specify a maximum amount of time to be spent by the law firm on client's affairs, beyond which additional fees will be charged.

retaining wall: A wall designed to block the natural flow and settling of earth and other solid materials, performing the same function as does a dam for liquids.

retirement community: A planned community, aimed at attracting those of retirement age, and therefore often providing modestly sized and relatively modestly priced dwelling units, as well as construction features, amenities, and locations throught attractive to such tenants; in the United States often located in southern and southwestern regions.

return: 1. Earnings on investment, expressed as a percentage of investment; sometimes used imprecisely to describe also dividends paid relative to the current market value of a stock, even though the stock itself has fluctuated since its acquisition. 2. A document supplying a taxing authority with information on matters relating to taxables and with tax computations accompanied by tax payments as necessary.

return on investment (ROI): Earnings on investments, expressed as a percentage of the amount of the investment; for example, an investment yielding a 4% yearly dividend and 2% in the form of increased market value in the year of investment would have returned 6% if that investment had been turned back into cash at the end of a year.

revenue: The total income received from all sources, but the term is used variously in business and government; for example, in government it includes tax and miscellaneous income but not appropriations, while in public utilities it generally means only sales.

revenue bonds: State and local bonds backed by revenues to be received from state and local income-producing facilities, such as port authorities and power plants, rather than backed by the full faith and credit of the governments issuing them.

revenue stamp: A stamp placed by a taxing authority upon a taxed item, indicating that taxes have been paid.

reverse leverage: See leverage.

reversionary interest: An interest that reverts to an owner after an interest granted to another has ended, for whatever reason; for example, real property occupied by another under the terms of a lease.

rider: A provision added by the parties to a basic contract, such as an insurance policy, which takes up some special question; such a provision may be signed at the time the contract is originally made or added later by the parties.

ridgeboard: The board running along the peak of a sloped roof, to which the rafters are attached.

right angle: See angle.

right of access: See access.

right of first refusal: The right to buy or rent property before all others, if that property is offered for sale or rent; for example, the right of a current lessee to renew a lease, if the leased premises are to continue to be rentable, or to buy if the leased premises are offered for sale; differs from an option to buy or lease in that the property must be offered before the right becomes operative.

right of way: A legal right to move over land belonging to another; for example, the right to use a lane on another's land as access to otherwise inaccessible land, as provided by deed, or the right to build a road as purchased by government from private landholders.

riparian rights: The rights of those owning land abutting waterways in regard to the use and enjoyment of those waterways and the land on which they flow.

risk: 1. The extent to which loss is possible. In a somewhat wider sense, the amount of danger of potential loss in a situation in personal and business terms. **2.** That which is covered by insurance, if it is insurable.

risk capital: Capital invested in high or relatively high risk securities and enterprises, in expectation of commensurately high returns.

risk of loss: In the law of contracts, a concept covering the question of property losses occurring during the period in which title to and possession of real estate are being conveyed. In states that have adopted the Uniform Vendor and Purchaser Risk Act, and in some other states, the seller carries the risk of loss, including loss due to government taking by eminent domain, and therefore pays insurance premiums covering losses until the closing. In most states in which that Act has not been adopted, risks pass to the buyer on contract signing, who is therefore obligated to pay for insurance premiums between then and the closing.

rod: A measure of distance, equalling 16.5 feet or 5.3 meters.

ROI: See return on investment.

rollover: 1. A refunding of debt by the replacement of existing debt by new debt; used by private parties and governments as a means of continuing debts, paying only interest on them, often while incurring new debts. **2.** A reinvestment of funds; sometimes, as in the reinvestment of pension funds or as in some moves to other pension forms, accompanied by tax deferral on gains so far realized.

roof: The top of a structure, and any smaller structures atop that; for example, a large apartment building may have a roof on which is a penthouse, which is part of the roof, although it has a smaller roof of its own.

roofing: 1. Any materials used as the outside surface of a roof. 2. The process of placing a roof on a structure.

row house: A house connected to a group of similar houses by common walls.

royalties: Amounts paid by one to another as compensation for the use of the other's property; for example, a percentage of revenue paid to a landowner for the right to extract natural resources.

RRM: See renegotiable rate mortgage.

rule against perpetuities: The common law rule that to be valid, a contingent interest in property must vest no more than 21 years after the end of the life in being at the time the interest was created. For example, a will granting an interest for life to one, plus a remaining interest to that one's heirs until they are 21, creates a valid interest in the heirs; but if the interest had been granted until they were 22, their interest would have been entirely invalid, although the original life interest would still be valid. The period limit is actually 21 years and 9 months, as life in being is deemed to have begun on gestation, rather than birth.

running with the land: Describing a covenant that is attached to the land, rather than to its owner, therefore passing with the land to future owners; for example, a legal restrictive covenant.

rural land: Land used for farming or in its natural state, located in an area so distant from population centers as not to be readily accessible and usable for suburban building purposes; an inprecise definition, and one that changes rapidly as population centers grow and spread.

S

sale: 1. A contract passing title to goods or undertaking an obligation to supply goods or services in return for stated consideration, usually in the form of a price. **2.** A lower-than-normal price offer of goods or services by a seller to one or more buyers; for example, the offering of a body of goods at cut prices for a limited time by a retail store.

sale and leaseback: The sale of a property by its owner to a financing organization, accompanied by the leasing of that property on a long-term basis by its former owner; a financing technique used to remove both ownership and debt obligation from the books of the former owner, while allowing full use of the property for business purposes. The technique is used in relation to both real and personal property.

sale on approval: A trial sale under a revocable form of contract in which the seller supplies goods to a potential buyer, who can return the goods to the seller for full refund or credit as specified in the form of contract; not really a sale or a contract, as no legally binding contract is made by the parties involved.

sales: Income from goods and services sold, appearing as such on financial records and statements.

sales agent: An independent organization or proprietor that acts as agent for the goods or services of one or more firms.

sales contract: See contract of sale.

sales tax: A tax on goods and services sold, normally a percentage of the actual selling price. As the tax may be placed on sales occurring anywhere in the chain of distribution, including retail sales, the final price paid by a buyer at retail may reflect several accumulated sales taxes.

salt box: See Cape Cod House.

salvage: 1. The estimated value of tangible property, if it were sold as scrap. **2.** The actual value of tangible property sold as scrap. **3.** To recover something of value, such as building material from a demolished building, or material from a wrecked ship. **4.** The value of recovered property when assessing the extent of compensable damage for insurance purposes.

salvage value: See salvage.

sandwich lease: A lease occupying the middle of three interests, in which the lease holder has leased from an owner and subleased to another.

sanitary landfill: Landfill composed of solid materials, including wastes, which are covered with earth periodically, to avoid the sanitation problems that would otherwise be encountered.

sanitary sewer: A sewer that carries waste materials, contrasting with a storm sewer, which carries runoff.

satellite city: See new town.

satellite tenant: A tenant in a retail area, such as a shopping mall, that is considerably dependent upon the ability of larger, or prime, tenants to attract business to the area; for example, a small restaurant in a mall containing one or more large department stores.

satisfaction: In law, the fulfillment of a contract or the execution of a judgment.

savings: Income held for future use, rather than being spent as received, forming a basis for accumulation and investment.

savings account: See bank account.

savings and loan association: A savings banking institution specializing in home mortgage loans, and organized on a mutual basis, with account holders actually shareholders holding equity proportional to the size of their accounts.

savings bank: A bank that holds depositor's money in interest-paying savings accounts and uses that money in the main to make mortgage loans, as well as making relatively small investments in high grade securities; but the distinction between savings and commercial banks is blurring, as savings banks undertake more and more service functions, such as checking accounts and life insurance sales.

savings bond; A United States government bond paying a fixed rate of interest and holding a fixed value; it cannot be traded on bond markets, and can be redeemed only by the government.

SBA: See Small Business Administration.

SBIC: See Small Business Investment Company.

scenic easement: An easement intended to preserve scenic property or property providing a scenic view in its natural state; may be privately purchased or taken by the state using its power of eminent domain.

schematics: Detailed, but tentative and incomplete architectural drawings; often prepared during the planning stages of a project, and before plans and financing have been completed.

scintilla of evidence: A very slight amount of evidence, but just enough to raise a question that should be decided by a jury.

scrap value: See salvage value.

seal: A metal die used to stamp a unique impression on material, such as that of a corporate seal upon paper; from ancient times, an essential component of official certification of a document, but no longer required for most transactions.

sealed bid: A competitive bid on work to be performed, offered to the buyer literally closed at some time before the date set for the close of bidding, to be opened by the buyer at the same time as all other bids.

seasonal variation: A change in economic activity that occurs regularly and relatively predictably in an industry, region, or country; for example, the surge in retail sales that occurs during the Christmas season, or the flow of business into ski resort areas during the ski season, and the employment swings that accompany and follow those surges.

seasoned: In real estate financing, describing a loan, usually a mortgage loan, on which payments have been forthcoming promptly for a number of years, and which, therefore, is a better purchase risk than one more recently made.

seawall: A wall protecting the shore from the abrasive and destructive action of the sea.

SEC: See Securities and Exchange Commission.

secondary mortgage market: The market for the purchase and sale of mortgage instruments created by mortgage loans in being, including those made by banks and savings and loan associations, other financial institutions of all kinds, private individuals, and such organizations as the Government National Mortgage Association (Ginnie Mae), and the Federal Home Loan Mortgage Corporation (Freddie Mac).

second mortgage: A mortgage on real property which already has a first mortgage. Such a mortgage is subordinate to the first mortgage, and in the event of foreclosure has no right to satisfaction until the first mortgage has been completely satisfied.

second mortgage bonds: Bonds secured by second mortgages and subordinate to bonds secured by first mortgages.

section: Six hundred forty (640) acres, one square mile of land, or 1/36 of a township, using the Federal Government land survey designators.

secured bond: A bond that is secured by some kind of collateral, such as a mortgage, thereby becoming more than a mere promise to pay on the part of its issuer.

secured creditor: A creditor whose claim against the debtor is secured wholly or partially by some property of that debtor, or by a mortgage on some such property.

secured loan: A loan that is secured by collateral or mortgage capable of being liquidated in the event of default in order to satisfy the debt created by the loan.

securities: Documents of ownership or debt, such as common and preferred stocks, bonds, and notes, some of which are negotiable and tradable in securities markets.

Securities and Exchange Commission (SEC): A Federal agency responsible for registering and regulating securities traded interstate and people and firms engaged in trading or counselling others as to any aspect of those securities; the SEC carries wide investigative, regulatory, and quasi-judicial powers to help it carry out its statutory charge.

security: 1. That which serves to act as a guarantee for payment of a debt, including all forms of collateral, such as instruments of value and tangible real and personal property; also includes an assumption of personal liability to pay the debt of another legal entity, as when an individual personally guarantees a corporate debt or co-signs another's note. **2.** Safety arrangements; for example, the arrangements made to safeguard a building from unauthorized entry.

security agreement: A document evidencing the existence of a lien upon property securing the borrowings of another.

security deposit: 1. A sum deposited by a tenant with a landlord, usually at the start of a leasehold period and usually for an amount equal to one month's rent, to be held by the landlord as security for performance of tenant obligations under the terms of the tenancy, to be returned by the landlord on termination of the tenancy, sometimes with interest specified by law or lease. The deposit is not taxable as income to the landlord as long as it is clearly only such a deposit, but becomes current income if it is treated in a leasehold agreement as money to be applied to the last month of the lease; then it is a taxable advance rental payment. **2.** A sum deposited as security for services to be rendered, as with a utility company, and returnable on termination of the service relationship, sometimes with interest specified by law.

seed money: See front money.

segregated cost method: See unit cost in place method.

seisin: A term found in real estate contracts which is, for all legal and practical purposes, synonymous with ownership.

seller's market: A market in which sellers can command higher than normal prices and better than normal conditions because of relatively high demand or short supply.

semidetatched: Describing a residence sharing one common wall with another, the two residences together making one freestanding structure.

senior bonds: Bonds carrying a primary claim upon a corporation, being secured by such assets as land and buildings, with no other bonds carrying prior claims; for example, first mortgage bonds, as contrasted with second mortgage bonds, which are junior obligations.

Senior Real Estate Analyst: See Society of Real Estate Appraisers.

Senior Real Property Appraiser: See Society of Real Estate Appraisers.

Senior Residential Appraiser: See Society of Real Estate Appraisers.

separate property: Property in which a spouse has no ownership interest; of significance in states in which community property is the main form of marital ownership.

septic system: A sewage system for a single structure or small group of structures, in which sewage is drained into a tank or cesspool.

sequester: To take possession of the property of another, by governmental process, holding that property for later return or disposition; for example, to hold rental income or a bank account by court order while litigation is in process.

serial bonds: Bonds that are issued at one time but mature serially; for example, a $5,000,000 bond issue that matures in five equal $1,000,000 installments over a period of five years.

service fee: In real estate, a service charge paid by a mortgage lender to a mortgage banker who physically services the mortgage loan, in such areas as accounting, collection, and tax payments.

service life: The anticipated useful life of an asset to its owner, forming a basis for computation of straight line depreciation. Physical life does not always equal anticipated service life, because an asset may become fully depreciated and still be in use, or an asset may be not yet fully depreciated when it is scrapped due to obsolescence. Also called economic life.

servient estate: See easement.

servient tenement: See easement.

setback: 1. How far from a specified building line a structure is built; usually the minimum required by local law. **2.** Sometimes used synonymously with failure or loss.

settlement: An agreement between parties as to the terms and conditions of a matter that has been negotiated between them; for example, a labor agreement, a dowry, or a dispute over interpretation of an existing contract.

settling: The process by which a building settles into the land on which it is built, as that land compresses under the weight of the building.

severalty: An ownership interest that is held by its owner alone, and shared with no one else during that ownership.

severance: 1. The termination of a joint tenancy. **2.** The separation of something from the land of which it has been part, as when crops are harvested, trees cut down, or minerals extracted.

severance damages: Loss of value in remaining property caused by partial state taking of property under its power of eminent domain.

sewage: Waste matter carried away by a sewer system; identical with what is carried away by a septic system, but a sewage system carries much larger quantities of waste, and usually much farther.

sewage system: A substantial body of drainage devices used to carry and dispose of waste.

sewer: A drain, usually covered, for carrying away water or waste.

sharecropping: A system in which a landowner rents land, equipment, and supplies to a tenant farmer, holds liens on future crops as security for those advances, and takes a large proportion of the tenant's crop as payment for advances; prices charged to tenants and paid for crops often bind those tenants to the landowner by a constantly growing burden of unpayable but legally enforceable debt. This was a popular system among landholders in the south for almost a century after the Civil War; though clearly not so popular among their former slaves and poor whites. It still exists to a limited degree in some parts of the United States.

shared appreciation mortgage: See appreciation participation mortgage.

shell: In real estate, a structure with a completed exterior, but without interior partitioning or other interior construction of any kind. Sometimes the shell is sold alone, with the buyer taking responsibility for all interior construction.

shell lease: A lease of only a shell structure, with the tenant completing the interior; a fairly common form of commercial lease. If the lease specifies that the interior work becomes the property of the tenant, rather than becoming part of the structure and therefore the property of the landlord, the tenant is responsible for a share of taxes payable on the improved structure.

shopping center: A group of retail stores offering a variety of goods and services and usually including joint parking areas, public access, and shared facilities; often constructed as a complex and owned by a single owner, functioning much like a market that rents stalls to sellers.

shoreline: The line formed by the high water mark on a shore, often dividing private from public property; a shifting boundary, as the sea changes the shape of the shore, unless more carefully defined in conveyances and other public records.

shortage: 1. A lower than normal supply, usually of a specific kind of product, such as natural gas at a time of withholding of supply. 2. A lower amount received than contracted for, as when a shipment of 100 cases actually contains only 98. 3. A smaller amount of funds than should be in an account, necessitating refiguring.

short form: Any document which is substantially shorter than the document normally used, often using the technique of referral to the longer document, such as a short form of lease or mortgage.

short rate: A higher periodic rate charged for a shorter term than that originally contracted, as when an insurance policy or subscription is cancelled in the middle of a contracted period.

short-term capital gain: For tax purposes, a capital gain that is treated as it it were ordinary income, because it has resulted from sale of an asset held too short a time to qualify for long term, more favorable tax treatment.

short term debt: 1. All debts and debt instruments maturing in less than one year. **2.** For accounting purposes, all debts maturing in less than one year, including long term debts coming to maturity in that period.

siding: Outside wall surfacing material, such as aluminum or wood.

sight bills and drafts: Negotiable instruments payable on presentation.

silent partner: A partner who is inactive in the conduct of a business and may be anonymous except to the other partners, but who is a general partner and therefore carries unlimited liability for the obligations of the business, as do all other general partners, whatever the extent of their activity; also called a sleeping partner.

sill: The bottom of an aperture frame, such as a window or door sill.

simple interest: An interest charge computed by multiplying the rate of interest by the principal, without any kind of compounding, or piling of interest upon interest.

single entry bookkeeping: A bookkeeping system requiring only one entry for each transaction, rather than the standard double entry bookkeeping system; it is the most usual non-business system, while the double entry system is the only one generally recognized as acceptable for business purposes.

single family dwelling: A structure with its own street access, heating unit, and other independent facilities, which is used solely as the home of one family; in recent years, a definition that has been extended in some jurisdictions to include unmarried people and their children living together as a family unit and small groups living together in extended families.

siphon supplier: An unethical contractor who steals from one site to supply another, either in order to fulfill a contract as budgeted, to maximize profits, or both.

site: A location, such as the location of a historic building or battlefield, or a place, such as the lot where a structure will be erected or a park built.

site plan: A formal development plan submitted by a developer to local authorities, which must by law review the proposal and accept or reject it before development may begin.

skin: See casing.

slab: A floor, usually of concrete, used as a foundation.

sleeping partner: See silent partner.

slum clearance: The demolition of slums, often but not always to replace them with new housing; often used to describe rehabilitation as well.

Small Business Administration (SBA): A Federal agency responsible for administering a wide range of loan and information programs aimed at fostering the growth of small businesses, pursuant to statute and public policy.

Small Business Investment Company (SBIC): An investment company supplying capital, loans and management advice to small businesses; such companies are partially financed by Federal money, but privately owned.

Society of Real Estate Appraisers (SREA): An association of real estate appraisal professionals, which publishes widely in the field and is heavily involved in educational activities, certifying participating appraisers as Senior Real Property Appraiser, Senior Real Estate Analyst, or Senior Residential Appraiser.

soft sell: An understated, empathetic selling style; usually contrasted with hard sell, which is thought to be an overly aggressive selling style.

soil bank: Land kept out of current use by farmers, who receive Federal subsidies for doing so.

soil conservation: See conservation.

solar heating: Any heating unit that wholly or substantially converts the rays of the sun into energy that can be used to heat buildings or water.

sole proprietorship: A major form of ownership, in which a single person is the only owner of a business, and carries both unlimited rights and liabilities in regard to that business.

Southern Colonial: A house style originating in the Southeast, often built of brick rather than wood, and featuring two story pillars and end wall chimneys; otherwise similar to New England Colonials, both being simple two story structures with entry halls.

Spanish style: A house style originating in Spain, and widely used in the Southwest; usually a single story building of stucco or adobe, and featuring tiled roofs, arcade verandas, and construction around an inner, private courtyard.

special assessment: See assessment.

special assessment bonds: Special purpose local and municipal bonds, issued to raise money for such projects as sewers, waterworks, and libraries, and backed by special taxes levied upon those within the area affected by those projects.

specialty store: A retailer carrying kinds of stock not normally found in most general merchandise stores; for example, cheese stores and pottery stores.

special use permit: A permit granted by local authorities to use land in a fashion which is specifically allowed by zoning laws if such a permit is granted, in contrast to a variance, which is a permit allowing a land use which is otherwise prohibited by zoning laws. For example, a special use permit might allow construction of a church in a residential area, a use mentioned in the local zoning law, while a variance might allow construction of an office park in a residential area, a use not mentioned or allowed by local zoning law.

specifications: Detailed, written, and drawn descriptions of work to be done or products in being, used for several purposes, including job performance evaluation, repair information, and standard setting.

specific lien: See lien.

specific performance: The legally enforceable performance of contractual obligations precisely as agreed upon in a contract, with no material deviation.

specified asset partnership: In real estate investment, a limited partnership in which all of the assets to be acquired by the partnership are known to the investor at the time of purchase of the limited partnership interest.

speculation: High risk purchases of any kind of property in hope of high profits at least commensurate with the risks; for example, purchase of volatile common stock in hope of quick, profitable sale or the purchase of land either for quick resale or coupled with willingness to hold it for a substantial length of time, but in either case risking large losses in hope of high profits.

speculative builder: A builder who has no purchaser before building starts, and hopes to sell that which is built at or before completion; a practice that is widely followed by both commercial and residential builders in boom times, when financing is relatively easy, but is rare in hard times, when financing is difficult.

split commission: A partial commission, resulting from the sharing of full commissions between two or more sellers.

split financing: The financing of two or more interests in a single property separately, usually with the aim of securing greater total financing than would otherwise have been available; for example, the financing of fee, improvements, and lease separately for a single property. Also called component financing.

split level: A house or apartment with three or more levels on two floors.

spot zoning: See variance.

spread: The difference between two related prices; for example, between the interest paid on deposits and the interest charged on money loaned, between the bid and asked prices of stocks traded over the counter, or between the price paid by a retailer and the price charged for the same goods.

spreading agreement: An agreement between lender and borrower to use more properties as security for an existing mortgage.

squatter's right: The interest in property held by one who is in adverse possession of that property; if there is no successful adverse possession, then no right exists.

squeeze: A general term for a wide variety of situations in which some are caught by economic circumstances. For example, one kind of squeeze occurs when mortgage money is expensive and hard to get, and home prices are high, driving potential buyers out of the housing market; an investment squeeze occurs when short sellers who have sold in expectation of declining securities or commodities futures prices are confronted instead with rising prices and must buy to cover at ruinous prices; a profit squeeze occurs when profits are curtailed by rising inventories and faltering sales during a recession.

SREA: See Society of Real Estate Appraisers.

stamp taxes: Taxes levied in the form of stamps that must be purchased and attached to items sold by sellers before legal transfer can be effected; examples include stamps on deeds, securities certificates, and cigarettes.

standard parallels: United States Geological Survey east-west map lines, 24 miles apart and parallel to the survey's base line.

standby commitment: A binding option sold for a nonreturnable standby fee by a lender to a borrower, providing that the lender will loan a specific amount on stated terms to a borrower at any time within a stated future period; the borrower may or may not exercise the option.

standby fee: See standby commitment.

standing loan: A loan on which only interest payments are being made, with amortization of principal to begin at some stated later date or with payment of principal to occur all at once on the final due date of the loan.

state bank: A state-chartered commercial bank able to perform all commercial bank functions, in contrast to federally chartered commercial banks; sometimes state banks are members of the Federal Reserve System and usually they are members of the Federal Deposit Insurance Corporation.

statement of record: A full description of land to be sold in interstate commerce and of the seller of that land, including the seller's financial statements, that must by law be filed with the Federal Government, when 50 or more lots are being sold.

statute of frauds: A body of state statutes, adapted from the English statute of frauds, providing that some kinds of contracts are not enforceable unless in writing and signed by the parties; all real estate contracts, except leases for one year or less, are so classified.

statute of limitations: A law providing time limits within which certain classes of civil and criminal actions may be legally pursued; such statutes cover a wide range of possible causes of action and time limits; but there is no statute of limitations on some kinds of criminal actions, such as murder and tax fraud.

statutory law: Law set by statute, within constitutional bounds, in contrast to the common law, which is developed by the accretion of case law; in many situations the practical distinctions between the two kinds of law blur.

steering: The illegal and unethical practice of directing some kinds of potential occupants to homes and apartments in some areas and not in others, usually with the aim of practicing housing discrimination.

stepup lease: See graduated lease.

stock: 1. An ownership share in a corporation, whether that corporation is publicly held, privately held, or both. Ownership is divided into shares of equal value, and the quantity of shares held indicates the proportion of ownership held. **2.** The inventory carried by a company, with particular reference to goods held by wholesalers and retailers for resale.

stock exchange: An organized securities trading market, such as the New York Stock Exchange, in which members trade on behalf of their own and customer accounts.

stockholder: One who owns some shares of a corporation, through ownership of one or more shares of company stock.

stockholders' equity: The value of total stockholder shares in a corporation, expressed as the net of assets minus liabilities.

stock insurance company: An insurance company organized as a stock corporation, in contrast to a mutual insurance company, in which those insured automatically become shareholders.

stock market: 1. Any stock exchange which is an organized market for trade in securities. **2.** The New York Stock Exchange, widely described as "the market" for stocks and bonds.

stop payment: An instruction to a bank from a depositor to withhold payment on a check drawing on that depositor's account, as when a check has been issued in error, or has been lost in the mail and must be replaced by a new check.

store: 1. A retail establishment, such as a grocery or department store. 2. A stock of materials, such as goods stored in a warehouse. 3. To put something, such as goods or information, away for future use.

storm door: A second door, outside a primary door, providing additional insulation.

storm sewer: A sewer carrying runoff, contrasting with a sanitary sewer, which carries waste materials.

storm window: A second window, outside a primary window, providing additional insulation.

straight line depreciation: A method of depreciating property that assigns equal proportions of value to each of the years it depreciates. For example, an asset worth $10,000 depreciating over a ten year period will depreciate at the rate of $1,000 for each of the ten years.

straight loan: A loan granted on the basis of the anticipated ability of the borrower to repay, without any kind of collateral.

straight paper: Any note, acceptance, or bill of exchange, that is secured by nothing but its issuer's promise to pay.

straw man: One who purchases land on behalf of an undisclosed principal, holding title, but passing effective control to the principal, as when one who is assembling a body of land for development uses several others as purchasers to hide the real purpose of the purchases and the identity of the real purchasers. Also called a dummy purchaser.

stucco: A kind of textured cement used for exterior walls.

stud: One of the vertical boards composing the framework of an interior wall, to which the wall is attached.

studio apartment: See efficiency unit.

subcontract: A contract to do work for one who has a larger contract to do a job; for example, the electrical work on a new house might be done on a subcontract with the contractor who has the contractual responsibility for the entire house.

subcontractor: See subcontract.

subdivision: The division of a single parcel of land into two or more smaller parcels, in accordance with local laws and regulations; also a smaller parcel of land so created.

subflooring: A layer of flooring attached to the joists beneath a floor, to which the finish flooring is attached.

subject to mortgage: A phrase in a conveyance of real estate indicating that the property sold is currently encumbered by a mortgage lien, and that the purchaser is taking over payments on that mortgage. Should the purchaser later default, purchaser incurs no personal liability for the mortgage; the lender must look to the original borrower for personal liability, if it existed under the terms of the mortgage.

sublease: A lease from a lessee, who in turn has leased from the owner, as when someone takes over the remaining portion of a lease; original leases normally specify that such a sublease requires the consent of the owner of the property.

subordinated debenture: A debenture which by its terms of issue becomes junior to such other debts as bank loans in the event of bankruptcy, reorganization, or dissolution.

subordinate interest: An interest in property which, by its nature and from the start, is of lower rank than some other interests; for example, a second mortgage which may be satisfied by sale of the property securing it only after an existing first mortgage is fully satisfied.

subordination: In real estate, the placing of one debt obligation or interest under another. Examples include an agreement continuing a second mortgage as a secondary or junior debt obligation, even when the first mortgage on a property has been paid, making it possible for a new first mortgage to be secured, rather than turning the former second mortgage into a first mortgage by operation of law; or an agreement by which a seller of land who holds a first mortgage on that land places a later construction loan ahead of that first mortgage interest.

subordination clause: A contract provision setting up an agreed-upon subordination of interests to those of another.

subpeona: An order to appear before a court to testify in litigation before that court.

subpeona duces tecum: An order to produce a document in court relating to litigation before that court.

subrogation: The substitution of one creditor or other claimant for another; for example, the substitution of one creditor for another when a note is made payable to another.

subscription: 1. An agreement to buy a new securities issue. 2. A contract to buy something which will be supplied in series.

subsidence: The sinking of a body of ground, usually because of subsurface action, such as a change in the course of an underground stream, or the extraction of subsurface material, such as coal, oil, and gas.

subsidy: Direct or indirect financial support by government of business organizations or individuals, as directed by public policy and statutory authority, including a very wide variety of supports and insurances for farming and farm prices, domestic producers, transportation companies, and public utility companies.

substructure: Any structure lying under another, and fulfilling support functions, as when a foundation supports a building.

subsurface easement: See subsurface right.

subsurface right: A right or interest in subsurface land held by one who is not the owner of the land, such as the right to extract oil, gas, or coal, or an easement granted for the passage of underground pipelines or cables.

suburb: A population center close to a larger population center, and considerably affected by the economy of the larger center; usually describing cities, towns, and villages near substantial cities, from which many commute to work in the cities.

summons: A notification that a court action has been started against a defendant, and that judgment against the defendant will be issued by the court if he or she fails to appear to defend the action.

sum-of-the-years'-digits method: An accelerated depreciation method in which the estimated life on an asset is used to figure progressively smaller depreciation amounts; for example, an asset estimated to have a depreciable life of four years will have these digits—4,3,2,1, totalling 10. First year depreciation will be 4/10 or 40%, second year 30%, third year 20%, and fourth year 10%.

sump: See sump pump.

sump pump: A pump used to drain a sump or drainage pit; such pumps are also used widely to drain all flooded building areas.

surety: One who agrees to guarantee the actions of another, usually the payment of a debt or the performance of a contractual obligation; such a guarantor may be an insurer acting for a fee or one acting without fee, such as the voluntary co-signer of a note.

surety bond: An instrument formally guaranteeing performance of an obligation, issued by an insurer to an insured for a fee.

surface: The top layer of a body of land or water, including that portion exposed to air and some distance down, that distance being defined by any conveyance of subsurface rights, rather than by any fixed measure.

surface right: Any right, interest, or easement on the surface of the land; normally used in connection with a grant of subsurface rights and describing surface rights necessary to the pursuit of subsurface rights, such as the building of necessary surface structures and access roads in connection with mining or drilling.

surface water: Water directly produced by precipitation and its runoff, rather than in the form of a stream or issue from a body of water.

surrender: In real estate, the act of giving up possession and a present interest in real property to one with a future interest; occurring by agreement when lessee and lessor agree to terminate a lease early, or by construction in law when a lessee abandons leased property and the lessor leases that property to another, thereby converting the abandonment into a surrender and re-leasing.

surrogate's court: See probate.

surtax: An extra tax, levied periodically on top of regular taxes; for example, excess profits taxes, which have been occasionally levied on top of regular corporate income taxes.

survey: The measurement of a body of land, conducted by and using formal procedures developed by professional surveyors and acceptable for official recordkeeping purposes, and the maps and supporting documents evidencing that measurement; includes measurement of boundaries, structures, other improvements, easements, and encroachments.

surveyor: See survey.

sweat equity: Time and work contributed by owners to the improvement of their property, usually but not always resulting in that property's growth in value, as when a homeowner spends substantial time and labor improving a single family residence, or a group of families spend time and labor rehabilitating a rundown multi-family residence.

sweetener: Additional consideration paid by borrower to lender to secure a loan; for example, an extra one percent of the entire amount of a mortgage loan, paid in a lump sum on granting of the loan, under conditions of tight mortgage money.

syndicate: 1. In the securities industry, a group of investment bankers joined to handle the marketing or placement of a securities issue; a means of sharing risk and sharing marketing strength when bringing a large issue to market. **2.** A popular name for organized crime.

syndication: An investment form, in which two or more investors own a single investment. In real estate, the normal form is that of the limited partnership, in which one or more general partners, the syndicators, who act as investment managers, sell participations to one or more limited partners, who act solely as investors.

syndicator: See syndication.

T

T account: A demonstration account physically set up in the form of a T, showing the accounting effect of a transaction, often for problem-solving purposes; the account name is placed above the T, with debits to the left and credits to the right below the T.

tacking: In real estate, the piecing together of consecutive periods in which adverse possession is claimed to create one period long enough to satisfy statutory requirements and create adverse possession.

take down: To borrow money which has been previously committed by a lender, as by use of a line of credit or construction loan commitment.

takeout commitment: See takeout loan.

takeout loan: A long term loan replacing short term interim financing previously advanced for a construction project; usually preceded by a takeout commitment, or agreement to advance a long term loan at the end of the project on satisfactory completion. Also called a permanent loan.

taking: Referring to expropriation, as by use of the government's power of eminent domain.

tandem plan: A mortgage market support plan designed to help provide liquidity in tight money periods, in which the Government National Mortgage Association (Ginnie Mae) buys mortgages, such as those guaranteed by the Federal Housing Administration and Veterans Administration, at full price rather than at the discounts at which they would otherwise be sold, and resells them to the Federal National Mortgage Association (Fannie Mae) at full price, with Fannie Mae later, if necessary, reselling at a loss and absorbing that loss.

tangible assets: Those assets that have physical being, such as machinery, in contrast to assets that are not physical and therefore are intangible, such as good will.

tangible value: The value to a business of such tangible assets as plant and equipment, while that business is in operation, in contrast to their value once that business has ceased to be a going concern.

tax abatement: See abatement.

taxable estate: That portion of an estate remaining and subject to taxes after all deductions of any kind from the gross estate.

taxable income: That portion of income remaining and subject to taxes after all deductions of any kind from gross income.

tax accounting: That part of the field of accounting primarily concerned with the tax aspects of transactions, including both the levying and administration of taxes by government, tax planning aimed at legally minimizing taxes paid to government, and compliance with tax laws and regulations.

tax anticipation obligations: Any of several interest-bearing financial instruments sold by governments to raise money in advance and in expectation of tax revenues, which aim to smooth out government income over the year, rather than having income concentrated in periods of high tax receipts.

tax avoidance: The legal minimization of taxes due government by application of a large number of tax planning devices; in contrast to tax evasion, which is illegal.

tax base: For tax purposes, the value of all the property within a jurisdiction subject to taxes; for example, the value of all taxable real property in a township, which would not include such nontaxable property as church-owned land.

tax burden: The extent to which a kind of tax or group of taxes impact upon a group, usually stated relative to other groups; for example, one of the aims of the progressive income tax is to lessen the impact of the income tax on the poor and disadvantaged, compared to the impact on those thought better able to pay.

tax credit: A sum that may be directly deducted in full from taxes due, in contrast to a deduction, which is subtracted from taxables; for example, an investment tax credit allows businesses to deduct certain sums spent for capital investment directly from corporate income taxes that would otherwise be due.

tax deduction: A sum that may be deducted from taxables, lowering those taxables; for example, certain sums spent for charitable purposes, taxes, and medical and dental payments are deductible from taxable income on Federal income tax returns.

tax deed: A deed to property taken by government for nonpayment of taxes and resold at auction pursuant to law; may be bought back by the defaulting taxpayer within a period specified by statute, on repayment of purchase price, costs, and interest.

tax equalization: The adjustment of property taxes payable among taxpayers in a taxing jurisdiction, in an attempt to fairly apportion taxes, usually by adjustments of valuations, rates, or both.

taxes: Charges imposed by government on those under its jurisdiction, including charges on income, imports, exports, sales, estates and trusts, gifts, licenses and fees, and property.

tax evasion: The illegal minimization of taxes due government; in contrast to tax avoidance, which is legal.

tax exempt bonds: Bonds paying income that is not taxable, including

Federal, state and local bonds that are not in any way taxable and Federal bonds not subject to state and local taxes.

tax exemptions: Sums deductible from Federal, state, and local taxable income for each taxpayer and each legal dependent of that taxpayer.

tax free exchange: See exchange.

tax fraud: Failure to pay taxes legally due, with intent to defraud the taxing authority, through such actions as failure to report income and misstatement of deductions; no statute of limitations applies to tax fraud.

tax haven: A country that levies little or no income tax on foreign individuals and businesses and so, under some conditions, offers foreigners the possibility of legal tax avoidance in their own countries; but in many situations the line between tax avoidance and tax evasion is a fine one, and is subject to considerable litigation.

tax lien: A lien placed on a taxpayer's property by government for nonpayment of taxes due; the lien is satisfied by payment of taxes due or by forced sale of the property for back taxes.

tax loophole: A provision of a tax law that makes it possible to avoid taxes that might otherwise be due, sometimes due to government inadvertence, sometimes pursuant to legislative intent, and often as a result of special interest legislation with applications far beyond the interests of the lobby that forced through the legislation.

taxpayer: 1. An individual or business liable for the payment of taxes, now or in the future. **2.** A property developed just enough to pay the taxes due on it, such as a single story row of stores on a piece of prime commercial property that is awaiting development into an office buiding.

tax rebate: Government return of taxes already paid to a class of taxpayers, usually as part of an attempt to stimulate the economy.

tax refund: Government return of taxes already paid, due to overpayment or error.

tax roll: A record of all taxable property within a taxing jurisdiction, with ownership and tax information.

tax sale: A sale of private property by government to satisfy unpaid taxes.

tax sharing: The sharing of Federal or state tax revenues with the governments of smaller jurisdictions; a means of moving some tax money into localities, sometimes to provide a higher proportion of that money to the needier localities.

tax shelter: A form through which income can be developed tax-free or in a tax-advantaged way, such as a pension or profit-sharing plan, an investment in tax-advantaged oil drilling activities, or certain real estate investments.

temporary injunction: A preliminary injunction restraining a defendant from doing or continuing to do an act until such time as the injunction is dissolved by the court or replaced by a permanent injunction.

tenancy: A legal right or interest in the holding and occupancy of real estate, which may be with or without written lease. Tenancy terms may very widely, including a specified lease period, month-to-month, and year-to-year terms; and tenancy may take many forms, including individual, joint and corporate tenancies.

tenancy at will: A tenancy stating no fixed period, in which either landlord or tenant may terminate the tenancy at any time, or in the time specified by statute, which is usually 30 days; or which automatically terminates on sale of the property or by the death of either party.

tenancy by the entirety: A kind of joint tenancy limited to spouses, in which wife and husband take conveyance of the tenancy interest in common, with that interest being treated as a single, indivisible unit, and with the survivor continuing to hold the tenancy as a matter of right.

tenancy for life: A tenancy by one who holds a tenancy interest for the rest of his life, or for the rest of the life of another.

tenancy for years: A tenancy by one who holds a tenancy interest for one or more years, as specified by the leasehold agreement.

tenancy from year to year: A tenancy by one who holds a tenancy interest for an unstated period, and pays rent yearly, each payment serving as renewal for another year; often resulting from the holding over of a previous specified term tenancy on which rental was paid yearly.

tenancy in common: A tenancy by two or more parties holding an interest in the same property, that interest being undivided, although not necessarily equal in each holder. A party's portion of an undivided interest may be conveyed to others in life and passes with the interest holder's estate on death, rather than directly to the surviving co-tenants.

tenancy in tail: A tenancy in which the right of inheritance is limited to a fixed line of succession, consisting of direct "issue of the body," or "blood relations." Property so limited is described as being in entail.

tenant: One who has a legal right or interest in the holding and occupancy of real estate, with or without a written lease.

tenant farmer: One who rents land from its owner and works that land, paying rent in crops, currency, or both. Sharecropping is one form of tenant farming.

tender: 1. An offer to pay a debt, perform a contractual obligation, or purchase real or personal property. **2.** An offer to purchase, often encountered in company takeover situations, in which one company makes an offer to buy the stock of another at a stated price.

tenement: **1.** Any ownership right in real property, tangible or intangible, although often used to describe only tangible property owned. **2.** A multi-story, multi-tenant apartment building intended for occupancy by those of low income, and a dominant feature in American big-city slums for the last century.

tenure: In real estate and in common law, and derived from feudal landholding forms, the kind of ownership interest held by one, subject to the superior right of another; now surviving only in common usage as an imprecise synonym for ownership interest.

term: Any time period, such as the length of time a leasehold, mortgage, or bond is in being.

termite inspection: An inspection of a property, or of one or more structures on a property, by a licensed or otherwise qualified exterminator, to assess the visible presence of termites or other wood-boring insects; usually conducted before a closing, as required by a termite inspection clause in the sales contract and a warranty by the seller that the structures are free of termites or termite damage.

termite inspection clause: See termite inspection.

termite shield: A shield running around the bottom of a structure, usually of metal, functioning to help prevent termite penetration.

terms of sale: The prices, arrangements for payment, and all conditions and guarantees attached to a sale, becoming part of the sales contract, including those implied by sales contracts that come under the jurisdiction of consumer protection laws.

terrace: A flat land area, cut out of or built up on a slope, for such purposes as crop raising, erosion control, and the creation of flat building lots.

terrazzo: A building material, consisting of marble or other stones embedded in cement; widely used for flooring and other construction purposes.

testament: A synonym for "last will," meaning the legally valid last will of a deceased person; therefore "last will and testament" is redundant.

testamentary: Pertaining to a testament.

testamentary capacity: That soundness of mind and memory necessary for one to be able to make a legally valid will.

testamentary disposition: Property given by the terms of a will, and not passed until the testator dies.

testamentary trust: A trust created by the provisions of a legally valid will, becoming effective after the testator's death.

testator: The maker of a legally valid last will.

tideland: Shore land between the high and low water marks.

tidewater land: Any body of low coastal land; an imprecisely used term.

tight money: A government policy that attempts to slow inflation by restriction of the amount of money and credit in circulation through exercise of a number of money-manipulative devices, especially manipulation of the Federal Reserve rate, which directly affects the prime rate.

tile: A term describing several kinds of building materials, including thin blocks or strips made of such material as plastic, glass, clay or other ceramic materials used to surface floors, walls, ceilings, roofs, and other structural components, as well as to form pipes used in some drains and some kinds of building blocks.

till: That mass of boulders, gravel, sand, and other materials carried by glaciers and deposited when the glaciers receded.

tillable land: Land that is cleared and fit to be cultivated.

timberland: Forest land, mainly covered with growing timber.

time certificate of deposit: See certificate of deposit.

time deposit: See bank account.

time is of the essence: A phrase found in contracts, indicating that timely performance of contractual agreements is essential to the continued existence of a valid contract, and that failure of timely performance is breach of contract, as when failure to complete a construction contract or pay a debt obligation on time constitutes breach or default.

time loan: A loan repayable in full at a specified future date, in contrast to an installment loan, which is payable in a series of equal payments.

time sharing: In real estate, the purchase of an undivided interest by two or more buyers, as when several buyers together buy a unit in a resort condominium, each agreeing to occupy the unit for a specified time or portion of available time; or when several sublessees lease shares in a resort tenancy for part or all of a summer.

title: Legally valid ownership of real or personal property, and the documentary evidence of that ownership, such as a deed, certificate of title, or bill of sale.

title abstract: See abstract of title.

title certificate: See certiticate of title.

title insurance: Insurance against losses resulting from the passage of legally invalid title, issued by a title insurance company after a title search by that company has established that legally valid title exists in the seller, who then is able to pass that title to the insured. One kind of policy covers owners, and can carry extended coverage against nonstandard defective losses; another covers lenders to the extent of their loan losses resulting from legally invalid title, with the amount of coverage diminishing as loan principal is amortized. Most title insurance policies are similar, and are issued by companies belonging to the American Land Title Association (ALTA).

title report: See preliminary title report.

title search: A search of public records to attempt to find any defects in a chain of title to real property; usually conducted by a title company or professional title abstractor, and resulting in issuance of an abstract of title, certificate of title, preliminary title report, or title insurance policy.

topographic map: See relief map.

Torrens system: A system of land title registration originated in Australia by Sir Robert Torrens, which has been adopted in some states, and which provides a landowner with the option of registering property owned with the state, having the state conduct a conclusive title search, and issue a certificate of title which is by state law deemed conclusive and incontestable, thereby eliminating the need for future exhaustive title searches on conveyances of ownership interests. From the time of such certificate issuance, no defect not already noted on the certificate will be accepted as valid, and all further conveyances, liens, and other encumbrances and encroachments must be noted on the certificate to become legally valid.

tort: A private or civil wrong to another, actionable at law for damages, such an unintentional harm to a person or property caused by negligence; such an action does not preclude a criminal action arising out of the same set of circumstances.

tortfeasor: One who is judged by a court to have committed a tort, that is an actionable private or civil wrong done to another.

townhouse: Any two-story, single-family residence attached to at least one other residence by a shared wall, as in a group of such houses in a suburban housing development or a group of attached houses on a city street.

township: By Federal land survey measure, 36 square miles, in a single 6 mile square piece.

tract: Any parcel of land, but normally connoting a large parcel suitable for the building of a development.

tract house: A residence built in a large development of similar or identical residences.

trade fixture: A fixture belonging to a lessee of commercial property, used in the normal course of conducting lessee's business, and considered personal property even though attached to the leased premises; therefore removable by the lessee on termination of the lease.

tradein: In real estate, the acceptance by a seller or broker of the home of a buyer as part of the purchase price of the home being bought; usually for resale by the seller or broker.

tradeoffs: The balancing of costs and benefits, when choices need be made between alternatives. Examples are a choice between quick delivery of a contracted job, which would involve high costs due to necessary overtime work, and somewhat slower delivery at lower costs; or a choice between the curative powers of a drug and its harmful side effects.

trading area: The geographic area to which a business sells, such as the neighborhood served by a retail store or the communities served by a suburban mall.

trading down: Buying something less expensive and of presumably lower quality than what is currently owned; for example, the purchase of a small house after having owned a much larger house.

trading up: Buying something more expensive and of presumably higher quality than what is currently owned, the classic instances being the purchase of a more expensive home or car than the one currently owned.

trailer: See mobile home.

trailer park: See mobile home park.

transfer: The legal conveyance of title to property from one party to another, whether by act of the parties or by operation of law.

transfer tax: A Federal, state, or local tax on the value of assets transferred; only state and local transfer taxes apply to transfers of real estate; also called conveyance tax.

trespass: A wrongful and violent entry upon the property of another, without the consent or authorization of that other; the law will imply such violence where only unauthorized entry exists.

trial balance: A listing and summary of all account totals in a double entry bookkeeping system, to determine whether total debits equal total credits, preliminary to balancing the books.

trial close: An attempt by a seller to determine how the prospective purchaser feels about purchasing the product or service; not necessarily a serious attempt to close the sale and often merely an attempt to produce reflexive agreement.

trial sale: A sale that is made subject to subsequent acceptance by a buyer, and that therefore is not really consummated until the buyer has either specifically approved the purchase or has by failure to disapprove the purchase after passage of a specified time, approved the sale.

trim: The moldings around doorways and windows, and the decorative moldings inside a structure.

triple A tenant: See AAA tenant.

triplex: 1. A three-dwelling unit residential building. **2.** A single apartment three story apartment.

truss: A framework, functioning to support such structures as roofs or bridges.

trust: **1.** A right or interest in property held by one or more for one or more others; the holders, or trustees, have the right and responsibility to handle that property in the best interests of the others, or beneficiaries. Also refers to the instrument creating that right or interest. **2.** An illegal monopoly, the intended target of antitrust activities.

trust company: A financial institution, usually a bank as well as a trust company, which handles many kinds of trusts and trust investments; sometimes as trustee and sometimes as agent for trustees; commercial banks perform all major trust company functions, and the line between then and trust companies has now blurred so much as to practically disappear.

trust deed: See deed of trust.

trust fund: A fund set up under the terms of a trust, in which the trustee holds the principal and distributes some or all of the trust's income to the beneficiaries. Such a fund is often for the benefit of a surviving spouse for the remainder of a lifetime, with principal then to surviving children or others, and often to surviving children until they have reached specified ages, with principal then to them.

Truth in Lending Law: One of a series of modern consumer protection acts, requiring lenders to fully disclose the rates of interest, other charges, and all terms and conditions of each loan, in writing and clearly stated.

Tudor: A house style originating in England in the 16th century, and featuring large, leaded windows; intricately carved wainscoting on many inner walls; and considerable ornamentation of the exterior walls.

turnkey lease: A lease providing that the landlord will turn the leased premises over to the lessee in occupancy-ready condition.

turnkey project: A construction project providing that the builder will turn the completed project over to its purchaser in occupancy-ready condition.

U

ultra vires: Describing corporate actions that are beyond the legal power of the corporation to take, as they are beyond the corporate charter, which sets forth the purposes and therefore defines the legal limits of corporate action.

umbrella policy: A major liability insurance policy, picking up coverage where other liability coverages end, functioning much the same as a major medical insurance policy.

unconscionable agreement: An agreement which a court will refuse to enforce because it is found by the court to be extraordinarily unfair.

underimproved: Describing real property carrying structures which are less than the most profitable possible; for example, a farm in the middle of a suburb, or a three-story apartment building where a six-story building would be more profitable, would be considered underimproved.

underinsurance: The carrying of too little insurance to cover potential losses, sometimes also resulting in failure to qualify for full insurance coverage under policy clauses requiring coinsurance.

underlying debt instrument: A debt instrument, such as a senior bond or first mortgage, which takes precedence over other debt instruments secured by the same property.

under the table: An illegal payment or bribe given to help consumate an agreement, such as a bribe given to a public official to influence a contract award.

undervaluation: 1. The placing of a lower than reasonable valuation on property; often the subject of insurance claim disputes. **2.** The lower than reasonable evaluation of securities being traded, or other property for sale, and consequent creation of investment opportunities.

underwriting: 1. The taking on of a debt or insurance risk by a lender or insurer; also the function of assessing and recommending a course of action as to the assumption of that risk, as performed by an underwriter, who is a person professionally qualified to make such recommendations. **2.** The guaranteeing of the sale of a securities issue by a firm or group functioning as purchasers of the entire issue of that security; to be distinguished from mere distribution, in which the distributor does not purchase the whole issue.

undeveloped land: See raw land.

undisclosed agent: One who acts as agent for another without informing others of the existence of that agency.

undisclosed principal: One who functions as a principal through an agent, rather than directly, without being disclosed by that agent to be a principal.

undistributed profits: Earnings that have been retained in the corporation rather than distributed to equity holders.

undivided interest: A property interest or ownership which is shared with others, though not necessarily equally, as in a tenancy in common or joint tenancy.

unearned income: 1. Revenue that has been physically received but is as yet unearned, such as payment for subscriptions not yet fulfilled, and therefore must be treated as deferred income for accounting purposes. **2.** For tax purposes, income that has not been earned for personal services rendered, such as rent.

unearned increment: An increase in the value of property that results from conditions out of the control of the owner of that property, rather than through additions to value brought about by action of the owner; but not including a general rise in property values due to the impact of inflation; for example, a rise in the value of real estate located near a superhighway entrance.

unearned revenue: See unearned income.

unencumbered: That which is entirely free of legal claims and obligations; for example, realty that is sold with clear title, and free of all debts and liens.

unenforceable contracts: Contracts which cannot be enforced by legal action, such as contracts creating obligations to do acts that are in themselves illegal, as well as contracts which are invalid for any of a wide range of reasons.

Uniform Commercial Code: A national codification of major laws concerning commerce and finance, which has been adopted by almost all states, covering a very wide range of matters, such as sales, contracts, commercial and bank paper, bank deposits, and receipts.

Uniform Residential Landlord and Tenant Act (URLTA): A model act, codifying the relations between landlords and tenants, which has been adopted by several states, and covers such matters as rents, security deposits, landlord and tenant obligations toward each other and the leased premises, and the conditions under which a tenancy may be terminated before expiration of the lease term.

Uniform Vendor and Purchaser Risk Act: See risk of loss.

unilateral contract: An offer by one, in fact constituting a unilateral offer rather than contract, that becomes a contract on occurrence of acceptance or performance on the part of another, as when one advertises or lists something for sale, and a bona fide buyer appears to accept the offer, that acceptance turning the unilateral offer into a binding contract.

unimproved land: See raw land.

uninhabitable: See habitable.

unissued stock: Stock that has been authorized but not yet issued by a corporation; such stock is not treated as an asset, in contrast to treasury stock, which is also held by the corporation, but which has been issued and repurchased by the corporation.

unit: A single definable piece, part of a larger whole; in real estate, a single rentable or salable property within a larger property, such as a unit in a housing development or condominium.

unit cost: The cost to a producer, distributor, or retailer of a single designated unit in a group of substantially identical units; for example, the cost to a tract housing developer of a single house, or the cost to the producer of plumbing fixtures of identical parts built on an assembly line.

unit cost in place method: A means of attempting to assess replacement cost, in which an appraiser estimates the cost of building components separately, developing a unit cost for each component, and including overhead and profit allocation estimates as well as direct labor and materials costs, and then adds all costs together to reach total cost and thereby replacement cost. Also called segregated cost method.

United States Coast and Geodetic Survey System: See geodetic system.

United States Government bonds: All bonds issued as debt obligations of the Federal Government.

United States Government securities: All securities issued by the Federal Government, including bonds, bills, certificates, and special debt issues.

unlawful detainer: The holding of property by one who was originally lawful, but who refuses to give up possession when that lawful right has terminated, as when a lessee holds over after lease termination and the landlord's demand for repossession.

unlimited liability: Liability that extends to all of a debtor's business and personal assets; the corporate and limited partnership forms of doing business substantially limit liability, but the sole proprietorship and general partnership forms generally carry unlimited liability.

unmarketable title: Title to real property that is so defective that it cannot be legally conveyed to another.

unsecured: Describing a debt instrument, such as a bond or note, that is not backed by any kind of collateral, but is backed only by the debtor's promise to repay.

upset date: A date specified in a contract, beyond which that contract may be cancelled by parties if other parties have not completed satisfactory performance of their contractual obligations; often found in construction contracts, with buyer able to cancel if seller has not completed work by that date.

upset price: The minimum price at which a sale will be made, such as the starting price set at auction, to be met by bidders or the item will be withdrawn from that auction.

urban homesteading: An urban renewal technique, in which people buy deteriorated government-owned dwellings at very low prices and rehabilitate them for personal residence purposes. The dwellings are usually multi-family houses in slum areas, which have been abandoned by their owners and taken by government for back taxes.

Urban Land Institute: A nonprofit national research and educational organization, which is involved in a wide range of educational and publishing activities in the areas of land use and development.

urban planning: The development of medium and long range plans for the rational development of city and metropolitan areas, in terms of land use, the economic and physical health of the area and its people, and the quality of life in the area.

urban renewal: Attempts to develop or redevelop sections of cities, often center city sections that have severely deteriorated; usually financed either directly by Federal, state and local governments or by private industry with substantial help from those governments in the form of direct payment of tax concessions.

URLTA: See Uniform Residential Landlord and Tenant Act.

usable area: See rentable area.

useful life: See service life.

usufruct: The right to use, enjoy, or take profit from the property of another, as long as that which is used is not substantially altered; for example, the right to use or rent a building belonging to another.

usury: The charging of illegally high rates of interest by a lender; such rates are governed by state laws, and allowable rates vary from state to state, creating some imbalances in periods of rapid inflation, when money may be available to borrowers in one state and very difficult to secure in another, because of higher allowable rates in one than another.

utilities: The continuing services associated with development and habitation, such as fuel, telephone, water, garbage collection, and electricity.

V

VA: See Veterans Administration.

vacancy factor: The percentage of rentable space in a structure or group of structures that is vacant in a given period, computed on either a space or rental percentage basis.

vacation home: A recreational second home; may be a house, mobile home, boat, condominium, apartment, or any other form of residence.

validation: Certification of the official or legal status of an instrument, such as the stamping of a newly issued passport.

valuation: 1. The process of establishing the value of an asset, usually for sales or tax purposes; for example, the highly formalized practices associated with setting real estate values for tax assessment purposes, or the process of evaluating items in an estate, including such items as antiques and collectibles. **2.** The value established for an asset, for sales or tax purposes.

value: 1. The worth of something, in terms of a reasonable assessment of what price it might bring if sold under current market conditions. **2.** The actual price paid for something just sold.

variable annuity: See annuity.

variable interest rates: See flexible rates.

variable payment mortgages: See flexible rates.

variable rates: See flexible rates.

variance: A permit granted by local authorities allowing a land use which is otherwise prohibited by zoning laws, in contrast to a special use permit, which allows a land use that is mentioned by and permitted by zoning laws, if local authorities issue a permit. For example, a variance might allow construction of an office park in a residential area, a use not mentioned or allowed by local zoning law; a special use permit might allow construction of a church in a residential area, a use mentioned in the local zoning law. Spot zoning, which establishes a special zoning classification for a single property or very small area, is a variance-granting technique.

vault: A security room, for keeping valuables; usually a literally armored room in a bank.

vendee: A synonym for buyer that is much favored in legal instruments.

vendor: A synonym for seller that is much favored in legal instruments and is also often encountered in general business usage.

vendor's lien: A lien on property sold to another that is retained in law or by contract by the seller until full payment has been made; for example, a lien on real property retained by its seller.

veneer: A thin layer of material covering other, usually less expensive material, as when a thin hardwood layer covers a board of much less expensive pine.

vent: An opening that allows the release of gases, such as air and exhaust fumes.

ventilation: The circulation of fresh air within a structure.

venue: The place in which an action is brought to trial, often the place in which the cause of action is alleged to have arisen.

verbal agreement: An alleged agreement between two or more parties, but not in writing, and therefore usually unenforceable as a contract; under some very limited circumstances capable of serving as evidence, which with proven actions might be used to successfully allege the presence of a constructive contract.

vested interest: In real estate, a legal right which is capable of being conveyed, although it may not take effect until some future date.

Veterans Administration (VA): A Federal agency responsible for administering a considerable range of Federal benefit and rehabilitation programs designed to aid veterans of United States wars, and administering a large number of hospitals and other physical facilities for veterans.

Veteran's Administration loan: A mortgage loan made directly to a veteran, which is insured or wholly or partly guaranteed by the Veteran's Administration, for the purpose of buying, building, or improving a home that the veteran intends to occupy.

Victorian: A house style originating in England in the latter portion of the 19th century, and featuring several stories, complex plans with many rooms, and considerable ornamentation inside and out. The Queen Anne, or Chateauesque, variation is characterized by steeply roofed towers and turrets.

virgin land: See raw land.

void: Describing an agreement, document, or evidence of obligation which is not legally enforceable.

voluntary bankruptcy: See bankruptcy.

voluntary compliance: Voluntary action by private parties to comply with government regulations, without threat of government sanctions for non-compliance.

voucher system: A mode of paying contractors and subcontractors on construction projects, in which a builder or developer issues vouchers to be paid directly by the construction lender, rather than taking cash advances from the lender and paying the contractors and subcontractors in cash.

W

waiver: The voluntary and unilateral abandonment of a right or claim which would have been legally enforceable, as when one agrees to give up the right to a mechanic's lien on work performed in connection with a construction project, or gives up the right to a jury trial in a civil suit resulting from breach of contract. Some rights may not legally be waived, where public policy insists on the protection of the rights of the weak as against the demands of the strong.

wallboard: A sheet of material, which when attached to studs or any other room-framing device, forms an interior wall.

ward: See guardian.

warehouse: A place used to store goods, whether those of others or those of the owner of the warehouse.

warehousing: In mortgage financing, the holding of a number of mortgage loans by such mortgage originators as mortgage bankers for sale as a group to other lenders in the secondary mortgage market.

warranty: An assurance by a seller or other contracting party, whether express or implied, that property transferred is acceptable, using generally accepted standards of measurement; while not the central matter of the transaction, such an assurance is very often so material as to invalidate a transaction if the warranty is breached or to give rise to successful damage actions.

warranty deed: A written statement accompanying a deed, stating that title to real property is clear, and that the property is unencumbered.

waste: 1. Injury or damage to real property or to the value of real property as security done by one in legal possession, but not holding ownership of land in fee, occurring through the act or omission of the possessor of the land, which will be recognized as fact or constructed by a court. For example, the destruction of structures, landscaping, or timber; the failure to do adequate maintenance and repair; or the failure to pay taxes, insurance premiums, or mortgage loans. 2. Unusable materials that are the byproducts of human industry or habitation, such as chemical and atomic industry residues or sewage.

wasteland: Land entirely unfit for human use, such as waterless desert areas; sometimes recognized as such by tax law, and subject to little or no tax burden.

wasting asset: An asset that by its nature diminishes with use, such as oil or natural gas, and that is recognized as such by tax law, which makes allowances for the progressive depletion of such assets, thereby also creating tax shelter opportunities.

water rights: See riparian rights.

watershed: An area creating the body of runoff which feeds a stream or body of water.

water table: The level of water in the ground of an area, which rises and falls with precipitation and natural or human drainage and use.

wear and tear: The loss of value caused by such normal factors as age and use.

weephole: A small hole in a wall, allowing drainage of condensation or precipitation.

wellhead tax: A tax on the value of oil or gas, as it leaves its producing well.

wetlands: Lands close to water, such as marshes, which are often important to the preservation of local flora and fauna, and therefore are protected from construction by local zoning laws.

wholesale banking: That aspect of commercial banking that handles accounts and transactions for large institutional and business customers and for wealthy individuals. Today most commercial banks handle both large and small customers, and the distinction between wholesale and retail banking has all but disappeared, except as a description of a commercial bank's thrust in building its business.

will: A legally valid document disposing of its maker's property after death; once accepted by a court of appropriate jurisdiction, the wishes of its maker are carried out as far as possible.

witness: 1. One who affirms the validity of a document by signing such an affirmation on the document. **2.** One who appears and testifies under oath at a legal proceeding.

work drawings: Draftsperson's drawings used in construction by those doing the actual construction, in the course of attempting to fulfill precise architectural intentions.

working capital: The net of current assets over current liabilities; a major factor in assessing a company's financial health.

working capital ratio: The relationship between current assets and current liabilities, expressed as a ratio; for example, a company with current assets of $1,000,000 and current liabilities of $500,000 has a working capital ratio of 2:1.

work letter: A letter from landlord to tenant, functioning as and often physically an attachment to a lease, specifying in substantial detail work to be done by the landlord as part of the landlord's lease contract commitments.

work-out plan: A plan by which a lender temporarily waives strict performance of loan obligations by a borrower, giving the borrower time to work out payment problems, by such devices as postponement of amortization payments and collection of interest only, or a longer term payment plan allowing smaller periodic payments.

wraparound mortgage: A second mortgage, in which the second mortgage lender both lends additional money to the borrower and takes over an existing first mortgage, treating both transactions as a single refinancing loan; depends upon the agreement, or inability to object, of the first mortgage holder, and upon a first mortgage that carries a considerably smaller rate of interest than that of the second mortgage.

writ: A court-issued document directing or empowering a sheriff or other officer of the court, an official body, or any citizen, to act in some specified way or within specified bounds.

write down: To cut the value at which an asset is carried on the books of a business, to conform it with current estimated value, for such reasons as obsolescence, unusual depreciation, or price decreases.

write off: To cut the value at which an asset is carried on the books of a business to zero, reflecting that estimate of the current true worth of the asset; for example, an uncollectible debt.

write up: To raise the value at which an asset is carried on the books of a business, to conform it with current estimated value, for such reasons as unanticipated price increases on stock in inventory.

writ of certiorari: See certiorari.

Y

yard: 1. The open space around a structure, as minimally required by zoning laws between the structure and the front, side, and rear borders of a property. **2.** More generally and imprecisely, any open space around a dwelling. **3.** A measure of distance equalling 3 feet, 36 inches, or approximately 0.9 meters.

yield: That which is actually returned by an investment, but not including the investment itself; examples are the rate of return on securities investments and the crops harvested from land under cultivation.

Z

ZBB: See zero-based budgeting.

zero-based: The idea that in planning nothing should be taken as a given; that even seemingly mandated and unavoidable costs and other factors should be re-examined thoroughly in each planning period, considering each plan as a fresh start.

zero-based budgeting (ZBB): The application of the zero-based concept to the budgeting process, with each cost treated as new, even though actually to a large extent historically determined; aims at taking a fresh look at each budget, creating the possibility of cutting seemingly fixed costs and finding new approaches to the solution of old problems.

zero lot line: A property line on which a structure may legally be placed, rather than a setback being required, as occurs in some special use permit situations.

zoning: The fixing by government of geographic areas in which specified kinds of buildings and businesses may be developed; for example, many local districts, as authorized by state laws, prohibit commercial building in residential areas, specifying in which areas commercial building is permitted, and what kinds of commercial activities are permitted.